SEX, DRUGS AND SOCCER

Maarten Bax

Aerial Media Company

Cover design: Kees Jongboom
Translation and editing: Danny Guinan, Wordforword
Illustrations: Tony Tati, pennestreek.nl
Design: Teo van Gerwen

www.eye4sports.nl
www.aerialmediacom.nl
www.facebook.com/Aerialmediacompany

ISBN 978-94-026-0082-7

© 2015 Maarten Bax
© 2015 English edition: Aerial Media Company bv, Tiel,
the Netherlands

This book is also available as e-book:
ISBN 978-94-026-0029-2

Aerial Media Company bv.
Postbus 6088
4000 HB Tiel, The Netherlands.

SEX, DRUGS
AND SOCCER

CONTENTS

INTRODUCTION

Before we go any further, this book does not include any stories about Messi, Ribéry, Piqué, Beckenbauer or Zidane. Their respective misdemeanors - tax fraud, sex with an underage prostitute (acquitted!), insulting the police, having an affair with their secretary, Heidi, and the small matter of a head-butt - are all simply too lightweight for inclusion here. Neither will there be any mention of one Nasser Al Shamrani. Who? Yes, Nasser Al Shamrani, the Saudi striker who was crowned 'Asian Footballer of the Year' in 2014 just after he had been suspended for eight duels for spitting and head-butting an opponent during the final game of the Asian Champions League. What about Marco Reus? Also a non-runner, even though the Borussia Dortmund striker drove around in his Aston Martin for three years without a drivers license. The Belgian keeper Jean-Marie Pfaff? Amusing character, but nothing more than a tax dodger. No room here either for Omar Ortiz, world famous in his native Mexico because of his use of anabolic steroids and being an accessory to kidnapping, but in international terms a complete nobody. Luis Suárez? Nope... after all Marco van Basten has already pointed out that there are worse things in soccer than biting your opponent. And indeed, a hickey here and there is not enough reason to place the Uruguayan at the top of the scandalous behavior heap. But surely Johan Cruyff, and the claims by people in his inner circle that he has had a mistress for years, deserves to be included? Not much point, I'm afraid, when this supposed indiscretion amounts to little more than a well-known public secret.

What we (the author and a number of soccer insiders) wanted to do was to dig out those characters who have really earned the title of bad boy, mainly due to their off-pitch antics. Players who reserved their displays of madness for on the pitch were mercilessly excluded. And there was also the minor precondition of being very famous. Not a star? Not a hope of your name appearing on these pages!
It was also interesting to see if we could find some kind of common thread. Are there one or more similar reasons for the excessive behavior of these (former) professionals? Most of them have a relentless will to succeed, an enormous readiness to sacrifice everything to get all they can get from their career. They want to win, always and at all costs. However, that's not true for all of them...
Dutch sports psychologist Martin Pet claims that it is the enormous pressure that makes

top soccer players derail. 'It causes a short circuit in the head.' You can see it everywhere in society where people are under pressure to perform: the artistic world, the business world and, of course, the sports world as well. According to Pet's fellow countryman and colleague, Bram Bakker, the number of sportsmen 'experimenting' with women and gambling has increased dramatically over the past few years. 'They believe in their own 'brilliance' and have a fierce craving for attention. Soccer players don't have to train extremely hard and if they are a little out of shape then there are always ten other people on the pitch they can hide behind.'

In 2000, when I was putting the finishing touches to the biography of the famous Dutch footballing twins Frank and Ronald de Boer, I provoked the latter by stating that soccer players actually have a pretty easy life. A big grin was his first reaction. However, Ronald was very serious when he said: 'Don't forget the pressure that's on our shoulders week after week. That pressure is immense, and unimaginable for the man in the street.' Psychologist Bram Bakker: 'There are all kinds of expectations in the minds of top athletes, but their parents and coaches contribute to this, too. And when things don't work out they try to escape from that fixation, from that focus. Time, attention, money and age are an explosive combination. It can happen that an athlete is not able to take the pressure anymore and ends up handing over control of his life to whatever means or substance that can offer them an escape.'

It will come as no surprise that young millionaires are more likely to fall for the many temptations that life has to offer. They are paid millions to strut their stuff on the field, but in between they happily fuck, drink and snort whatever they can in their spare time. After their life in the spotlights, some seek compensation for the loss of attention and admiration. The black hole that this leaves behind is huge. Does this have anything to do with their background? Is there a common thread? After all, the majority of soccer players manage to walk the straight and narrow after their playing career has drawn to a close. Do the *bad boys* always come from the gutter; is winning all that counts; do they succumb under the pressure of success and feel misunderstood afterwards? In any case, once a party animal, always a party animal it seems. Fact: these kinds of soccer players have as many friends as they have enemies. Fans idolize them or dismiss them mercilessly. And it is also a fact that their behavior is often so controversial that we cannot resist reading about their trials and tribulations...

The Author

ROMÁRIO DE SOUZA FARIA

Tony Tati

Nationality: Brazilian

Born: 1966

AKA: O Baixinho (the little one) and O Gênio dagrande área (the genius of the penalty area)

Known for: not being very tall (5 feet 6 inches), innocent brown eyes and his perpetual look of fatigue

'NO DANCING, NO WHOOPIE, NO GOALS'

I t is the summer of 1994 and *O Globo*, the biggest-selling newspaper in Brazil, decides to dedicate a full page to a story about the women whose affections Romário had won up to that point in time. 25 women were featured, a small selection from the rumored total number, complete with photos and full names. The article reveals how long the soccer player – the star of the Brazil team – was 'associated' with these women (i.e. was sleeping around). Of course, his wife, Monica, also appears on the list. She has already been cheated on so many times by 'O Baixinho' that the article will come as no surprise to her.

His friend and teammate at FC Barcelona, Hristo Stoichkov, once said that Romário only cared for two things in life: scoring goals and getting laid, fact that the Brazilian child prodigy was only to glad to confirm. He even admitted to being a *womanizer*. 'I once had sex with three different women on the same day' and he claimed to have slept with over a thousand women (and that he was a member of the Mile High Club). He has even done 'it' in the famous Maracana stadium, though the seasoned playboy was unable to recall the girl's name or when it happened exactly. 'It was a golden opportunity. After the game against Corinthians I was the only one that had to stay behind for a doping test. Everybody else had left when a friend just happened to show up. There was an official fast asleep outside the dressing room door but he didn't notice a thing.'

Monica, now his ex-wife after seven years of marriage, would later expose Romário's love of excess in all its gory detail. The last straw was the moment she caught him in the act with a cabaret dancer in Barcelona. 'The more famous he became, the more women he had following him around. And in the meantime he acted like a dictator at home, a real dog. I always had to wear high heels and short skirts. I also had to wear lipstick all the time, even though I hated lipstick.'

Monica was only seventeen when she married her childhood sweetheart in a ceremony held on a soccer pitch. This was just before the extremely young couple moved camp to PSV in Eindhoven, the Netherlands (and just after his bachelor party in a strip club). An upcoming fashion model from a well-to-do family, she got to know Romário when he still was unknown and living in the Jacarezinho slum in Rio de Janeiro. He spent his days wandering the streets where, despite his chronic asthma, he would play soccer for hours on end. His father, Edevair, worked as a paint mixer in a paint factory and the family struggled to make ends meet. They lived in a shack they had constructed themselves. The daredevil Romário was regularly beaten by his father whenever he got himself into trouble. Nevertheless, every day, before going to work, his father would get up at four o'clock in the morning and wake up his son to kick a ball around the field alongside the railway track that ran next to their home.

The young Romário - who, according to his mother, weighed less than four pounds at birth and fitted perfectly into a shoebox - turns out to be an outstanding jumper and could easily have pursued a career in volleyball. Instead he signs for Rio's second biggest soccer club, Vasco da Gama. It isn't long, however, before he has earned himself a bad reputation. He regularly misses training sessions and sometimes even fails to turn up on the day of a match. Why? Because he believes that the club management doesn't have enough faith in him, and so he rebels. During matches he stands around waiting for the ball to come his way. 'Sometimes I just pretend I'm asleep,' he jokes; this stubborn teenager is also not afraid to open his mouth. Despite everything, he makes his professional debut on February 6th 1985, but remarkably enough he fails to score on that occasion.

Romário's trademark was scoring goals and he put many defenses to the sword throughout this career. After his successful appearance for Brazil at the 1988 Olympic Games, where he is the top scorer, the Dutch team PSV snap him up. The club's main sponsor, Philips, offer him a very lucrative deal but make optimum use of the generous exchange rate when doing so. On top of that, PSV are the first club ever to claim the international imaging rights for a player. Over the course of five years, the Brazilian wins three national titles and two domestic cups with PSV. He is also crowned top scorer of the premier division three times. Romário can score like no other, but at the same time he also frequently fails to deliver. PSV coach Bobby Robson tells him this to his face: 'Sometimes you play like Pelé, other times like Mickey Mouse.' The highly talented *enfant terrible* misses training sessions, fakes injuries and stays on holiday in his native country for longer than has been agreed (his reasons include homesickness, personal problems, carnival time and even a mosquito bite...). Complaints concerning Romário do not flow exclusively from the Dutch side. In Brazil, the coach of the national team, Sebastião Lazaroni, curses his fellow countryman when he pulls out of an international game yet again. *'It's a shame, players who choose their holidays over the honor of their country. They are useless, and don't deserve to be selected at all.'*

A bunch of journalists get the surprise of their lives when they see Romário illegally lining out for a friendly match for the Brazilian club Estrela. In Eindhoven they can only shrug their shoulders. They know that their star player regularly plays matches, contrary to agreement, for his 'family' team. He is lucky that the PSV manager, Kees Ploegsma, never complains. Ploegsma even defends him by saying: 'The coaches shouldn't complain. When we bought him we knew what we were getting into.'

PSV even had to form a special committee to find out why he traveled to Rio so often and for so long. Their probing didn't yield any results however. So all the club can do is focus on the behavior of the little Brazilian on the fields of *Holanda*, where he is not always flavor of the month. 'He lets people down all the time without even flinching.' Many of the PSV players are completely fed up with him. Erwin Koeman: 'It's all just me, me, me. Even his wife is treated like a slave.' And colleague Wim Kieft: 'He often said: "Give me the ball, then I'll dribble past five opponents and give it to you to score." That never happened, of course. He just scored all the goals himself.' Kieft, who frequently hung out with the Brazilian away from the club, but whom Romário also 'forgot' just as often, eventually tells Romário straight to his face that he is an 'asshole'. Another teammate and friend, Stan Valckx, calls Romário a 'super ego'.

Romário's only reaction is to shrug his shoulders. And when he is told that everyone has to play by the rules, he counters this by saying 'I'm not everyone'. He denies that he is spoiled and believes that it is ridiculous to expect the players to train the day after a game. Romário knows exactly who his critics are within the players' group. He ignores their criticisms and sneers at their 'wooden' style of playing.

The club finds it increasingly difficult to handle him. They can just about tolerate him parking his car right in front of the dressing room instead of in the car park like the rest of the team, never mind the fact that he often cheats at card games. But the club is less happy with his refusal to learn to speak Dutch, a liability that makes communicating with his teammates very problematic. He avoids the team bus and the players' quarters. He also leaves camera crews waiting for ages and then fails to turn up, and he ignores all of the bills and tax assessment forms that arrive in the post. Manager Kees Ploegsma is frequently kept waiting at the airport for nothing. The striker visits practically every nightclub in the Netherlands, where he is often found enjoying himself until three or four o'clock in the morning (though he only drinks Coca-Cola). When coach Hans Westerhof introduces a penalty system, the Brazilian immediately pulls out his wallet: 'Here coach, I'll only be in on time on Friday so.'

Whenever he is asked how he is feeling, the Brazilian invariably replies: 'Romário bit tired.' He goes out a lot but sleeps just as much, on average fourteen hours a day (usually in the company of yet another blonde). PSV even has to employ someone to get him out of bed in the morning. All the sleep must be doing him some good, however, because every time the players are asked to undergo a physical examination he turns out to be fit as a fiddle. He waves goodbye to PSV in 1993 after five seasons and 165 goals (in 167 matches). He plays for Barcelona for two years, but leaves because of a conflict with Johan Cruyff, the Barcelona coach. Cruyff was not very happy when his striker failed to turn up for pre-season training prior to the 1994/95 season as he had not given him permission to stay in Brazil. The Brazilian thought he deserved some time off after the World Cup, in which he had played so well (see further on in this chapter). Instead of returning to his club, he partied on like a rock star in Rio.

Nevertheless, Cruyff still thought Romário was the best player he had ever worked with in Spain. Once he even substituted him early because Romário was anxious to return to Brazil to celebrate carnival in Rio. Of course, Cruyff would normally never have entertained such an idea, but he told Romário that if he scored two goals in the game he could leave immediately. Within twenty minutes the striker had scored twice and was able to catch his plane. Later, Romário said of Cruyff (surprise, surprise) that he was 'by far the best coach' he had ever played under in his career.

Their love affair comes to an end after two years and Romário returns to his home

13

country to happily continue his hedonistic lifestyle. While playing for Flamengo, Romário, Savio and the highly flammable Edmundo – nicknamed 'The beast' because of the number of cards he receives and his aggressive playing style – are known to one and all as 'the Bad Boys'. They are more worried about finding booze and women than they are about playing soccer. Because, to quote Romário: 'No dancing and no whoopie means no goals.' His first match after returning to Brazil turns out to be legendary. He is paraded in front of a Maracaña stadium that is sold out for the first time in years. The camera crews and photographers trip over each other trying to catch a glimpse of him when he steps out onto the field and the fans go mad. But in the match against archrivals Fluminense, he literally doesn't take one step more than is necessary. The Brazilian newspaper *O Globo* rewards his 'efforts' the next day with a rating of 1 out of 10.

With the alarm bells going off all over the hotel, she spots her husband sprinting to the emergency exit along with his most recent conquest...

A month before the start of the 1994 World Cup his 64-year-old father is kidnapped. The criminals demand a ransom of six million dollars. In a letter to the editor printed in the national newspaper *Jornal do Brasil*, Romário begs the kidnappers to release his father. The Barcelona striker says that he understands the kidnappers' motives, but he also adds: 'I have given the Brazilian people many wonderful moments. I don't deserve to have my father kidnapped.' In the end, his father is found and freed, thanks to the efforts of over one thousand cops and the support of the drugs mafia in the slums. Later it is claimed that Romário's brother and his bodyguard staged the kidnapping in an attempt to force the Brazilian football association to pay the ransom.

A couple of days before the World Cup semi-final against Sweden, the hotel where the Brazilian squad is staying is in utter turmoil. Monica, Romário's blond childhood sweetheart has long since passed the stage of enjoying his exclusive and eternal commitment. Her husband has been going astray ever since his time at PSV; and she knows. Romário's authorized biography 'From gutter to god' provides a candid account of his extra-marital activities. But the last straw for Monica is when she is denied access to Romário's floor in the players' hotel. When the security guards stand firm on denying her access, she becomes blinded by jealousy and sets off the smoke alarm with a cigarette lighter. With the alarm bells going off all over the hotel, she spots her husband sprinting to the emergency exit along with his most recent conquest...

The day after Brazil win the World Cup, the fans in Rio de Janeiro wait until six-thirty in the morning for their heroes to arrive back home. Romário has been voted player of the tournament, and later he is even proclaimed 'Best player in the world' by the FIFA. He scores five goals at the World Cup. Again and again the cry of 'Romáriooooo!!! 'Romáriooooo!!' resounds in living rooms and bars around the country when the samba star puts the ball in the back of the net one more time. At the end of the nineties he wins the Copa América twice with his country. In the meantime, Romário continuously switches from one club to another. For instance, he joins and leaves Flamengo on three separate occasions and does the same four times at Vasco da Gama. His behavior remains incredibly egocentric during this time. He doesn't care about his teammates at all, regardless of where he plays. When playing for Valencia, his salary is apparently being paid 'under the counter', a rumor that is eventually confirmed by Francisco Roig, the club president at the time. The predictable outcome is even more trouble for Romário.

To achieve his ultimate ambition of scoring 1000 goals in professional soccer, Romário roams from continent to continent, including spells in Qatar, Australia and the United States. He ends up playing – if you could even call it that; he only ever moves when he thinks he might score – mostly in near-empty stadiums. He feels completely at home again on the beaches of Miami. Latino women, who often recognize him straight away, look on in admiration whenever they see him kicking a ball around on the beach. Romário calls it literally 'playing outside' with a twinkle in his eyes. Here the days are long, just like in Rio. In Holland, the days were always short and cold. He also indulges greedily in the Miami nightlife. 'I'm a stray cat, and the night is my friend. When I think back on earlier periods, between my 18th and 30th birthdays, also when I played with PSV, I can't remember sleeping a lot. I danced, had breakfast and trained. It didn't seem to do me any harm.'

On 20 May 2007, the longed-for moment finally arrives. Romário – who by then is 41 years old – scores his 1000th goal. In the forty-sixth minute of the match against Sport Recife, he nonchalantly dispatches a penalty kick to the back of the net. He is immediately buried under a heap of players and journalists. The game has to be stopped for sixteen minutes. In *Esporte Interative* he says that he has now achieved more than Maradona: 'Pelé is the undisputed number one in my eyes, after that comes me.' There is some dispute as to the validity of Romário's own tally. Critics allege that goals scored in underage, amateur and friendly matches have been included in the count. Moreover, his club, Vasco da Gama, apparently organized a lot of matches against inferior opponents just so that he could add to his total. It is even said that Romário paid teammates to let him play as a striker in the year he reached his target. A little-known fact is that he was caught for doping in the same year. He claimed that the banned substance finasteride came from a hair growth agent he had been using around that time. He also has to deal with a rumor that he used banned substances while at PSV. In *de Volkskrant*, a Dutch newspaper, he firmly denies this: 'The only thing that came anywhere near doping was the glasses of vodka my fellow team members at PSV drank during the half-time break at a couple of games.'

With his career as a player winding down, O Baixinho slowly but surely moves into the world of coaching and even into politics. This doesn't mean the end to all his troubles however. In 1998 he insults the coach of the national team, Zagallo, and his assistant Zico after they decide to leave him out of the squad for the World Cup finals. The official reading is that they leave Romário at home because he is carrying an injury, but in reality they fear that Romário's presence might damage the team spirit in the squad. The superstar of the previous World Cup calls Zico, who participated in three World Cup tournaments himself (without winning), a 'born loser'. But Romário doesn't leave it at that. In an act of revenge, he orders a few of his staff to paint the toilet doors of a nightclub he owns with unflattering images of the two men. In one of them, Zagallo is shown sitting on the toilet with his trousers around his ankles, while in another one Zico is shown waiting his turn, holding a roll of toilet paper in his hand.

His absence from the World Cup four years later is down to his age (36), stubbornness and unrealistic image of himself. 'I am still the best striker in Brazil,' he claims. However, he had recently refused to play a match against Colombia, making the coach of the national team, Scolari, very angry and unwilling to select him anymore. In response to the question as to whether he will watch the World Cup on television, he replies: 'They start at six in the morning, right? Perfect, that's usually the time I get home.'

As manager of the club América he fires his coach and good friend Bebeto, the player with whom he formed the highly successful striking partnership at the World Cup back in 1994. And according to Romário, the great Pelé is now a museum piece and mentally ill. Pelé is not amused and makes this unmistakably clear by saying: 'I'm a Catholic and I believe that God always forgives the ignorant, so I forgive the ignorant.' Romário counters: 'He is a poet when he doesn't speak. He always talks nonsense. I don't believe he is as Catholic as he claims. If he would have been, he would have recognized his daughter by attending her funeral.'

As for his decision to get into politics... the move is a strange one to say the least. He becomes a member of the city council in Rio for the socialist party (PSB) and even wants to become mayor, though the latter ambition is thwarted. Later on he becomes a federal representative for the party. Rumor has it that he only does this so that he can get out of debt. He has been dodging the tax authorities form some time now. But unfortunately for him, the judge doesn't buy his story and orders him to pay a fine of 550,000 dollars. He is forced to sell his apartment in Rio. 'Everybody thinks I'm a crook, but I'm not. I pay four alimonies and that's not easy,' the ex-player objects. Romário, who in the meantime has fathered six children with four different mothers, even ends up spending a night in jail when he refuses to pay the alimony owed to his ex-wife Monica. He is furious: 'I have to pay 22,000 dollars a month, even though I think 15,000 would be more than enough.' A short time later he is sentenced to three and a half years in prison for tax evasion. In the end he gets away with doing two and a half years of community service.

In closing, before the 2014 World Cup, which is being held in Brazil, Romário is frequently at loggerheads with the powers that be at FIFA and their 'puppets' in the organizing committee, his fellow countrymen Ronaldo and Pelé. According to him, the public doesn't have the faintest idea how much money their country is wasting on the World Cup. In relation to Ronaldo he says: 'He publicly promised free entrance for handicapped people. And so far, nothing.' When Ricardo Teixeira, the infamous president of the Brazilian football association, flees the country because of an enormous corruption scandal, Romário says he is happy to be rid of this 'cancerous tumor'. He calls for demonstrations, says the amount of money that has been wasted is 'a crying shame' and states that 'it has been enough with all the theft and humiliation. They only come to build up their stuff, take their profit and disappear just as quick. FIFA doesn't even pay taxes. They ought to be prosecuted.' He calls the president of FIFA, Sepp Blatter, a 'son of a bitch' and secretary-general Jerome Valcke an 'extortionist'. Romário: 'They are corrupt, are guilty of blackmailing. The tickets are almost two times as expensive as at the World Cup before this one in South Africa. Let me guess where the money went... We can't expect anything from the FIFA. The country of Brazil will be the big loser after the World Cup.'

One thing Romário never has to worry about is a lack of beautiful women. Nightclubs were often closed off to the public whenever he showed up. Once, after he had been selected for the national youth team for the first time, he had the nerve to urinate over the balcony of his hotel. And as a lauded member of the Divine Canaries he regularly visited prostitutes before a game or had sex in the toilet of whatever airplane they were flying in. In Eindhoven, Romário even had a room permanently booked in the Holiday Inn so that he would always have a place to retreat to with a girl in privacy. He was as stubborn a character as they come. And these days? He hasn't changed a bit: he continues to strut his stuff on the beaches of Rio, has gotten married for the fourth time and is still 'enjoying life to the fullest', as he says himself.

LOTHAR MATTHÄUS

Tony Tati

Nationality: German

Born: 1961

AKA: Screwing Machine, Judas, Mister Schwalbe, Der Lothar, Der Loddar and Der Grosse (the big one)

Known for: big mouth, square head and self-righteousness.

'I'M DEFINITELY NOT PROUD TO BE GERMAN'

Not many players have been vilified as much as Lothar Matthäus. In his heydays he was loathed all over Europe for screwing other players over. His teammates, opponents, club officials, women and whole nations even hated the German, notwithstanding the fact that he broke many records as a defensive midfielder. So how did it all come to this?

Matthäus calls himself a son of Puma in his biography *Ganz oder gar nicht* ('All or nothing'). He grows up in Herzogenaurach where the factories of Adidas and its rival Puma are only a stone's throw from each other. The young Matthäus lives right next to the Puma factory, together with his deeply religious parents and his brother. His father works as a janitor in the Puma factory, where his mother sows football boots and balls every day from five in the morning. They never go on vacation, as they are constantly paying off debts. 'I came from a real working class family. My parents were always working. They never got anything for free. That's what they taught me as well.' Matthäus is a small boy. Later on he will say: 'By fighting, opening my mouth and training hard I have become what I am now. I'm proud of that. I deserve to be a little self-righteous. After all I've earned it.'

Puma is the main sponsor of the soccer club Borussia Mönchengladbach, and the Matthäus family naturally supports them instead of the much bigger Bayern Munich, which is sponsored by Adidas. Lothar Matthäus starts playing soccer at FC Herzogenaurach (also sponsored by Puma) at the age of nine. He plays as a striker and scores over one hundred goals for the club each season, year after year. But his lack of height is a disadvantage. At regional selection matches he isn't picked out as a player with potential. Even though he is a pretty good student, he leaves school at the age of fourteen. He is more interested in cigarettes, girls, and soccer, in particular. He earns his living as a painter and decorator until he eventually joins the professional ranks at his beloved Mönchengladbach,.

Matthäus is 23 when he plays in the German cup final (the DFB-Pokal) against Bayern Munich. It is his last game for the club, as he is set to join Bayern the following season. The game comes down to a penalty shoot-out and he is the only player who fails to score. Many of the faithful Borrusia supporters believe that he did this on purpose. Matthäus denies this, of course, but in the years that follow he will be subjected to constant verbal abuse from the Borrusia fans and called a Judas.

At Bayern, Matthäus wins trophy after trophy. He has already booked his summer holiday when he hears that he has been called up for the German national squad, *die Mannschaft*, for the 1980 European Championships. He makes his international debut in the group match against the Netherlands. He gives away a penalty which the Netherlands score to get themselves back into the game. However, the Germans run out 3-2 winners in the end. Twenty years later he plays his final game for the national team – in the Kuip stadium in Rotterdam – having chalked up 150 international caps, a record at the time that he shared with the Mexican Carbajal. Later he will say in *Bild* magazine: 'I would have preferred to have broken the record in a home match. Or in Italy where I played for six years (for Inter Milan). Or even in Croatia, where I'm hugely popular. But not in the Netherlands because that's where all my biggest enemies are.' He could even have added to his impressive total of international caps were it not for the fact that he missed the European Championships of 1992 because of injury. And after a bust-up with the coach of the national team Berti Vogts and the captain Jürgen Klinsmann at the 1994 World Cup, the defensive midfielder wasn't called up to the squad for quite a long time.

Trouble: a word that is as synonymous with Matthäus as grass is with a cow. This self-assured, arrogant, theatrical soccer player has more enemies than the President of the United States has Facebook followers. He turns provocation into an art form, both on and off the field. In his own words: 'I let my heart speak (too) often, when I would have been better off using my brains.' In his columns for the tabloid *Bild* he lashes out regularly and scores cheap points by writing provocative stories and anecdotes aimed specifically at certain people in the footballing world. 'It all went to my head a bit after winning the European Championships in 1980,' he will later admit. 'Honesty was often my downfall,' before adding 'but you should remember that every top athlete or soccer player has a direct line to some journalist or other.' In the meantime, the average German has long stopped taking him seriously and he has become the butt of their jokes - 'there goes Lothar again...' - and his fellow national team members are increasingly exasperated at his tendency to mock even them. 'Even when we were discussing something as simple as meal times, he would insist on upsetting the apple cart,' according to Erich Ribbeck, who was assistant coach of *die Mannschaft* at the time. His international teammate Rudi Völler advises him to reserve his opinions for the toilet bowl, and Uli Hoeness starts calling him 'our new press officer'. At the 1994 World Cup the pot finally boils over when Matthäus is found to have leaked the details of dressing room conversations to the newspaper *Bild*. The coach of the national team, Berti Vogts, who even has Matthäus's phone bill checked, is furious and it proves an absolute blessing when their 'press officer' suffers a bad injury during the tournament.

Even at the start of his period with Borussia Mönchengladbach, he regularly clashes with coach Jupp Heynckes. Matthäus is far too fond of the nightlife, often gets completely wasted after a game (and sometimes before) and even manages to demolish his brand new Mercedes 190 while drunk - the car is a total write-off, he gets to spend a night in the hospital, is handed a fine of eleven thousand dollars and loses his drivers license for eight months. At FC Hollywood, i.e. Bayern Munich, Matthäus often feels he is being treated 'like a six-year-old child' because of its strict regime. He is allowed to continue wearing his favorite Puma boots in the beginning, however, even though Bayern use the Adidas kit. He has a series of quarrels with Søren Lerby, and he and Stefan Effenberg – who is no angel himself – are sworn enemies. The latter calls him a turncoat with a big mouth. For example, he says that Matthäus was afraid to take the penalty kick in the 1990 World Cup final even though he was the team's nominated penalty taker. Matthäus claimed to have torn his shoe. Effenberg: 'Nonsense. He just didn't have the balls.' Luckily (for Matthäus and his country) Andreas Brehme scores from the penalty spot and the Germans beat Argentina 1-0. Nine years later, Effenberg is raging mad at his colleague once again. In the magazine *Der Spiegel* he accuses Matthäus of cowardice during the Champions League final against Manchester United in 1999. 'Who would allow himself to be substituted ten minutes before the end of the game with your team defending a 1-0 lead? I would only have done that if I had a broken leg.' And we all remember the dramatic end to that game, with Bayern losing 2-1.

Despite his cowardly behavior, the World Cup final of 1990 is the highlight of Matthäus' career. Whereas the 1982 World Cup was all women and booze (Matthäus: 'We had models coming into the hotel room all the time but the last thing we were interested in was their clothes'), there is a much more disciplined atmosphere in Italy in 1990. As team captain he leads Germany to the world title at the expense of an Argentinian team featuring Maradona. He is voted world footballer of the Year and even the best sportsman in the world in 1990. In his biography, Maradona calls Matthäus 'the most difficult opponent' he has ever come up against. Matthäus for his part has the temerity to have a pop at Helmut Kohl, the German Chancellor: 'He has never once shown his face at any of our games but still thinks he has to the right to walk into our dressing room after we have won the World Cup. He should be ashamed of himself.'

Matthäus comes in for particular criticism from the Dutch, especially when the European Championships of 1988 are the topic of discussion. The tournament is being played in *die Heimat*. Tensions are high, especially in the Netherlands where people still haven't entirely forgotten the Second World War. The Germans, and Matthäus in particular, make the front pages of the Dutch newspapers when it turns out that the team visited a brothel during run-up to the finals. At the end of the night in question they are presented with a bill amounting to a couple of thousand Deutschmarks, but none of the players has the cash to pay it, at which point Matthäus produces his credit card... When word of the incident reaches the ears of head coach Franz Beckenbauer, he is furious. Matthäus – whom Beckenbauer has always considered to be something of a loose cannon – is singled out: 'You always seem to be around when this kind of thing goes on!', Beckenbauer complains. In his biography, Matthäus laughs it all off: 'It wasn't the fact that we visited a brothel that made him so angry, but rather that we went there wearing our official World Cup suits...'

At the European Championships, Germany and the Netherlands meet each other in the semi-final. Matthäus knows only too well what to expect. 'I remember a previous match in Rotterdam where their fans compared me to Hitler on one of their banners. And on another occasion we were woken up in the middle of the night by a bomb scare.' When the two teams are out on the pitch warming up, the entire stadium is a sea of orange. Matthäus: 'We thought: *Mensch*, this is like a bloody away match!' The team captain wins a penalty and opens the scoring: 1-0. This time he isn't afraid to take it. However, the Dutch go on to win 2-1 thanks to a late goal by Marco van Basten. Matthäus is less than impressed when Ronald Koeman pretends to wipe his arse with the shirt he has swapped with the German player Olaf Thon. 'I had never seen anything like it. Scandalous! An insult!' He also has a few words to say about Jan Wouters, his

23

direct opponent in the semi-final: 'A very mean player. Usually he went for your legs before going for the ball.' And on the Dutch keeper, Hans van Breukelen: 'He spent the entire match shouting at us about the war...'

But, as mentioned already, Matthäus is no goody-two shoes himself. In the Netherlands, *Der Lothar* receives the dubious honor of being the most hated player in soccer. This is largely because of his *schwalbes* (diving to win a penalty) and his ability to get other players booked. His *schwalbes*, when he would act like he had just been mercilessly hacked down by an opponent, made him world famous (or more appropriately: world infamous). Despite his bad image, or more likely because of it, he constantly tried to improve his standing among Dutch soccer fans. 'I never go out to deliberately provoke, but I do intimidate, it's nothing but pure survival instinct,' Matthäus once said in the *NRC*, a Dutch newspaper. 'I don't have anything against Dutchmen, so why are they so against me?' Fact: at the 1986 World Cup he was responsible for getting Frank Arnesen, the Danish defender who was a PSV player at the time, sent off thanks to yet another infamous *schwalbe*. It immediately spelled the end of the tournament for Arnesen. And during a Bayern-PSV game the Dutch international Mark van Bommel also quickly became acquainted with the German's antics. After an innocent push, Matthäus falls to the ground like a dying swan. Van Bommel has to leave the field. Later the PSV player later had this to say about the incident in a Dutch TV show: 'I spoke about it with Matthäus afterwards. He said: "That was a really easy red card all right. All I had to do was fall over."' When the return game is played in Eindhoven, Matthäus is unsurprisingly the target of the fans' hate and aggression. Every time the German touches the ball he is jeered by the crowd, and they spend the entire game hurling oranges and cigarette lighters in his direction.

'Matthäus personifies everything that the Dutch hate in Germans,' is the conclusion of the average Dutch soccer fan. 'Arrogant' is the word that is heard most often when he is the topic of discussion. Take for example Matthäus' reaction during the Oktoberfest in 1993 in Munich when he spots a Dutchman filming him and isn't one bit happy about it: 'Adolf forgot to deal with you,' he snaps at the amateur cineast. He forgets, however, that the camera is still rolling and it doesn't take long before half the world knows what he has said. Matthäus has put his foot in it again. And when his remarks aren't racist they are usually sexist. For instance, at an airport in Germany he jokingly shouts at a female basketball team passing by that 'our black boy (meaning his fellow team member Adolfo Valencia) has a really big one'...

After winning many honors, Matthäus finishes his career in the United States. Even though he had always been taken serious as a player, as a human being that had never been the case. And this move is no different: his reason for crossing the ocean, in the opinion of many, has less to do with the standard of soccer in the USA than it has with the amount of cash on offer. But Matthäus insists that it is because his girlfriend wants to enroll in a theater school in New York... his move to the *Big Apple* is typical Lothar. At the press conference he says in his best English 'I hope, we have a little bit lucky' at which remark the assembled journalists can barely stifle their laughter. It turns out to be a disappointing adventure in which he get to play only sixteen times for the Metro Stars. It's a taste of what is to come in his future as a coach. His first job is in Austria at Rapid Wien, with the team lying in sixth place when he takes over. They end the season in eighth place, only two places above the relegation zone, the Austrian *Recordmeister's* worst finish ever in the league. The fans demand his head on a plate. Immediately after the last game of the season Rapid Wien decide to fire the German. He didn't even last a year in Vienna. Matthäus, who was to be found more often in the gossip columns than in the sports section in Austrian newspapers because of his endless list of scandals, has this to say: 'In the past I've always maintained that Bayern was one big snake pit, but at Rapid it was even worse.' The Rapid keeper Ladislav Maier: 'He has no cause for complaint. Matthäus was just too stubborn and his training sessions were unbelievably boring.'

What followed wasn't exactly successful either. At Partizan Belgrado, Matthäus suddenly ups and leaves to assume the position of head coach of the Bulgarian national team. He fails to lead them to the 2006 World Cup however. At the Brazilian club Paranaense, he is suspended for a month after giving a referee the finger. Again – after only five weeks in the job – he resigns, this time without winning a single game. He flies back to Europe after giving some lame excuse or other, leaving a telephone bill of almost six thousand dollars behind him...

And so he stumbles from one fiasco to the next. His burning desire is to coach a German club, but the awful truth is that there isn't a single team in the country that wants Matthäus as their coach. Whenever rumors spread that their club is being linked to him, supporters, such as those at Eintracht Frankfurt and 1. FC Nürnberg, are quick to raise their voices as one in objection. The fallen star, who doesn't even want to live in his country of birth anymore, complains in *Bild* about the lack of interest: 'I don't understand what they've got against me in Germany.' A strong link to Bayern and the fact that he frequently makes negative statements in the tabloid *Bild* seem to scare away the Bundesliga clubs. For example, at one point HSV chooses the Dutch coach Bert van Marwijk over him. Later, when Van Marwijk is fired, Matthäus is quick to comment: 'Without him and Van der Vaart the club finally started playing as a team again.' He even calls the latter 'a blemish on the reputation of HSV.' However, this doesn't prevent the powers-that-be in Germany from ignoring him when the job of head coach of the national team becomes available in 2004 and again in 2008. The German association even decides to appoint his arch-enemy, Jürgen Klinsmann. His 'own' club, Bayern, has shut the door in his face, too. After criticizing the team in *Bild*, manager Uli Hoeness says 'he wouldn't even be allowed to mow the grass in the stadium.' Highly offended, the former player reacts by sending the $30,000 gold watch he had been given when he left back to the club. Matthäus: 'Hoeness hasn't had a clue about soccer for the past twenty years.' Happy days in Munich...

'We had models coming into the hotel room all the time but the last thing we were interested in was their clothes'

When it comes to women, however, Lothar Matthäus, the most capped international player of all time, has a very successful track record. Though, on second thoughts, 'turbulent' might be a better word to describe that record. He is linked to one model after the other in his 'love career' and he enters the bond of marriage no less than five times. After having cheated on his childhood sweetheart Silvia, next up is the former Miss Switzerland, Lolita, with whom he moves into the house Dennis Bergkamp used to live in, in Civite (Italy). This marriage, which soon ends up on the rocks, is even the subject of a documentary that puts him back into the national spotlight as the subject of national ridicule in Germany again. After

Lolita he proceeds to put a ring on the respective fingers of Marijana, Anastasia and Liliana. He calls Anastasia his personal Mona Lisa in his biography. 'We are having a wonderful time together and have many things in common. I've finally found a woman who doesn't just like shopping, but who is interested in culture and even soccer as well. I haven't felt this happy in a long time.'

The 21-year-old Ukrainian model Kristina Liliana Chudinova is the successor to 'Mona Lisa'. Matthäus is 47 when they marry in Las Vegas. They met during the *Oktoberfest*, the German beer festival. And no, he wasn't drunk at the time. With the German nation still recovering from the sex scandal surrounding Franck Ribéry – the Bayern player who was accused of having sex with an underage prostitute – Liliana causes quite a stir when she is photographed half naked on a yacht with another man. *Was ist los mit unserem WM-stars?* ('What's wrong with our World Cup heroes?') asks one of the headlines in a German newspaper at the time. Matthäus is distraught and subsequently refuses to pay for Liliana's breast reduction and liposuction procedures. The scandal – which is well documented in his favorite newspaper *Bild* – costs him the job as coach of the national team of Cameroon. When the wife of the president hears about what has happened, she advises her husband to remove him from the list of possible candidates. He even gets embroiled in a court case with his ex-wife. Matthäus' divorce from Liliana was apparently not legally binding. The public prosecutor threatens to put him in prison for forgery. To top it all off, he is declared dead after a court sends him alimony papers and he fails to reply. Matthäus is furious, of course, but his fellow countrymen, and Dutch soccer fans, in particular can't stop laughing their heads off...

EDGAR DAVIDS

Wraf Wrraf
edGrrr wraff Wraf
Waff Wraf

Tony Tati

Nationality: Surinamese

Born: 1973

AKA: Piranha, Pitbull, Il Mastino (the dog), Edje Kadetje (little bread roll) and Tubarão (the shark)

Known for: rude behavior, wandering hands, dark glasses and dreadlocks

'I WEAR MY HEART ON MY SLEEVE, ALWAYS'

Davids was always widely recognized as being a very driven professional. By contrast, his behavior off the field left an awful lot to be desired. Edgar Davids gradually came to be seen as a bit of a thug afflicted with wandering hands. But he didn't seem to mind at all. He has a thick skin, stays out of the limelight and prefers to live his life behind a pair of dark sunglasses.

The Dutch TV program maker Harry Vermeegen once took a walk with Davids, who was a young and upcoming talent at Ajax at the time. Vermeegen's casual approach did the trick; the burgeoning soccer talent was very happy and willing to chat. That all seems like such a long time ago now, and it is absolutely unthinkable that such an opportunity will ever present itself again. From the time of his international breakthrough at the end of the nineties on, Davids considers pretty much everyone and everything to be 'the enemy'. He avoids journalists like the plague, and the rare times that he is available for interviews he either arrives late or keeps it all frustratingly brief. His general behavior can be summed up as extremely rude. He rarely looks anyone straight in the eye and his answers to questions are short and blunt. In 1995, after undergoing eye surgery, he takes to wearing dark glasses designed especially for athletes. This provides him with a tough image that turns out to be very attractive when it comes to sponsorship deals and thus a handy source of extra income. He once said: 'I like sportsmen with a dangerous look. Mike Tyson is my favorite. That body, that look...' Dennis Rodman, the eccentric troublemaker and bad boy of American basketball, is also one of his big heroes. More on that later.

So what is the reason behind Davids' uncouth behavior? Maybe he has just always felt misunderstood everywhere he goes. According to his nephew, Harvey Esajas, who also played with him in the Ajax junior team, his unwillingness to open up is partly down to his past. 'From the very start of his career Edgar was typified as a little brat and a bragger. Things were said and written about him without anyone ever having asked him anything. That's the end of it then for him. If journalists know everything already, he figures, why bother talking to them at all?' And: 'Ed has always been reluctant to talk, he didn't talk much either when he was young. That's just the way he is.'

Born in Paramaribo in 1973, Edgar Davids moves to the Netherlands when he is only two years old. His father is a welder and his mother cleans airplanes at Amsterdam Schiphol Airport. He has one brother. From an early age he is a fierce, rebellious little guy who doesn't like taking orders. During his time as a junior at the Schellingwoude soccer club, he manages to get himself suspended for a month. At soccer camp, the skinny Edje Kadetje (little bread roll) throws a whole plate of food over the head of another player after getting into an argument. He then runs away into the forest and the others have to spend the whole night looking for him. It is on the street, in the squares of Amsterdam, that he develops his winner's mentality. The small youngster has to slug it out with the bigger boys and he learns to defend himself in the process. His favorite game is *broko bana*, Surinamese for 'anything goes'. When he plays this game he goes wild, chasing the ball and the opponent like a madman. His youth coach once said: 'When Edgar was a junior I could already see that he had no problem kicking the hell out his opponent while laughing in his face at the same time.'

In 1992, after nine years at the amateur club Schellingwoude, he joins Ajax. At the famous talent scouting days organized by Ajax he has already been turned down two times, but at the age of thirteen he finally gets the call he's been waiting for. However, he is quickly dropped to Ajax's A2 team after the coach of the A1 team brands him unmanageable. 'He had a big mouth and never listened to us.' The young Davids is also very prone to receiving red cards, mainly because he can't hold his temper. An official at the club takes him to AC Milan and Juventus to show him how wonderful the life of a professional player can be, as long as he can behave in a professional manner. 'He was a real rascal,' according to youth coach Dick de Groot. 'I was forever trying to put manners on him. He argued about everything, never did what he was told and always wanted to know why, why, why.'

A little known story concerns an incident that tales place one evening when he is watching his teammates take on the FC Utrecht A1 team. Davids has his arm in a cast and is unable to play. When he hears one of the Utrecht fans shout 'take the Moluccan out of it!' in reference to the Ajax player Innacio Tuhuteru, Davids (of Moluccan extract himself) loses it. The fists start to fly and he clobbers the fan with the cast on his arm. The police have to be called and Ajax briefly consider throwing him out of the club.

But the boy has talent, that's for sure. He is only eighteen years old when he makes his debut for the first team. He even scores on his debut, something only the big names ever do at Ajax. When Leo Beenhakker is replaced by Louis van Gaal as head coach he becomes a regular in the team. But he remains difficult to manage. As a result he has to sign up for a physically draining irritation management training program. Assistant coach Bobby Haarms, nicknamed 'The kind executioner', makes him run around in the sand dunes wearing an armored vest for extra weight. Davids is furious, doesn't see the point of it at all, but puts his head down and keeps on running. He also does a few boxing sessions to boost his strength. He ends up playing for Ajax for five seasons. In 1992 he wins the UEFA Cup with the club and in 1995 the Champions League and the World Cup for club teams. His success takes him to AC Milan and from there to Juventus, Barcelona, Inter Milan and Tottenham Hotspur. This is what he has always wanted, a career as a top soccer player, because there is nothing he loves more. It is rumored that he has a ball in every room in his house and that he even plays keep-up when he is brushing his teeth...

Things start to go wrong in 2001. On March 4, after the match between Juventus and Udinese, a player is held on suspicion of doping. For a moment, confusion reigns: is Davids the player that has been caught, or is it his teammate Filippo Inzaghi? It isn't long, however, before the anti-doping commission of the Italian Olympic Committee confirms that it is the Dutchman who has tested positive for the use of the prohibited substance nandrolon. The Italian and international media can't get enough of it. Davids denies the accusation: 'I'm innocent. Really. I've actually had trouble with the club management before because I refused to take aspirin or get a flu injection.' Nevertheless, further tests also show up traces of the prohibited substance. Davids is faced with a suspension of two years and a fine of 14,000 dollars. He continues to protest his innocence and he feels that his reputation is being sullied. The traces of the substance in his blood are barely above the accepted norm of two nanograms per milliliter. He also believes that the substance must have been in the eye drops that he takes for his eye condition. And for those drops he had already received an exemption from the anti-doping committee.

In the meantime, however, the club doctor at Juventus states in the Italian sports newspaper *Corriere dello Sport* that Davids hasn't been using the eye drops for some time... Luciano Moggi, the chairman of Juventus, insinuates that the doping may have been administered in the Netherlands because Davids was there for a week at the end of February to play an international match against Turkey. The Dutch football association, the KNVB, vehemently denies the allegations. Later, the FIFA president Sepp Blatter angers Davids by declaring in a TV interview that there may be more to Davids' case than the high nandrolon values alone. Davids demands an apology and even initiates judicial proceedings against Blatter. While all this is going on, experts, including the sport scientist Harm Kuipers, express their doubts as to whether taking nandrolon has any performance-enhancing effect at all: 'It can even make a player heavier and thus slower.'

So how does it all pan out in the end? The Italian football association initially suspends Davids for a period of eight months, but the sentence becomes shorter the longer the story drags on. After Davids' appeal, his punishment is a four-month suspension plus a fine of 60,000 dollars. As a result he misses the Netherlands' crucial World Cup qualifier against the Republic of Ireland. The Dutch, coached by Louis van Gaal, lose the game 1-0 and fail to reach the World Cup finals of 2002.

In his first game after returning from suspension, a Champions League match against the Scottish club Celtic, Davids manages to get himself sent off. And a few days later, in an Italian league game against Lecce, he punches an opponent full in the face. He is suspended on the basis of television images. In early 2002 he is once again the center of attention. An ex-girlfriend – the 23-year-old model Sarah H., mother of their two-year-old child – goes to the police claiming Davids has serious assaulted and threatened her and that this has happened on more than one occasion. Her injuries were sometimes so serious that she couldn't go to work for weeks on end. The assaults were said to have become more frequent after the nandrolon scandal broke. According to Sarah's own account, Davids had once kicked her extremely hard in the face and, on another occasion, he had choked her so hard that she thought he was going to kill her. Davids had ripped the clothes from her body and said: 'No one leaves me, you fucking whore! I will kill you if you warn the police and I will take your son away from you.' The public prosecutor in the Netherlands and the justice department in Italy begin separate judicial inquiries. Half of the eight assaults were alleged to have occurred on Italian soil. However, due to a lack of evidence the case is eventually thrown out.

The 'Pitbull' is alleged to have pushed one of the two women in the back and punched her in the face.

That doesn't mark the end of Davids' run-ins with the fairer sex, however. In 2009 he divorces his wife Gladys Celosse. When she refuses to pay back a loan – which she used to open a spa – Davids takes her to court. Worse still is his assault on a female visitor to the Tuschinski cinema in Amsterdam. A fierce row develops between Davids and two women over reserved seats.

The 'Pitbull' is alleged to have pushed one of the two women in the back and punched her in the face. The whole incident is recorded by the security cameras in the cinema. The police confirm that they are investigating reports of an incident in the Tuschinski cinema, but decline to say anything about the identity of those involved. Davids himself files a report for assault on the same day. He denies hitting the woman, though he does admit to pushing her, according to his lawyer. He claims that the woman punched him after he had shoved her. His fiancée Olcay Gulsen, who was a witness, backs up his story. 'He is a good man (even though she will later say he cheated on her). How that woman got a black eye is a complete mystery to me.' Numerous sources confirm to the Amsterdam TV station AT5 that Davids was the one throwing the punches. After the incident Davids runs out of the cinema. And according to the Tuschinski, a number of its employees were so upset by what they had witnessed that they were unable to carry out their work.

Davids is often in trouble on the field of play as well. In August 2002, while playing for Juventus, he is suspended for two games after getting into a fight with the AC Milan defender Cosmin Contra during a friendly match. Several security guards are required to prize the two apart. When word leaks that Davids was involved in a fight with Mark van Bommel after the international game against Austria (in October 2002), the coach of the national team, Dick Advocaat, denies the rumor: 'It was only an argument. Just a case of one of them raising his voice a little bit more than the other.' Apparently, it all started when the PSV player criticized Davids after the game. He had tried to take on the role of 'holding player' once again, while that was supposed to be Van Bommel's job. Davids was said to have lost it completely after Van Bommel's comments.

During his holiday in Rio de Janeiro in 2005, the Dutchman gets himself into another fight. This time, during a friendly game, he punches his opponent in the ear and spits in his face. It was reported that Davids and his teammates confiscated the cameras of a TV channel that happened to be on the scene, only giving them back after being promised that the images would not be broadcast. And to stay in the Brazilian mood, at an Ajax training session in 2007 Davids gets into an argument with his teammate Leonardo and goes for the Brazilian's throat when he objects to a remark made by Davids. A couple of other players have to intervene to keep the two of them from killing each other. The coach, Adrie Koster, makes light of the incident: 'It's a good thing when the whole group is kept on their toes by something like this.' While playing for the English club Crystal Palace in 2010, Davids loses it once more when his teammate Julian Bennett criticizes him during a training session. Davids grabs him and screams: 'I'm the boss around here!' Again the rest of the team has to jump in to separate them. In similar fashion he tears the golden chain Lorenzo Staelens is wearing from his neck, but he gets away with it without further repercussions. That happened one year after Patrick Kluivert had received an undeserved red card at the World Cup because of the Belgian's antics.

All of the above involved 'only' his fellow players. He has also had major clashes with various coaches, the most infamous being that with Guus Hiddink, the coach of the Dutch team at the 1996 European Championships in England. Hiddink even has to send the player home after Davids insults him during a press conference: 'The coach has to quit putting his head up some of the players' asses,' are the words that are soon broadcast all over the world. 'He might be able to see a bit better when he does.' He seems to have taken the words right out of the mouth of his idol and super *bad boy* Dennis Rodman, though Davids later denies any such thing. The same night, the player is put on a plane to Amsterdam. He tells the press that though he may have been a bit emotional at the time, he refuses to withdraw one word of what he said. According to Hiddink, Davids was unable to accept not being in the starting line-up for the second group match against Switzerland. That much is true. He lost his place to Danny Blind, who had been suspended for the opening match. When Clarence Seedorf is substituted during the game against the Swiss and takes his place on the bench next to Davids, 'The pitbull' loses it. 'He wanted to punch Hiddink and said all kinds of things that were really inappropriate', Ronald de Boer would say years later in the Dutch TV program *Andere Tijden Sport*. Davids believes that De Boer and Blind influenced the coach when he was picking his team. Davids mistrusts Hiddink, as do his fellow team members Seedorf, Michael Reiziger, Winston Bogarde and Patrick Kluivert. They come out in support of Davids. The term 'De Kabel' (The Cable) begins to circulate in the Netherlands – a reference to the belief among the dark-skinned (Surinamese) guys at Ajax that they are less valued by their club, especially in terms of their salaries when compared to what their white team members earn.

Davids adopts a policy of self-censorship for two years after the incident at the European Championships. He believes he has been treated badly by the press and calls the journalists at the newspaper *De Telegraaf* 'assholes'. At Juventus, for whom he signs in December 1997, he develops into a genuine star on the world stage. The dispute with Hiddink, who is still coach of the national team, is resolved at two subsequent reconciliation meetings. Davids: 'I said to him: "Beautiful words are not always true and true words are not always beautiful." Guus apparently thought it was a good line because he wrote it down.' Hiddink also managed to come up wit a nice one-liner as well: 'Whatever happened, happened.' And: 'I'm a fan of Edgar. He has more passion in his little toe than some other international players have in their two legs.' Davids is told that he has to sign an agreement with eight rules of conduct he must follow if he wants to play for the Dutch team again. A year later, Dutch soccer fans find themselves scratching their collective heads as they watch Hiddink and the 'reformed' Davids hug each other in delight after the match against Yugoslavia at the World Cup finals in 1998. This is after Davids buries a long-range shot in the back of the net that ensures the team's progress to the quarter finals. After the World Cup Davids had this to say: 'Everyone left their egos at the door of the dressing room, bringing only their pride and desire to be the best onto the pitch with them.'

He also has a bust-up with Marco van Basten... Thanks to his outstanding performances at the World Cup in France, the Dutch public has embraced Davids wholeheartedly once again. In the fall of 1998 Hiddink's successor Frank Rijkaard even names him vice-captain of the Dutch team. He plays for the Netherlands at the

European Championships of 2000 and 2004. When Van Basten is appointed as coach of the national team he even makes him team captain. In the meantime, however, Davids gets left on the sidelines after his transfer to Inter Milan. He rarely gets to play. Sometimes the coach, Roberto Mancini, doesn't even grant him a spot on the subs bench. As a result, Davids is dropped from the Dutch squad. A year later, and still furious, he moves to Tottenham Hotspur. But to no avail. Van Basten doesn't select him for the World Cup finals in 2006.

Van Basten leaves it until the closing press conference of the 2006 World Cup to explain why he didn't call Davids up to the squad and won't be selecting him anymore in the future. 'I don't select Jan Wouters anymore, do I?' by which he insinuates that Davids (33) is too old. Davids reacts furiously: 'I think that Van Basten has crossed a line in terms of decency and respect,' the midfielder says in an open letter to the Dutch weekly magazine *Voetbal International*. 'With his remarks he has shown a huge lack of personal class. Especially because this doesn't seem to be an isolated incident. In the past he has spoken condescendingly about other players with a successful international career.' Davids also reveals that he has serious doubts about Van Basten's ability as a coach. 'The choices he made seem to be based largely on romanticism and idealism. How can the supporters and the media of a country that is third in the FIFA rankings accept this? You take part in the finals of the World Cup with only one aim in mind, and that is to become world champions. The World Cup should never be used as a kind of glorified training camp under the pretext of a so-called learning process because the team will be expected to perform well at the European Championships two years later. In answer to the question as to whether my qualities as a player were badly missing in the squad right now, Van Basten replied that I hadn't had such a good season (at Tottenham Hotspur), after which he tried to make light of the situation in a rather cheap way, and at my expense.'

In 2011 Ajax announce that Davids is to be appointed to the club's new board of directors. 'Surprised? Of course,' he says. 'You could compare it to having Patrick Kluivert on the management board of the Dutch Road Safety Commission (a reference to Kluivert's infamous car crash). Why they asked me? Johan (Cruyff) proposed me,' says Davids. And he doesn't foresee any problems? Davids shakes his head. Not much later all hell breaks loose. Cruyff is furious at Davids. The head of the youth academy, Wim Jonk, has had to ban trainee coach Davids from De Toekomst, the club's training center, because of 'indecent and unacceptable' behavior. The former midfielder also wanted, together with the other members of the board, to make Cruyff's long-time rival, Louis van Gaal, managing director of the club. Cruyff accuses the former midfielder, of being the first to approach his former coach, Van Gaal, with the offer of a return to Ajax. Davids denies this and even goes a little further. According to the ex-international, racism has raised its ugly head in the board of directors on more than one occasion. 'It's like being in a movie sometimes, one in which some people (meaning Johan Cruyff) are forever crossing the line.' This is a reaction to comments that Cruyff made in which he insinuated that Davids was only appointed to the board 'because of the color of his skin'. In the end the board of directors has to resign en masse.

Davids ends his career in style... Back in 1995 Guus Hiddink had to take Davids out of the Dutch squad before a friendly match after the player had received his umpteenth red card during an Ajax game. And now, in the autumn of his career, he is still as petulant as ever. In 2008, for example, while playing for Ajax against PSV, he commits two really nasty fouls, leaving the referee with no option but to send him off. In the Champions League he collects the most red cards ever handed out to a player in a single season. While wearing the Juventus shirt he has to leave the field four times. It is almost as if Davids needs to make enemies to get the best out of himself on the field. Gianluigi Buffon, a teammate at 'Juve': 'Davids flips out sometimes. When he is in a difficult situation you never know what's going to happen.'

In Milan he makes the front pages once again when he gets involved in an argument over a parking spot. Three Italians are on the wrong end of his fists this time. On another occasion in Italy, he lashes out at a photographer. And while playing for Tottenham he gets into a fight with his teammate Robbie Keane during a training session. At Ajax he yells insults at a ballboy when he takes too long to retrieve the ball and at a charity match for Unicef (of all things) he takes a swing at an opponent. He gets into a conflict with the KNVB, the Dutch football association, when he wants to take a course to become a professional soccer coach. He then suddenly changes his mind and decides not to do it anyway. 'It's already the third time the KNVB has changed the rules for the course,' Davids says on a Dutch TV show. According to the KNVB, Davids wants to get the same preferential treatment that Clarence Seedorf had looked for. But the KNVB are unwilling to play along. After all, Mark van Bommel,

Ruud van Nistelrooy and Jaap Stam, amongst others, are all taking the usual route to becoming a coach. So why should he be any different?

Davids' last club is the obscure FC Barnet, located in a deprived neighborhood in London. Exactly why he becomes a player and coach there still remains a mystery to most people. But Davids lives around the corner from the stadium and apparently just wants to learn more about the profession of soccer coach. He doesn't receive a salary but plays for a 'token fee' so to speak. At *The Bees* he yells at and insults his players on a regular basis. They also have to address him as *Sir* or *Mister*. Davids even gives himself the shirt number 1 to emphasize his role as leader of the team. He doesn't get along with fellow player-coach Mark Robson. The team captain (Robson) is soon fired and one year later the next captain (Davids himself) leaves on his own initiative because, as he says himself, he 'is being sought by the courts.' In the short time that he turns out for the club he is sent off five times. In his first season in charge Barnet are relegated and the year after that he refuses to take his feared team of kickers to away matches when it is necessary to stay the night. And as for poor old Barnet, they're just happy that peace finally returns to their club...

PAUL GASCOIGNE

Tony Tati

Nationality:	English
Born:	1967
AKA:	Gazza and G8
Known for:	sense of humor, smell of whiskey, lines of cocaine and depression

'I'M EASILY BORED, ALWAYS HAVE BEEN'

It's not by any means the first alarming newsflash concerning the Brit that the ANP press agency reveals to the world at the end of January 2014: Paul Gascoigne is fighting for his life. He has been admitted to a rehab center for his alcohol addiction, for the seventh time. Gascoigne and alcohol are often mentioned by many in the same breath by now. According to insiders, he could easily put away forty glasses of alcohol in one night if he put a bit of effort into it...

The gifted soccer player could probably have gotten a lot more from his already impressive career if only he had been able to stay away from the booze. That would also have saved him a fortune in fines for being drunk in public, suspected drug dealing, violent behavior (such as attacking a bus conductor, his coaches and other officials), charges of rape, traffic offenses, head-butting a bouncer and also his wife, etc., etc.

For much of Gazza's life it has been a case of one step forward, two steps back. *'Was life good? No it wasn't,'* is Gascoigne's stark conclusion when halfway through one of his many rehab periods. But he was also convinced that he was very boring when he wasn't drunk. This outlook on life would eventually lead him to the edge of the abyss. However, one must not forget that the Brit became one of the most colorful players ever to grace the footballing world, in large part because of his clownish behavior.

He was named after the ex-Beatle Paul McCartney. His father was usually either jobless or awol, while his mother did her best to support the family by holding down three jobs. Gascoigne fought regularly with his sister and brother, and at school, where he could never concentrate, he was always in trouble with everyone. He stole from slot machines, stole candy from shops, and tried to hide the poverty of his family by wearing stolen clothes. But every time he came home, the first thing he would do was tell the family the latest joke he had heard. That way there would always be a little bit of light on his predominantly dark horizon.

At first he seems to have been born to lead a wonderful life. He gets his first football when he is seven years old. His hero is Johan Cruyff. On the flipside, however, he gets drunk for the first time when he is only fourteen. Shaken by the consequences of his foolishness, he promises that it will never happen again. He makes a big effort at Newcastle United. But his penchant for speed and his gluttony quickly become a problem. Gascoigne is almost removed from the youth academy after he crashes a motorbike (without a drivers license) and is hospitalized. Gascoigne develops several nervous tics – no less than nine in fact – including making a slurping sound when speaking, not unlike the sound pigeons make. His love for the ball is outstripped only by his obsession with death, which becomes even stronger when he sees his best friend's younger brother get run over by an ice cream van and die right before his very eyes. He had been asked to keep an eye on the boy and this tragedy will haunt him for the rest of his life.

In the meantime, the talented midfielder makes his debut for Newcastle at the age of seventeen. In a game against Wimbledon three years later in 1988, the infamous Vinnie Jones – who once received a red car after only three seconds in a game; still a record – approaches him while the teams are warming up. *'I'm Vinnie Jones. I'm a fucking gypsy. It's just me and you today, fat boy. Just you and me.'* Gascoigne shits his pants. Later, when they are waiting for a free kick to be taken, Jones grabs Gascoigne's balls and almost twists them off. The photo of the incident becomes world famous and Gazza probably still winces at the memory of it. A lesser-known fact is that after the game ended Gascoigne got someone to deliver a rose to the Wimbledon dressing room and Jones's response was to sends him a toilet brush in return with the text *'Fuck off, fat bastard'*. Remarkably enough, the two become good friends later and frequently go off fishing or shooting together.

After four years his sojourn at Newcastle comes to an end. Sir Alex Ferguson, the Manchester United manager, is extremely disappointed when Tottenham Hotspur pilfer the gifted player from right under his nose. His salary is ten times what he earned at Newcastle. But it is the 'extra benefits' that really seal the deal for Gascoigne. The London club has promised to buy his parents a new house and he insists that his sister be given a fancy new *chaise longue*. A new Mercedes and an expensive fishing set for himself are almost beside the point. The Brit celebrates his transfer with a close friend by drinking eight bottles of expensive champagne and then jumping into the hotel pool stark naked. 'A real shame,' says Ferguson in his biography. 'I would loved to have signed him. He was the best player of his era. And our older players, like Bryan Robson and Steve Bruce, could have taught him some discipline.'

Not long afterwards he makes his international debut for England. Rumor has it that on trips abroad Wayne Rooney couldn't fall asleep at night without hearing the noise of a vacuum cleaner and that Gascoigne liked to leave the lights and the television on. There is a lot of gambling and drinking, too, like after the game against the Netherlands at the 1990 World Cup, during which Gascoigne calls Ruud Gullit a hairy monster and even pulls his hair in jest. In another moronic incident, *Gazza* falls overboard along with Gary Linker's wife during a boat trip. *Gazzamania* really grips the nation when the creative midfielder lets his tears flow after losing to Germany in the semi-final. The sympathy of millions of TV viewers in England is his reward. When he returns to England, 100,000 fans are screaming his name at the airport. One fan manages to give him a pair of fake plastic breasts, which the born joker immediately straps on of course. Gascoigne can do no wrong now and is looked upon as the ideal son-in-law...

Immediately after crying his eyes out at the World Cup, Gascoigne's head is spinning from all the offers he receives, ranging from appearances on TV shows to promoting clothing brands and recording a pop single (which goes on to sell over 100,000 copies). But he slips into true *Gazza* mode when a journalist asks him at the presentation of a new Brut aftershave whether he ever uses it himself. No, he answers honestly, unwittingly and instantly nullifying his million-dollar contract. He remains enormously popular, however, so the contracts keep flooding in. The question though is whether he knows how to deal with all this newfound attention. The answer is quick in coming when his transfer to Lazio is endangered after he injures his knee in a bar fight. In the end, he is welcomed to Italy in style by a banner saying *'Gazza's Boys are here. Shag women and drink beer'*. He returns the compliment by farting into the microphone when he is introduced to the fans.

He quickly wins the hearts of the supporters, even though his performances on the pitch for Lazio are often less than convincing. His coach Dino Zoff is also very fond of him and recalls that 'he ate ice cream for breakfast, drank beer for lunch and when he was injured he looked like a whale. But as a player? Marvelous, marvelous...'

Gazza never forgets how to act the clown, even in less than humorous circumstances. Take for example the time he broke his cheekbone during an international game against the Netherlands when Jan Wouters elbowed him. He has to wear a protective mask for weeks as a result. It doesn't bother him. On the contrary, he starts calling himself the *Phantom of the Opera*. The fans frequently see him riding about on one of his nine Harley Davidsons, a fat cigar in his mouth. And the clown doesn't hesitate to drop his pants for the photographers. When he comes up against Maradona in a match he whispers to the Argentinian that he is suffering badly from a hangover. Maradona's face breaks into a wide grin and he replies that he is feeling exactly the same. Gascoigne is always good for a laugh and, of course, is as mad as a hatter. However, when the Italian parliament is less than enamored by one of his jokes after he burps loudly into a reporter's microphone for all the world to hear, the politicians soon find themselves in the middle of a hot Gazza debate. And when asked by a Norwegian journalist after an international game if he has anything to say to the Norwegian viewers, he replies: 'Yeah, sure. Fuck off, Norway!'

All joking aside, he was also a real bad boy at times. He brings all of his bad habits – booze, junk food, pills and fighting – to Glasgow after he signs for Rangers. The move ushers in the best period in Gascoigne's career as a player. However, he frequently arrives for training still drunk and he needs a couple of sips of brandy before going out to play a game. He is threatened with the sack three times in as many seasons. When he pretends to play the flute before a match against archrivals Celtic, he receives death threats from the IRA. It's the worst possible insult for the Catholic fans at Celtic. It is also one of the few times he admits to being in the wrong: 'It was stupid, almost suicidal. But the fans were harassing me so badly...' On the advice of the police, Gascoigne has to check his mail and his car for explosives every day for weeks and months afterwards. 'Also, someone pulled up next to me in his car and told me he was going to cut my throat.' In a documentary about his life broadcast in 2015, Gazza says that he lived in fear of his life for six months. He only felt safe after the IRA sent him a letter saying that he would be left alone (for the time being) because he had behaved himself in the intervening period.

The death threats only make him drink even more. He also starts taking sleeping pills and becomes a chain smoker. His growing fear eventually forces him to flee Scotland. When he hears he is not in the final squad for the 1998 World Cup he barges – drunk, of course – into the office of coach Glenn Hoddle. He tears the place apart and throws the furniture around the room. The day before that, he and the singer Rod Stewart had their photo taken by the British paparazzi brandishing beers and kebabs. In the midst of all the fuss about what Gascoigne did to Hoddle's office, his wife Sheryl files for divorce. She has had it with his constant drinking and cheating. And to top it all off, *Gazza's* regular drinking buddy dies of alcohol poisoning.

While playing for Middlesbrough he has to be committed to a mental institution after drinking 32 glasses of whiskey during a flight in an attempt to 'liquidate' his fear of flying. In his biography 'Gazza, my story' he talks about his fascination with death. He tries to commit suicide several times. He cannot deal with all the attention he is getting and is frustrated by a series of injuries. On one occasion, he hangs out of a window completely out of his mind on drink and acts as if he is going to jump. Another time, he waits on a platform at a train station for two hours to jump in front of the next train, only for a railway worker to eventually tell him that there won't be any more trains that evening.

He tears the place apart and throws the furniture around the room.

It is often said that Gascoigne could have easily packed out theaters if he had chosen a career on stage instead. In actual fact he did take to the boards late in his career and enthralled his audiences with his practical jokes. And there was no shortage of jokes where Gascoigne was concerned. For example, he once dived into an aquarium in a restaurant in an attempt to select a lobster for himself before returning to the table and finishing his dinner soaking wet. He was also spotted one time in a pub, only one hour after an international match, still wearing his full kit and boots (supposedly 'to watch the highlights'). The list of shenanigans goes on and on, like when he took an ostrich, complete in Spurs shirt, for a drive through the middle of London, eventually dropping the poor bird in the middle of his astounded teammates on the training field. Or when he jumped behind the wheel of a bus filled with tourists and drove them round and round Piccadilly Circus until they were dizzy. He also turned up once at a meeting with Sepp Blatter wearing a Santa Claus costume and was known to urinate over sleeping teammates and smell the armpits of referees after they had given him a yellow card. Gascoigne even dishes out yellow cards to referees when they accidentally drop one onto the pitch. He once walked stark naked into the canteen at Middlesbrough before ordering his food as if it was the most normal thing in the world. And he causes over 10,000 dollars worth of damage to an airplane when he decides to display his king-fu skills to the rest of the team during a flight.

Despite all the apparent hilarity, his destructive side eventually gets the better of him. He is convicted for rape and driving under the influence of drugs. In 2005 he ends his active career with Boston United in the USA, where he also worked as a coach for a while. Gazza is not particularly successful in that role, however, whether in China, the USA or at Kettering Town. In the case of the latter club, who play in the lower leagues in England, he is fired after only 39 days. Alcohol turns out to be the problem once again. Gascoigne is furious and decides he is going to buy the club, but to no avail. The year 2008 marks one of his lowest points when his cocaine and alcohol abuse almost cost him his life. He becomes a regular inmate of rehab clinics, especially in Arizona in the USA. One of the doctors there subsequently describes his detoxification period as the worst he had ever seen. On another occasion, in his own home, six cops have to drag him from his bathtub - completely wasted from booze and pills – when he tries to drown himself. As for cocaine, he says 'I snorted at least sixteen lines a day.' And whiskey? 'At least four bottles a day.'

During the final years of his career, the immensely popular Gascoigne sells his story many times over to whoever might be interested. He was and is public property. The naive young boy who was crazy about soccer eventually turns into a confused, depressed, lonely man who feels sorry for himself and his never-ending list of injuries. He never really reached his full potential during his career, lost his wife and frittered away over eleven million dollars. He is plagued by delirious thoughts. Sometimes he thinks he is Bin Laden or is convinced that he has invited George Bush over for a game of chess. He has no clue as to how it has all come to this. At thirty-seven, already completely destroyed by alcohol and drugs, he continues to offer his services to any club that will have him. It is a wonder that the man is still alive. It seems he has more lives than his cat and the two parrots that he regularly feeds with booze. Early in 2013 a bunch of former teammates, including Gary Lineker, Frank Lampard and Steven Gerrard, come up with the money to pay for his treatment in an intensive care unit. Even Mike Tyson offers to help him. Nothing or no one could help him however...

One small mercy was the 250,000 dollars that the Mirror Group Newspapers was ordered to pay him in 2015 for hacking his telephone - a welcome donation. Before that he had been almost declared bankrupt after squandering an estimated fifteen million dollars on alcohol, drugs and careless investments.

CARLOS TÉVEZ

Tony Tati

Nationality: Argentinian

Born: 1984

AKA: El Apache, Carlitos and Scarface

Known for: neck-warmer (especially in cold weather) and third degree burns running from his right ear to his chest

'I COULD HAVE ENDED UP AS A DRUG ADDICT OR A CRIMINAL'

C arlos Tévez was only 24 years old when a film producer decided to make a documentary about his life. The aim of the film was to show the impact the Argentinian rebel had made on soccer in England up to that point.

Immediately after playing the Champions League final in which his club Manchester United beat Chelsea on penalties, Tévez flew to Argentina, where he was born in 1984, to shoot the first scenes for the film in Ejercito de los Andes, better known as Fuerte Apache, one of the poorest and most dangerous suburbs of Buenos Aires, a place ruled by gangs and where even the police were afraid to set foot. He was only six months old when he went to live with his aunt and uncle because his mother could not take care of him and his father never recognized him as his own. When Tévez was only ten months old he was badly burned by a kettle of boiling water. It left him with a huge scar on his neck. 'My mother and my aunt were drinking mate (a traditional Argentinian drink) when I knocked the kettle over. I was rushed to the hospital, where they treated me for third degree burns.' Tévez was lucky to survive the accident and spent the next two months in hospital recovering from his injuries.

Today, the Argentinian wears those scars with pride. 'That accident defined my life. It reminds me every day of my past, of the neighborhood I grew up in. I could have easily gotten into drugs, but I fought my way up out of the gutter and built a successful life. Still, I have fond memories of my youth. I learned everything about the values that help me now: respect, humility and sacrifice'. Tévez has never considered having plastic surgery: 'People have to take me as I am. The same goes for my teeth. Better teeth won't make me a better Carlos.' However, Tévez almost changed his mind when his club Boca Juniors offered to pay for having the scars treated. But when he heard that he need six weeks to recover, he turned it down. One and a half months without being able to indulge his passion... that was just too long for a guy totally in love with the ball.

The young Tévez, who like everyone else in Argentina idolizes fellow countryman Maradona, will later become an idol himself. Today you can find his image everywhere in Fuerte Apache. The walls are covered in graffiti proclaiming his greatness, like *Carlitos Tévez – el jugador del pueblo* (the boy from the village). Nike even films a commercial based on the boy who will never disown his background: *'Tévez is the people'*, and the Argentinian even sets up his own foundation through which he hopes to help the poor from the disadvantaged neighborhoods by building schools, hospitals and sports facilities. 'I want to be an example for them,' he says.

So, Tévez a *bad boy*? You can bet your bottom dollar! But where did it all go wrong for the technically gifted kid who scored thirteen goals in his first game for the Boca Juniors youth team? The young talent who made such a name for himself in the international soccer world at the U-17 World Cup. It may have started to turn sour somewhere between 2001 and 2004, a period when each success led inevitably to another. For example, he wins the award for best player in South America three times in a row and big clubs are queuing up for his signature. One of those clubs, PSV in the Netherlands, is prepared to pay more than eleven million dollars for him. Their offer comes too late, however. The Brazilian team Corinthians outbids the Dutch club. Tévez has just led his team to victory in the Copa Libertadores and he also finishes as top scorer at the 2004 Olympic Games. He receives a hero's welcome when the team returns to Argentina. Together with Maradona, who had checked himself out of rehab for the occasion, he gets to walk the walk of champions into the immense Boca Juniors stadium, *La Bombonera*. Maradona gets completely carried away, kisses Tévez full on the mouth and shouts in the microphone that Carlitos is a phenomenon.

Corinthians pay fifteen million dollars for him and they go on to win the league that season. However, all this success is starting to go to Tévez's head. For example, he is puzzled when his club reacts furiously after he is seen wearing a Manchester United shirt during an interview. 'It's like showing up in a River Plate shirt' (the arch rival of Boca Juniors), vice-president Andrés Sanchez says in *Folha de São Paulo*. 'You just don't do that.' Corinthians hand him a fine of 100,000 dollars. And even for Tévez that's a lot - about twenty percent of his salary.

Not much later, Tévez leaves South America for Europe, primarily as a result of his excellent performance at the 2006 World Cup. The fans of Corinthians have been blaming him for their bad start of the season. They boo him, insult him and even surround him in his car. Tévez starts missing training sessions. He is obviously terrified of the fans. The Argentinian says that he wants to leave the club and go to Europe and hopes that his refusal to train will force a transfer to Chelsea or Manchester United. Tévez's gets his way eventually, but only partly. Instead of signing for a big European club, he has to make do with joining West Ham United. The move doesn't prove a huge success. Even though the fans choose him as their player of the season, his relationship with coach Alan Pardew isn't exactly what you would call smooth. In Pardew's words: 'He never said a thing, never even talked to the other players.'

'I cover myself with vanilla and chocolate essence so they want to eat me whole.'

Eventually it transpires that his transfer to West Ham (and not only his but also that of fellow countryman Javier Mascherano) was illegal. It turns out that they are not the property of the club at all but of the Spanish company Media Sports Investment. FIFA gets involved in the case. At the end of the season the already relegated Sheffield United start an arbitration case against The Hammers. For a while it looks like West Ham will be deducted a number of points and will be relegated instead of Sheffield, but in the end, after two years of arguing, West Ham are ordered to pay Sheffield United twenty million pounds in compensation to settle the matter - a record fine in the history of English soccer.

Tévez' dream eventually does come true. After endless negotiations, he moves to Manchester United in the summer of 2007. But this adventure will not be a great success for the diminutive striker either. In 63 matches he scores only nineteen goals. He believes that the coach, Alex Ferguson, isn't giving him enough playing time but neither does he want to let the Argentinian leave. Negotiations on an extension of

Tévez' two-year contract are delayed time and time again. Tévez is fed up with the situation, especially after comments made by Ferguson. 'He claims that my manager and I have rejected their offer. What a load of nonsense. We haven't even received an offer yet!' Tévez is also having a difficult time in the Argentinian team. In three matches he gets sent off twice and he starts to consider quitting soccer altogether. 'I've already won so much anyway...'

The footballing world is shocked when Tévez signs for United's arch rival Manchester City for a fee of 25 million pounds. Tempers flare on both sides of the Manchester divide. Former teammate Rio Ferdinand expresses his relief at the Argentinian's departure: 'He never contributed anything to our training sessions.' Another United colleague, Gary Neville, feels much the same: '25 million pounds for Tévez? Isn't that a bit over the top?' Tévez, who never felt welcome at United, feels terribly insulted. In a cup match between United and City he silences his critics by scoring two goals. After the first goal he makes 'big mouth' gestures with his hands in Neville's direction. Neville returns the compliment by giving him the finger. Tévez: 'Neville shouldn't say such stupid things. I've always had a lot of respect for him. Now he's being just like Ferguson with all his chat. He's nothing but yes-man.' And: 'Did I go too far? No, not at all.'

Tévez also has a score to settle with Ferguson. He never understood why the manager left him out of the first team so often. After the first match between City and United since his transfer, the Argentinian viciously bites back when a journalist asks him about his feelings on Ferguson. 'I wouldn't even look at him. He never asked me how I was doing back then, did he?' Things go from bad to worse when Tévez is linked to a sex scandal. Manchester City had given him a couple of days off to be with his pregnant wife in Argentina. When he returns in England he tells reporters that he has spent all his time there looking after his newborn daughter, Katie. 'Family always comes before soccer.' But on the very same day that his child leaves the hospital, the Argentinian is spotted with the sexy model Mariana Paesani. They even fly back to England together from Argentina. It turns out they had had a fling a couple of years ago. Paesani is known as a WAG in England, a member of the so-called *Wives and Girlfriends* club that make it their business to attract the amorous attentions of professional soccer players. 'I die for football players. When I want a player I simply become a goddess. I cover myself with vanilla and chocolate essence so they want to eat me whole.'

Interestingly, barely a week before the incident, Tévez had criticized the Chelsea player John Terry when they squared up to each other during a league match. It had been revealed that Terry was guilty of cheating on his wife and Tévez accused him of a lack of respect and wore a shirt to support Terry's teammate Wayne Bridge, whose wife Terry had slept with. After the game Tévez was merciless: In my opinion, Terry has no moral code for what he did to Bridge. If you acted like this in Argentina you'd be dead.'

Driven by resentment, Tévez bags goal after goal for City. At the end of the season Tévez is even voted the third best player in England, after, Wayne Rooney and Didier Drogba. Nonetheless, the notorious *party pooper* threatens to jump ship again and move to another club. This time, however, he has good reason to do so...sort of. Tévez believes that Roberto Mancini's training regime at City is far too demanding. 'The game of Manchester City requires too much from my body. I am 26 years old, but I feel tired and old. I've been playing in England for five years now and I haven't been with my family once at Christmas or New Years Eve. That hurts me.' He also cites the extreme physical training as one of the reasons why he wants to quit playing for his country as well. And to top it all off he complains that the Argentinian football association does not pay him enough respect. 'After the World Cup (of 2010) we couldn't even fly home *business class.*'

Tévez gets sent off twice during the qualification campaign for the 2010 World Cup. But at the finals in South Africa he more than makes up for this: his two goals against Mexico take Maradona's men into the quarter finals. His first goal is the subject of endless discussion. He is clearly offside when Messi passes the ball to him. However, the assistant-referee is the only one in the stadium who fails to spot the offence and Tévez is free to head the ball into the goal. After the game Tévez admits to the error, laughing: 'I know I was offside, I know it was selfish but as long as they say it was a goal it's okay for me and the team.' In the meantime, his half-brother isn't making life easy for him either. He gets sentenced to jail for sixteen years for the armed robbery of a money transport van. But not before he tries to get Tévez to shoulder some of the blame too, saying that he had given him shelter. Tévez' alibi checks out, however, and he is freed of any involvement.

Back in Manchester, Tévez doesn't have any trouble picking up where he left off in terms of his poor behavior. Again he tries to break his contract with City, doing all he can apart from going on hunger strike. According to the club their best-paid player is demanding a much-improved offer, though the player himself denies this. He says he is homesick, especially since his family returned to live in Argentina. He has become so depressed in the 'eternally wet' city of Manchester that he even has to spend time in a clinic. The relationship between the club, coach and player reaches a new low when he refuses to come on as a substitute during the Champions League game against Bayern Munich, which they end up losing. '(Mancini) was in the middle of an argument so then he tells me to keep on warming up and treats me like a dog.' Mancini is livid. 'I've completely had it with him.' Tévez is suspended for two weeks. When, despite endless promises, his attitude doesn't change in the following months, the fines start mounting up. The tabloids calculate that the conflict eventually ends up costing Tévez almost fifteen million dollars.

Speaking of fines... Tévez doesn't exactly show his best side either when driving around in his glitzy Hummer. He puts the pedal to the metal a little too often, insists on having an Argentinian license plate and 'forgets' to pay his speeding fines. In the end, a judge bans him from driving for six months. Tévez is nonplussed. He continues to drive around (this time in a Porsche Cayenne) until he is caught again and barely escapes a six-month jail sentence. He gets away with a hefty spell of community service that the Argentinian dismisses with a laugh and manages to 'buy off'.

In the spring of 2012, Manchester City are crowned champions of England after a long 44-year wait. A victory parade through the city in an open-top bus is organized during which thousands of fans witness a joyful Tévez holding a sign above his head with the text: '*R.I.P. Fergie*', as if to say 'You probably never thought we were going to become champions, Ferguson? Well, dream on!' His protest has him hogging the headlines once again. The club management is furious. After the celebrations die down Tévez offers his apologies to Ferguson. However, it soon turns out that the Argentinian *bad boy* hasn't learned a single lesson. His third and final season playing for City is nothing but trouble. Tévez brags about the endless list of offers coming his way from other clubs, but City refuse to let him go without a fight. The Argentinian is even offered a move to Real Madrid, but in the end he plumps for Juventus. When he arrives in Turin he promises to behave himself. 'I know that at the beginning of my career I used to be a hothead whenever I was substituted. But I have changed and

I behave like a professional now.' This is the source of much amusement in the press, especially when he proceeds to kick the Fiorentina goalkeeper in the head during a game not much later. He is lucky to get away with only a yellow card. Nevertheless, Pope Francis is prepared to give the rebel a warm welcome during a team visit. The pope is overheard whispering in his fellow countryman's ear, 'You are a champion. People look up to you, and through their admiration they learn from you.'.

Another hero of the people, his friend Diego Maradona, can barely believe his ears when he hears that Tévez may not feature in the selection for the upcoming Copa América in 2011. It appears that the coach of the national team, Sergio Batista, is planning to overlook him. Messi is his favorite as the team's number nine and Higuaín is his second choice. 'Ridiculous,' is Maradona's verdict. 'You either have to be very drunk or just plain stupid not to select Tévez. I came in for a lot of criticism when I was coach of the national team. Now we have a complete idiot as coach and nothing is being said.' The battle for the Copa turns out to be a big disappointment, both for the organizing country, Argentina, and for Tévez, who was selected after all. When the diminutive striker is the only one to miss during the decisive penalty shoot-out in the quarter final against Uruguay, Batista probably feels justified in his initial doubts.

After the disappointment of the 2011 Copa, Tévez is not called up for the national team again. This is not so much because of the missed penalty at the Copa as because of the fact that Alejandro Sabella, the successor to Batista, believes that Tévez is a disruptive factor in the squad. Pro-Tévez demonstrations in Buenos Aires don't do much to help the player either. Tévez's wife is also furious and goes to the press saying that her husband is better than any other player in the new 23-man Argentinian squad. But it is all to no avail and he ends up missing out on the World Cup finals of 2014. None of this seems to bother the player too much, however: 'For the people who think my time is over, don't forget that I came from a place where they said you could never win. I wish the team the best of luck.' Even though the Argentinian has previously said that Lionel Messi is one of three players for whom he has a lot of respect, Messi for his part is apparently not a great fan of Tévez. The difficult relationship between the two is said to be detrimental to their cooperation on the pitch. Tévez dismisses this as nonsense. The top scorer at Juventus says, 'For some reason the coach of the national team is just afraid of me.' But it was Sabella who proved his mettle by resisting the loud calls of the fans to select their favorite.

At the Copa América in 2015 Tévez exacts revenge for the missed penalty four years earlier. After coming on as a sub, he scores the winning penalty in the shoot-out against Colombia. The Argentinian is so happy he lets his tears flow. Messi embraces him warmly. Tévez, who has just confirmed that he will be playing for his childhood favorite Boca Juniors the following season, is well aware of the implications: 'Football always provides the opportunity for revenge, but what happened four years ago is over.'

PAOLO DI CANIO

Tony Tati

Nationality: Italian

Born: 1968

AKA: Pallocca (fatty), The Animal, Rambo, The Volcano and The Barbarian

Known for: Nazi salutes, a tattoo on his right arm that spells DUX (the Latin name for Benito Mussolini) and a large fascist tattoo on his back, including an eagle and a portrait of Mussolini

'I WILL NEVER CHANGE'

F ew soccer players have been the source of as much commotion as the Italian Paoli Di Canio. His explosive remarks both on and off the field are infamous and he isn't called 'The Volcano' for his polarized opinions alone. He seems to have had a run-in with nearly everyone at some time or other - with fellow players, referees, coaches and supporters. It's almost a miracle that a statue hasn't been erected yet in his 'honor'... this Italian is a genuine master at the art of the provocation.

However, Di Canio is also a great artist with a football. Even Sir Alex Ferguson nearly signed him for Manchester United on two occasions. And the well known English coach Harry Redknapp once said: 'He does jaw-dropping things with the ball. Other players would pay to see him practice.' And all that despite being born with a gammy leg in 1968, which was only one of a number of physical defects. As a kid he was small, fat and addicted to Coca-Cola and other sugar-rich drinks. No wonder he earned himself the nickname 'Palloca' in his neighborhood.

Born in Rome, Di Canio grows up in Quarticciolo, a poor working-class area. His family struggles to make ends meet. His father, a construction worker, is your average temperamental Italian. He gets up at four o'clock in the morning and only gets home after a hard day's work at five in the afternoon. Being the youngest son, Di Canio has to share a bed with his oldest brother Antonio, who is not happy with the arrangement. Di Canio remembers that 'when I had to pee, I couldn't get out of the bed to go to the toilet. I continued to wet the bed until I was about eleven years old.' Not surprisingly, he gets into frequent fights with his brother. When his other brother, Giuliano, sells Paolo's bike to a trader, Di Canio takes revenge by stabbing him in the back with a fork. 'He was hopping mad, but I was couldn't stop laughing because it looked so ridiculous.'

Di Canio is often depressed as a child. Apart from his obesity, he also suffers from being cross-legged and has to wear orthopedic shoes. As a youngster he experiences chronic panic attacks ('Really terrible. It's like going completely blind.'), as well as a fear of flying and nervous breakdowns. Despite all of this he has one burning ambition: to become a professional soccer player. The Italian spends most of his time out on the streets in a neighborhood full of AS Roma fans. Being the rebel he is, however, he chooses to support Roma's archrivals Lazio instead. This immediately grants him the freedom to side perpetually with the underdog. Di Canio will later even become a member of the *Irriducibili*, the extreme right, hard core of Lazio, which is feared all over Europe. They wear swastikas and runes and worship former dictator Benito 'Il Duce' Mussolini.

Di Canio starts his soccer career at Rinascita '79 where his talent is quickly discovered by Pro Teverne Roma, a satellite club of his beloved Lazio. Di Canio is the best player on the pitch, week in week out, gammy leg or not. When he turns thirteen Lazio come calling. It is a dream come true for the young Di Canio. In the meantime, he carries on hanging out with the *Irriducibili*. During battles between rival supporters he throws stones, is the target of teargas and gets into trouble with the police. He even witnesses a police chief being stabbed right under his nose. His involvement with the *Irriducibili* puts his career at Lazio at risk. One of the first team's medical staff recognizes him in the crowd when he is treating a player for an injury just off the pitch. Fortunately for Di Canio the attendant keeps his mouth shut, but it is clear that the Italian will have to make a choice, which is not as simple as it sounds...

Di Canio makes his debut for Lazio's first team against Cesena in October 1988. He only manages to find the net once in thirty games that season. That one goal, however, is hugely significant because it proves to be the winning goal against AS Roma. He celebrates his goal extravagantly and provocatively in front of the Roma fans, an act that earns him a massive fine. His undying love for Lazio is tempered somewhat the following year when the club decide to sell him to Juventus, completely against his will. His salary demands at Lazio are said to be too high...but his fans know better. Di Canio calls it a disgrace and even says that he would have played for nothing for his beloved club.

At 'Juve' a discussion with coach Giovanni Trapattoni almost turns into a fistfight. His teammates have to jump in to separate the two protagonists but the incident still makes the headlines. Di Canio's bad reputation is now firmly established. He goes on to play for Napoli and AC Milan, where he gets into trouble with his coach as well – on one occasion he even pushes Fabio Capello to the ground after a row – but then his career threatens to fizzle out unspectacularly. He is rescued from obscurity by the Scottish club Celtic, where he forms an attacking duo with Pierre van Hooijdonk. The volcano remains active however and he bemoans the ability of his teammates regularly. After an 'Old Firm' game, the traditional battle between Celtic and Glasgow Rangers, he causes a massive brawl on the pitch. The fans love it and it seems they can't get enough of their fearless wacko Di Canio. However, they don't get to enjoy their hero's antics for much longer. Preparations of his second season at Celtic are not even a couple

Di Canio seems less than impressed after his meeting with a number of survivors of the Holocaust.

weeks old when coach Wim Jansen decides to drop the unmanageable forward from the squad after Di Canio expresses his unwillingness to travel with the team to a training camp. And Jansen isn't all that impressed with his commitment either when he does decide to train with the squad. Di Canio subsequently gets into an argument with the club's management and is eventually given permission to leave, but only after he called them 'a bunch of liars and traitors!'

He's not finished yet, however. Not by a long shot. In his first season at Sheffield Wednesday, Di Canio grabs the headlines again when he drops his shorts in front of the supporters of Wimbledon FC. He turns it up another notch in the game against Arsenal when referee Paul Alcock sends him off after he deliberately kicks an opponent. In a rage he pushes Alcock to the ground. Di Canio calls him 'a drunken clown' because of the ease with which Alcock fell over. But the clown will have the last laugh. Di Canio is suspended for four months for *the Push* and handed a huge fine. There are questions asked in the British House of Commons about the incident. England, it seems, has had enough of him. He flees to his native Italy and is fined again by Sheffield Wednesday for leaving without permission.

West Ham United are the next to sign him and, of course, he makes the tabloids there too when the team's repeated penalty appeals are turned down while trailing 4-2 to Bradford City. It doesn't take much to light Di Canio's very short fuse again. The Italian walks to the bench to ask to be substituted, as if this is the most normal thing in the world. But coach Harry Redknapp refuses to take his best player off the pitch. When their team is eventually awarded a penalty Di Canio insists on taking the kick, even though his teammates are very reluctant to let him do so. He scores, the game turns in West Ham's favor, and they end up winning 5-4. The storm seems to have blown over for the moment. Better again, as is revealed later on, Manchester United make an attractive offer for his signature. In an interview in *The Independent*, Di Canio says that he doesn't want to disappoint his fans: 'Football has never been business. Football is a passion.' West Ham are also reluctant to let the talented forward leave; the striker who teammate Rio Ferdinand calls 'an absolute idiot' after he makes yet another Nazi salute on the pitch.

In the same season that Di Canio openly expresses his support for the fascist leader Benito Mussolini in his autobiography ('He was completely misunderstood), he receives the plaudits of FIFA president Sepp Blatter. The reason for this gesture is his uncharacteristic display of fair play in an away match against Everton. With the score at 1-1 the Everton keeper, Gerrard, gets injured just before the referee is ready to blow for full-time. With the keeper lying on the ground in agony, Di Canio's teammate Kanouté passes him the ball. The Italian has the easiest of chances to score and win the game for West Ham, but instead he catches the ball and points at the injured keeper who he believes badly needs treatment. His actions earn him a standing ovation from the crowd. For a brief moment 'The Animal' is the hero of all England. Blatter gives him the FIFA Fairplay Award for the season; the same Blatter who up until then had wanted to impose a worldwide ban on the player because of his repeated Nazi salutes – how quickly one's sins can be forgiven.... Later, however, Di Canio seems less than impressed after his meeting with a number of survivors of the Holocaust. The fact that six million Jews were killed during the Second World War is horrendous, he says - and he promises never to make the Nazi salute again - but at the same time he is of the opinion that Mussolini achieved a lot of good things for Italy. The Italian Prime Minister, Silvio Berlusconi, no stranger to controversy himself, rows in behind him: 'Di Canio has a heart of gold, at worst he's an exhibitionist.'

When Di Canio returns to play for the almost bankrupt Lazio on a much-reduced salary in 2004, seven thousand fans are waiting to welcome him back at the training field. He thanks them, as only he could, with a by now all too familiar Nazi salute. In his first game he grabs the ball from Simone Inzaghi when the team is awarded a penalty. He scores, grabs the white-hot Inzaghi by the throat for not joining in the celebrations, and laps up the praise of the fans. Lazio win the game 1-0. He can do no wrong in the eyes of the club's supporters. A couple of months later he greets the hard core of the club with a Nazi salute once again. Lazio have just beaten their old rivals AS Roma. Underneath his shirt he reveals the text: 'There are only two ways to leave the field: with the head of the enemy or your own.' On this occasion, having scored the opening goal himself, it is the enemy's head that Di Canio carries off the pitch. A fine of more than 11,000 dollars follows. Again he denies that his salute has anything to do with politics. His explanation is short and simple: 'This is just my way of showing my commitment to the fans.' The neo-fascist party Alleanza Nazionale immediately organizes a collection among Lazio fans to pay his fine. However, his contract is terminated shortly thereafter when things get so out of hand at a dinner hosted by the president of Lazio that Di Canio topples the table at which they are sitting. The president is left sitting there with pasta dripping from his suit...

After a short period of reflection Di Canio decides to become a coach ('A lion can't stay in a cage. A lion has to be on the pitch.'), starting at Swindon Town in England, the country where soccer is always 'pure, intense and a battle', according to him. The fourth division club immediately loses the backing of one of its sponsors as a result of his appointment. He soon lives up to his reputation when he makes racist remarks directed at the colored player Jonathan Tehoué. The club denies the incident in a press release, but many of the squad are witness to Di Canio's derogatory remarks. He also gets into an argument with Wes Foderingham when he substitutes the keeper after he makes two mistakes. The game is only twenty minutes old. The goalie responds by calling his coach 'arrogant and ignorant'. Not to be outdone, Di Canio retorts by saying: 'Foderingham is one of the worst players I've ever seen', adding that 'With some players, if he has a chihuahua character, I can't make a chihuahua into a rottweiler.' In other words: if a player doesn't have it in him to fight for every ball, he as coach can't do anything about it. Di Canio eventually resigns after a series of run-ins with the management. A couple of days later he breaks into the club to collect some of his stuff. He also tears down all the photos on the wall portraying his achievements with the club. The management takes no further action however; they are happy enough that the coach who had been so aggressive towards his players has finally left. They don't even issue a press release, though they do decide to change all the locks in the stadium...

Even before he has taken his first steps inside the stadium as coach of his new club Sunderland, a fresh scandal has broken out. The vice-president, Miliband, immediately resigns when he hears that Di Canio has been given the job. 'His appointment is a disgrace and a betrayal of all who fought and died in the fight against fascism.' Di Canio's response is to shrug his shoulders and say that although he might be a fascist he is not a racist. His true colors are made painfully clear when his attendance at the funeral of Paolo Signorelli is recorded on camera. Signorelli, an extreme-right politician, had been held on remand for eight years under suspicion of being involved in a terrorist bombing at the train station in Bologna in which 85 people died. When the casket is being carried out of the church, the mourners, including Di Canio, give the Nazi salute. Later it is revealed that Di Canio had visited the politician on several occasions in the last years of his life.

Di Canio quickly adapts to the peculiarities of working as a coach in England. At least the frequency with which he is involved in controversy at Sunderland equals the frequency with which the rain falls on that northern town. The players have nothing good to say about their controversial coach. He is extremely hard on them and regularly calls them fools. The Italian introduces a double training session every day and not only forbids his players from consuming beer, cola, ketchup and mayonnaise but also from eating sausages and beans as well. Any player who seems to be just a little overweight incurs his wrath immediately. Cellphones are forbidden, too. 'If anyone comes in here with one of those, I'll throw it in the North Sea.' The players are not even allowed to sing under the shower anymore. The coach claims that this disrupts their concentration. That this usually happens *after* a game is beside the point in the Italian's opinion. He demands absolute dedication. Those who refuse to listen will soon feel the consequences. Di Canio often seems to be just one step away from literally whipping his players.

The Dutchman Etiënne Esajas calls Di Canio 'a true dictator', and his voice is not a lone one. The coach for his part doesn't agree. On the contrary, he thinks he is 'one of the best coaches in the world.' But one look at his resumé paints a different picture. Despite the fact that he has submerged himself in the spiritual culture of the Samurai over the last couple of years, the Italian's behavior on the sidelines is not much better than that of an aggressive and idiotic hardcore fan. He does what he likes and he says what he thinks. When his team scores he often celebrates in the most curious fashion for a manager, with a knee slide over the grass for example. He says that scoring against Manchester United is like 'having sex with Madonna'. Sometimes his press conferences last for hours. He allows himself to be photographed bare-chested or posing with a pig's head. Sunderland fire the Italian after only six months in the job when the players revolt against him. 'He was unreasonable in his approach. Everyone was relieved when he left.' His answer? 'I will never change.' In the end, Di Canio receives a fitting accolade when the English press proclaims him to be the most idiotic manager ever in the history of British soccer.

WAYNE ROONEY

Tony Tati

Nationality:	English
Born:	1985
AKA:	Wayniac, The white Pelé, Wazza (the urine man), Roo, Roonaldo, Shrek, The Wonder Boy and Hustler
Known for:	his fleet of cars, a tattoo of the English flag on his left shoulder, and hair transplants

'MY LIFE OFF THE FIELD WAS A HELL'

Wayne Rooney wasn't the first and he won't be the last. Just like his famous colleagues John Terry, Ashley Cole, Ryan Giggs, Dwight Yorke and David Beckham, he has been involved in all kinds of sex scandals. And that's only the start of it...

Rooney grew up in Croxteth, a suburb of Liverpool where the population was made up almost entirely of the unemployed, drug dealers and murderers. His father was a construction worker, but he lost his job as a result of a severe back problem. He was forced to try and make some money on the side as a boxer. Ma Rooney had a job in a local canteen. These were hard times for the family. The young Rooney rarely bothered going to school. Luckily for him though he was pretty nifty when it came to soccer.

He is a die-hard Everton fan. When he goes for a trial at Liverpool FC he refuses to take off his Everton shirt. When he is nine, and after having struggled for a long time with being overweight, his dream finally comes true. The young Wayne signs his first professional contract with Everton. The signing doesn't go unnoticed... The local mafia, always on the lookout for some extra income, tries to intimidate Rooney by shooting a couple of bullets through his agent's front door. After this incident the club decides to hire a couple of bodyguards to protect their talented young player.

When he does bother to attend school, Rooney spends most of his time staring out the window. He will leave without any kind of qualifications. His talents lie elsewhere. At the age of sixteen he makes his debut for Everton and immediately makes a name for himself by working himself into the ground for the full ninety minutes in the derby against Liverpool. He spares nothing and no one while doing so. The Liverpool goalkeeper, Kirkland, is left nearly broken in two after Rooney steamrolls into him. An apology is not forthcoming. This is Rooney's signature, and not just on that particular day. For him, winning is everything, he will later repeat ad infinitum. He is only seventeen when he earns the dubious honor of being the youngest player ever to receive a red card in the Premier League. And at the age of seventeen years and 111 days be becomes the youngest debutant ever in the English national team. All landmarks that will epitomize his career.

In the meantime, Rooney has proclaimed his eternal loyalty to Everton. After scoring against Aston Villa he reveals a t-shirt that says 'Once a blue, always a blue'. However, even Rooney turns out to be a mere mortal when after two seasons he joins Manchester United for a record fee of 27 million pounds (42 million dollars). The swords are quick to come out and the 'traitor' is repeatedly set upon by Everton fans. He hides out at his aunt and uncle's house and they drive him from Liverpool to the training field in Manchester. When he returns as a United player to the Everton stadium Goodison Park, he is endlessly booed. And despite his obvious ability the United fans are at first slow to warm to him - a *Scouser* at Man Utd, always a difficult combination.

On his debut for the club, against Fenerbahçe in the Champions League, he gives an outstanding performance, scoring three goals. He turns into a genuine scoring machine season after season. His explanation is simple: 'I don't aim. If I don't where the ball is going, how is the keeper ever going to know?' However, the child prodigy loses the run of himself time and time again on the pitch. Sir Alex Ferguson, the manager, even sends his nineteen-year-old forward to a therapist after he is caught swearing no less than a hundred times during a game against Arsenal. His perpetual outbursts of anger, rough tackles, elbows and a series of yellow and red cards aren't doing the image of the proud club any good... And off the pitch, in the dressing room, he curses practically everything and everyone around him after the team has lost a game. His teammates have great difficulty dealing with him. Ferguson compares him to another genius madman, Paul *Gazza* Gascoigne, who is also the inspiration behind Rooney's nickname, *Wazza*, which is slang for urinating.

He is constantly getting involved in skirmishes with England teammates and the team's fans. For example, he takes David Beckham to the cleaners with a stream of verbal abuse during an international game against Northern Ireland. And many of the team's supporters have had more than their fill of him after he kicks Ricardo Carvalho in the crotch (and is sent off again) in the World Cup game against Portugal in 2006. He is despised by practically the entire nation but this doesn't seem to bother Rooney too much. He is more upset by the fact that his Manchester teammate Cristiano Ronaldo tried to get him sent off. After the foul, the Portuguese star was seen excitedly waving an imaginary red card and then giving the bench a sneaky wink after Rooney was dismissed. Rooney is livid. When Ronaldo next puts a foot on English soil Rooney vows to 'cut him in two'.

It never comes to that, however. They even go on to become good buddies. But his love-hate relationship with the English supporters remains unchanged. At the 2010 World Cup he insults the fans when they boo the team after a disappointing draw against Algeria. 'Nice to see your home fans booing you. That's loyal supporters,' he snaps in the camera when walking off the field after the final whistle. A year later he gets sent off again during a World Cup qualifying match. As a result he misses the first two games at the finals. The coach of the national team Fabio Capello is being generous when he calls him 'crazy', and the English press have a field day questioning his mental state of health. Rooney continues to behave like a hooligan. His pub brawls are not even newsworthy any more. Neither are his clashes with

The engagement party gets completely out of hand (surprise, surprise)

the paparazzi and journalists. Rooney reverts to Twitter as his favorite place for venting his anger. For instance, he reacts fiercely to a tweet by a Liverpool fan who calls him a 'fat whore'. Rooney's stone cold reaction: 'I'll put u asleep within ten seconds.'

He becomes a much-loved subject in the infamous English tabloids when they discover that he used to frequent brothels ('massage salons' in his own words) in his younger years. He was just fourteen when his father gave him a very special gift: a trip to the prostitutes. A signed check is produced as proof. The surrounding scandal explodes exponentially and becomes known as *Rooneygate*. Rooney starts to drag several other well-known professional players into the affair. At the end of August 2004, The Sunday Mirror publishes seven (!) pages detailing Rooney's sexual escapades. And that is after he has already paid to take possession of other damning evidence (including video images) held by several figures in the underworld (who threaten to blackmail him).

It turns out that he likes 'kinky' sex. It is revealed that the sixteen-year-old Rooney had sex in a brothel (for 60 dollars an hour) with the chain-smoking, PVC-wearing prostitute Patricia Tierney, who was thirty-six years his senior. Nicknamed 'Auld Slapper' and the mother of seven children, she was already a grandmother at the time. When a certain Jennifer Thompson sells her story to a national newspaper, the bomb really goes off. Prostitute 'Juicy Jen', who already has a string of English soccer players behind her ('six defenders, three midfielders and four forwards'), reveals that Rooney has been with her no less than seven times. And that while Rooney's wife Coleen is pregnant with their first child. Coca-Cola abruptly terminates its sponsorship deal with the fallen star, also because he had committed blasphemy during a TV show. Result: a fall in income of 850,000 dollars a year.

And, on the subject of Coleen... She is Rooney's childhood sweetheart and they marry in 2008. Rooney proposes in a most romantic setting: a gas station. Their engagement is celebrated in a much more salubrious manner however. The engagement ring costs 40,000 dollars and his bachelor party on the island of Ibiza, which lasts for four days, costs him even more, according to insiders. The engagement party gets completely out of hand (surprise, surprise) when the two families end up going for each other's throats. Coleen's clan know that Rooney had recently been caught with a well known escort lady, Charlotte Glover. The fact that Rooney had already confessed to this affair doesn't make any difference.

When the dust has settled the wedding dress is ordered in New York. At the famous Marchesa fashion house, Coleen splashes out 150,000 dollars for the dress (four days salary for her husband). However, there is a slight setback when it turns out that Coleen, who has been on a diet, doesn't fit the dress anymore just before the happy day. The solution is simple: they fly to New York again and the dress is adjusted accordingly. When the two marry – with the dress fitting like a glove – another seven million dollars has to be shelled out. But for that price they get a hell of a party in a luxurious villa in the classy resort of Santa Margherita Ligure in Italy. And, completely against the will of their priest, they hire a deconsecrated church near Genoa for the ceremony. So, does Coleen end up staying true to her whore-loving husband? She certainly does, whatever about him keeping his side of the bargain...

As for cars, Rooney adores them. So much so in fact that they are often the victim of his penchant for driving at high speed. An Aston Martin and a Range Rover Overfinch can be counted among the expensive wrecks, while a Lamborghini Gallard 'only' ended up in a ditch on the wrong side of the road. According to insiders, the star player – having learned his lesson through trial and error – now obeys the traffic laws a little more often. This transformation may also have something to do with the birth of his son, Kai Wayne Rooney, in November 2009, an event that ushers in a milder, quieter life for Wayne Sr. The chain-smoking, drink-driving, car-wrecking whoremonger and gambler is a bit washed out...

In 2011 Rooney's father is arrested on suspicion of being involved in a bribery scandal in the Scottish soccer league. Soon afterwards, the brilliant soccer player embarks on a series of hair transplants. He is fed up with being called 'Bobby Charlton' – after the very famous and very bald ex-United player – by his teammates. His rapport with Alex Ferguson, and with his successor David Moyes, is far from ideal. Before being appointed manager of Manchester United, Moyes is described by Rooney as 'unbearable'. Unsurprisingly, the one season that they have to work together is far from harmonious. In 2010 Rooney demands that Ferguson sign Mesut Özil from Werder Bremen. 'Mind your own business,' is all the Scot has to say to him in reply. Ferguson regularly expresses his doubts regarding the fitness and focus of his star player. Pictures of Rooney smoking or pissing in a back alley after a night of clubbing don't do 'The Boss' any favors either.

Rooney attacks Ferguson from time to time as well. He is fed up with playing in midfield. He wants to go back to his old spot up front. The argument becomes so heated that Rooney announces his decision to leave the club. He soon starts receiving death threats as a result. Ferguson, who has stuck with him through thick and thin, now calls him an ungrateful dog. Rooney has the opportunity to move to Real Madrid, but insiders wonder at the wisdom of such a move. After all he got a grade of zero for Spanish on his school report... Above all he will surely miss his clan, including his father and his uncle, both of whom are facing charges of gambling on games (but who will be acquitted later). Archrivals Manchester City also flirt with him. Chelsea offer United 60 million dollars for his signature, but in the end Rooney remains loyal to the club and stays on. He signs a contract for five years with a handsome salary of 400,000 dollars a week. Fans start calling him greedy and accuse him of pushing the club to the limit purely for the sake of more money. When he looks back at these years in his biography he says: 'My life off the pitch was a hell. Whenever I got into my car, I had to look in the mirror to see if I was being followed. And the enormous expectations made the barrel of gunpowder explode from time to time.'

RONALDO (LUÍS NAZÁRIO DE LIMA)

Nationality:	Brazilian
Born:	1976
AKA:	The real Ronaldo, O Fenómeno (the phenomenon), El Gordito (the fat one), Dadado, O Menino de Ouro (the golden child), R9, Robocop, and little Millio
Known for:	the gap between his front teeth and his triangular hairdo (at the 2002 World Cup)

'IT'S A SHAME THAT ROMÁRIO HAS SO MANY PROBLEMS OUTSIDE OF SOCCER. I DON'T LIKE THAT.'

A bout half of the six to nine million dollars that the Brazilian club Cruzeiro gets from PSV when they sign Ronaldo in 1994 is paid under the table...

It is 1994 when the seventeen-year-old super talent comes to the Netherlands. Coach Louis van Gaal is determined to secure his signature for Ajax, who already have six million dollars put aside in the bank and Ronaldo's word that he will join the Amsterdam club. But in the end, upon the advice of Romário, he plumps for PSV instead. It turns out that Romário did have a soft spot for his former club after all, despite the cold weather and the strict regime when he played there.

Initially they are 'incredibly happy' with him in Eindhoven, according to technical director Frank Arnesen. But the smile soon vanishes from their faces. Just like Romário, the seemingly shy Ronaldo is in constant trouble with his coaches. First up is interim-coach Kees Rijvers, who thinks the Brazilian needs to change his attitude. He is constantly late for training, refuses to participate in group activities like golf outings, and won't learn to speak Dutch. Rijvers also thinks that Ronaldo shouldn't link his name with a beer brand until he has reached the adult age of eighteen. On top of that he wastes way too much energy between the sheets with his girlfriend Nadia. Rijvers even claims that the reason he played so well in the Champions League game against

Leverkusen was because he hadn't seen his girlfriend in five days. The PSV coach also calls his star player stubborn and questions his fitness levels. And he says that his poor fitness is detrimental to the rest of the team. 'He has the fitness of a veteran and the least amount of effort sends his heart pumping like crazy.' Teammate Arthur Numan says: 'When Ronaldo isn't eating or training, he is sleeping or on the phone. Or busy playing some computer game. He only gets up for a game of foot volley.' Numan is fed up with the gentle treatment his teammate is receiving. The successor to Romário soon earns himself the name 'little Millio' (soccer jargon for millionaire).

Ronaldo is soon fed up with being compared to Romário: 'You'll rarely find me on the Copacabana, I'm not a member of any carnival association and I can't dance the samba. Actually I prefer to stay at home. What more could PSV possibly ask for?' The cheerful Brazilian does like to go for a drive now and then, preferably in a big shiny Chrysler Cherokee. He frequently trades his expensive car in for an even more expensive one. Nádia, of course, is only delighted.

When the coach of the Brazilian team, Mário Zagallo, comes to the Netherlands to watch Ronaldo play, PSV's new coach, Dick Advocaat, decides to start him on the subs bench. Ronaldo is furious and in the days that follow he openly flirts with FC Barcelona, who have shown an interest in him: 'I'll play there for free if I have to.' Advocaat reacts angrily: 'He is being childish, isn't showing any character and is a victim of his own agents.' In the meantime, the striker has started to experience problems with his knee. Is it because of the extra training that his upper leg muscles have expanded in diameter by three centimeters in a very short space of time? Or is it maybe down to doping? Twelve years later the head of the anti-doping department of the Brazilian football association (CBF), Bernardo Santi, accuses PSV of giving him anabolic steroids at a very young age to strengthen the sinews and ligaments around his knee. Initially this resulted in extra speed and strength, but later in his career the knee injuries seem to come one after the other. 'The bill for the use of steroids shows up 10, 15 or 20 years later,' Santi says in a Brazilian newspaper, adding that Ronaldo's muscles were growing faster than his joints could handle. The statements will cost Santi his head. The CBF fires him immediately and PSV dismisses the story as 'totally absurd'. Ronaldo also strongly denies the use of doping.

However, Santi repeats his accusations two years later in his biography. He says his information is based on sources at PSV. 'What an idiot,' is the reaction of an annoyed Ronaldo, who has been struggling with knee problems at all of his employers – Barcelona, Inter Milan, Real Madrid and AC Milan. Santi: 'They gave supplements to Ronaldo, who was very thin, and among those supplements they included some anabolic substances which could make him grow a bit more. At seventeen he was already undergoing treatment in the Netherlands. A man is only full-grown by the age of twenty.' Years later, in February 2008, Ronaldo has surgery for the sixth time in his career, this time in Paris. The three-time 'World footballer of the Year' has torn the ligaments of his left knee while playing for AC Milan. The same thing happened to him in 1999 and 2000 as well, and also to his other knee. The injuries keep Ronaldo on the sidelines for years.

Sex, drugs, gambling and gluttony soon become synonymous with the name Ronaldo. Not to mention controversy. For instance, it's still a mystery what exactly happened on the night of the World Cup final in France in 1998. Host country France is facing Brazil in the final, which is being played in the Stade de France in Saint-Denis, a suburb of Paris. Exactly 72 minutes before kick-off, the team sheets are sent to the FIFA. No surprises on the French side, but when the 2700 journalists present see Edmundo's name in the team instead of Ronaldo's, all hell breaks loose. Everyone is at a loss to explain his absence. Over 200 million Brazilians hold their breath. Ronaldo Luis Nazário de Lima, their phenomenal center forward, is not playing! What is wrong with the star of the 1998 World Cup and the tournament's top scorer? Is it his ever-troublesome knee? Or is it the injury to his ankle, the result of Frank de Boer's hard tackle in the semi-final against the Netherlands?

When a new team sheet is presented to the press not much later, it turns out that Edmundo's place will be taken by Ronaldo after all. The assembled journalists have their doubts, however. Why this sudden turnaround? A blunder by FIFA or by the Brazilian manager? Surely not? A more plausible explanation is that the wily old coach of Brazil, Mário Zagallo, 'The Old Wolf', is trying to confuse his team's opponents. But an hour later, as the frustrated and annoyed Edmundo looks on from the bench, Ronaldo is playing abysmally in the final. He looks slow and apathetic. He walks around the pitch like a lost soul, but he isn't substituted. France win the game easily 3-0. The streets are deserted in Brazil; the defeat is a disaster for the soccer-crazy country.

Not surprisingly, all eyes are on Ronaldo after the game. The official story is that he was hindered by the ankle injury he picked up in the semi-final against the Netherlands. But when later that night Roberto Carlos declares that his teammate collapsed under the immense pressure, the media start buzzing with activity. What's the real story here? Did the Brazilian super striker faint before the match? That becomes the most plausible story when Ronaldo offers his own explanation a couple of months later to the BBC. 'I had convulsions after lunch. I passed out for a couple of minutes. Nobody knows why. Maybe it was the pressure or the nerves. I don't know. The doctors told me I had had convulsions and that I wouldn't be playing. I replied that that was impossible, that I had to play. We went to the hospital, where I was examined for hours. They didn't find anything wrong with me, so I was okay. I went straight back to the stadium and when I got there it turned out that Edmundo had taken my place in the team. I could understand that, but I immediately said to the coach: "Please let me play. I'm fine".'

Dr. Toledo, the team doctor, gave a slightly different interpretation of events, however. Apparently Ronaldo had swallowed his tongue a couple of hours before kick-off. His teammate Edmundo even thought he was going to die. Ronaldo had lost consciousness completely for a while. Did he have an epileptic fit? Even more sensational is the explanation offered by Dr. Da Matta, Toledo's assistant. He claims that the player may have suffered 'an overdose of doping or painkillers'. The coach, Zagallo, and the two aforementioned doctors are fired after the World Cup. In the meantime, the doctor at Inter Milan, Ronaldo's employer, is hopping mad. 'It is very unwise to let somebody play a soccer match within 24 hours of having convulsions.' So what was the actual cause of these convulsions? Reporters at *The Guardian* discover that on the morning of the final Ronaldo wasn't just given painkillers but also an injection of cortisone.

So what was the upshot of all of this in the end? In Brazil, two parliamentary inquiries are held into the true causes of the nightmare of '98. Was there some kind of conspiracy going on? Did Ronaldo's sponsor Nike force him to play? After all they had a heavy interest in his lining up for the team. *O Globo* claims that Ricardo Teixeira, the head of the Brazilian football association, changed the team sheet almost singlehandedly an hour before the game. Nike, head sponsor of the *Seleção* for ten years to the tune of 400 million dollars, and also Ronaldo's sponsor (they paid him 1.5 million dollars per season), may have put enormous pressure on the association. The ex-coach of the national team, Zagallo, categorically denies this but he has been guilty of many 'untrue' statements in the past. The fans stand firmly behind Ronaldo, who incidentally was voted 'Best player of the World Cup' in the end. Teixeira is made out to be a traitor and a clown. And the truth? That, unfortunately, will never be known.

Ronaldo is only seventeen when he first wins the World Cup with Brazil, without playing a single minute on that occasion, however. He grows up in a family of three children, not far from Rio de Janeiro. The family lives in a rundown house only forty square meters in size. Luxury is an alien concept to them. His father is addicted to cocaine and his parents divorce when he is only four years old. His mother tries to complement the meager alimony payments with a job at an ice cream shop. She sees her son more often there than she does at home. Ronaldo, always called Dadado by his brother, is a street kid. He becomes a member of the Social Ramos Club, an indoor soccer club established to keep youngsters off the street and out of juvenile gangs. He is bullied a lot because of his buckteeth. On the pitch, however, this Skinny Joe is feared by many. His sudden acceleration, his obsession with scoring... He is even more dangerous when he becomes equally able with both feet. In his first season at the club Cruzeiro – he is only sixteen years old at the time – he can't stop scoring. People begin to compare him to Pelé. Soon, however, his biggest shortcoming also becomes apparent: his laziness, which is the main reason why the shy, skinny boy never manages to finish even primary school.

'He is always in the mood and is as passionate as seven gorillas combined.'

His laziness also adversely affects his body and it is the source of much complaint. When he is playing at PSV the young Ronaldo – still wearing braces on his teeth – is a regular and welcome guest at McDonalds. At Inter Milan, president Massimo Moratti advises him to seek psychological treatment for his eating habits. Even president Lula of Brazil calls Ronaldo 'too fat' in public. During the 2006 World Cup the striker's weight is discussed more often than his performance on the pitch. His weight problems follow him everywhere. He embarks on the one strict diet after another, but his visits to fast food restaurants are just as frequent. In the run-up to the 2010 World Cup – in which he is desperate to take part – Ronaldo has 700 milliliters of fat drained from his belly. The striker, now playing for Corinthians, is clearly in decline and even his own fans have resorted to calling him 'Gordito' (Fatty).

Over the course of his career Ronaldo's attitude in general leaves a lot to be desired. Among his critics are Pelé, his coaches and the fans of Real Madrid, Inter and AC Milan, most of whom think that Ronaldo has been focusing too much on the wrong things down through the years. To put it in a nutshell, girls were more important than soccer to him. As a teenager he is already a frequent visitor to nightclubs. In his time at PSV he has a relationship with the daughter of PSV's technical director, Frank Arnesen. When he falls in love with Susana Werner, the TV Globo beauty, he spends more time waiting at the airport to take another 'love trip' to Brazil than that he does working up a sweat at a training session. Ronaldo travels to Rome and Moscow to see Anna Kournikova, the tennis player with whom he is madly in love. And an ex-girlfriend, Favyola Francois, calls him 'a sex machine' in her book. 'He is always in the mood and is as passionate as seven gorillas combined.'

Ronaldo and women – quite a saga. He marries the Brazilian blond Milene Domingues, a professional soccer player herself and the queen of keep-up. The have a son, Ronald (named after Ronald McDonald in honor of Ronaldo's favorite fast-food restaurant) but they divorce after four years. A couple of flirts later, Ronaldo starts dating the model Daniella Cicarelli. They marry, but it only lasts for three months. He embarks on his third (and last?) marriage in 2008. Another relationship, this time with the model Michele Umuzu, doesn't get as far as the altar before it too fails, even though he has to admit to being the father of her son after a paternity test. He is accused of having sex with minors, and a compromising photograph is published showing Ronaldo sitting in the lap of a Brazilian brothel owner. The lady in question is clad only in a suspender belt. 'A feast of orgies, cocaine and an awful lot of dollars,' according to German magazine *Der Spiegel*. Ronaldo defends himself by saying: 'Thousand of pictures are taken of me with someone else every day. Even my phone number is easy to find.'

He doesn't deny the incident, however. And the game is well and truly up for the by-now infamous *womanizer* – the man who at that point was the all-time top scorer at the World Cup with fifteen goals – when he gets caught with three prostitutes. After Ronaldo has dropped his girlfriend off at home, he picks up the trio and they drive to a motel. He is in for a big surprise, however. The prostitutes turn out to be transvestites.

The AC Milan star is reputed to have offered them five hundred dollars each to keep their mouths shut. Two of the three 'ladies' accept the offer, but the third one demands 20,000 dollars... Eventually, the police have to step in. It turns out that the trio have filmed the whole incident and posted it on the internet. They accuse Ronaldo of asking them to buy drugs for him in the nearby favela Cidade de Deus. The scandal costs the former world footballer of the Year dearly. Mobile phone provider TIM, with whom Ronaldo has a sponsorship deal, immediately terminates their lucrative agreement. In his defense, Ronaldo could muster no more than this: 'It was a bit stupid of me.'

Ronaldo's naivety often gets the better of him. In a TV interview with the Brazilian TV host Xuxa, he admits that he sometimes still wets his bed. And he says that the incident with the transvestites will haunt him forever. He insists that he isn't gay and says, 'I didn't know they were transvestites.'

In 2011 Ronaldo finally gives up the fight against premature retirement. His knees are creaking worse than ever before and his beer belly has become a major hindrance. 'No matter how much I'd love to keep going, I can't carry on like this.' His participation in a TV show called *Medida Certa* ('The right size'), in which he tries to shed a few kilos, has little effect. 'I know I'm too heavy. But everyone looks three kilos heavier on television. I often have five cameras pointed at me. That adds up to fifteen kilos,' jokes the former professional player, who is now at least forty kilos overweight. Now working as an intermediary between soccer players and corporations, Ronaldo says he is enjoying his freedom. 'I can do whatever I please now. I don't have to worry about photographers or newspapers any more. And I don't have to hide my beer in a soda can either.'

AHMED HUSSEIN ABDELHAMID HOSSAM (MIDO)

Nationality: Egyptian

Born: 1983

Nickname: Mido

Known for: idiosyncratic behavior and a string of clubs

'I'M NOT 100% NORMAL'

H e could have made a name for himself at the 2006 Africa Cup. His country, Egypt, reached the final and beat Ivory Coast to claim the title. Mido, however, was nowhere to be seen. Two days before the final he was suspended by his country's association for no less than six months. The reason was his furious reaction to being substituted during the semi-final against Senegal.

The game is in its 78th minute when the Egyptian coach, Hassan Shehata, decides to take Mido off. The score is 1-1 and Shehata believes his team has a better chance of winning if he brings on Amir Zaki. The crowd is obviously behind the decision. Then a remarkable spectacle unfolds near the sideline. Mido is furious that he has to come off and swears at the coach. The ensuing scene lasts more than a minute and the cameras capture every second of it. The striker is only one step away from physically attacking his coach. Another sub has to come between them. The Belgian teletext service gets a lip reader to interpret the conversation:

Mido: 'Why are you taking me off?'

Shehata: 'I'm the coach here.'

Mido: 'You are taking me off. You're a donkey'

Shehata: 'You're a donkey yourself, now get off the pitch!'

Even before Mido has time to disappear into the catacombs of the stadium, his replacement Zaki scores the winning goal. His teammates say that they want to keep Mido in the team and the *enfant terrible* apologizes for his actions ('I did it for the team and for Egyptian soccer. I was convinced that I would score one more time.'), but association president Zaher declares that the striker has to leave the squad. On top of that he will be suspended for six months. Assistant coach Shawki Gharib adds: 'Egypt is more than just Mido. We have 23 players in our squad.' Shehata does offer Mido the chance to pick up his medal, but the striker refuses to do so, saying, 'Shehata is an amateur, a joke.' And with regard to the national association: 'They think they know everything, but they are clueless.'

Mido has been a source of trouble just about everywhere he has played. A year before the Africa Cup he had clashed with the coach of the Egyptian team at the time, Marco Tardelli, after he called his international teammates a bunch of amateurs. The trigger for this outburst was his failure to make himself available for a World Cup qualification match, claiming that he had a knee injury. However, this didn't stop him from playing a friendly game for his club, AS Roma, 24 hours later. The Egyptian fans are completely fed up with him. Tardelli considers never selecting him again. Team captain Hossam Hassan supports his coach: 'Playing for the national team should be an honor. No one can expect special treatment.' Mido later apologizes for being impolite to the Egyptian press. 'I still have a thing or two to learn.'

Seven months after his run-in with Tardelli's successor, Shehata, at the Africa Cup, Mido is accepted back into the fold. But the peace is only of a temporary nature. When the coach leaves Mido out of the Pharaohs' squad for the 2010 Africa Cup because his fitness levels are poor, he reacts furiously. Mido, who finds out about his omission on the internet, criticizes Shehata and refuses to play for the national team ever again. 'I don't understand Shehata's motives at all. He's thrown me out of the squad after only four days. He just doesn't like me. They don't treat top players like Drogba and Eto'o like that in their countries, do they?'

There are few players with so much potential who have made so little of their career as Mido. And seldom has a player played for so many clubs in such a short space time or left so many of them so rancorously. The first big club to show interest in him is Paris Saint-Germain. As a seventeen-year-old talent he impresses during his trial period by scoring two goals in four friendly games in succession. The club immediately offers the young player from the Egyptian club Zamalek a contract. But when he hears that he will have to live in dorms he reacts angrily and refuses to sign. 'Together with three others in one room! Not a chance.' The striker opts to sign for AA Gent instead. In Belgium, the teenager – who still goes by the name Hossam – is initially very homesick. But when his father hears that he wants to return to Egypt he forbids it.

The Hossam family isn't exactly rich, more upper-middle class (Mido: 'We were pretty well off.'). This doesn't stop him from driving a car through the densely populated city of Cairo at the age of thirteen – without a drivers license. School is patently not for him. He is fortunate that together with his brother Tamer he is able to enroll at an expensive language school, while most families can't pay for school at all. An additional advantage is that he doesn't have to do military service. He graduates from school thanks to the help of his corrupt teachers. Even back then he is getting used to the idea of privilege.

At AA Gent he turns out to be unmanageable. He believes he is far better than his teammates and is helped in this belief when he is awarded the 'Ebony Shoe' for the best African player in Belgium. Anderlecht want to buy him but the deal falls through.

'Every coach has to deal with a completely impossible player at least once in his career. For me that was Mido.'

The Anderlecht chairman, Roger Vanden Stock, calls him a 'shitty kid' when Mido suddenly decides to sign for Ajax instead of his club. The Belgians, who had just lost their top striker, Jan Koller, believed that they already had a deal with his intended successor and that there already was a verbal agreement between Anderlecht and AA Gent. Anderlecht publish a press release in which the club makes it very clear that they don't want Mido any more because his signature is not worth the paper it is written on. Vanden Stock is fuming but Mido is seemingly unmoved: 'Ajax is like a Ferrari, Anderlecht is only an Alfa Romeo.'

Ajax has always been his dream club, even as a child, and Patrick Kluivert his idol. When their attempt to sign Arjen Robben from PSV is not successful, the Amsterdam club switch their attentions to Mido and eventually sign him on a five-year contract. Technical director Leo Beenhakker says that the arrival of the Egyptian will finally give his team some flair again. But within one season the first problems are already brewing. Is Mido turning out to be a second Dani, the Portuguese player who was very popular with the ladies and whose wild parties in his apartment were legendary, but who never really had the will to get the best from himself and his career? After his transfer to Ajax, Mido becomes a megastar in Egypt, especially in Cairo where his image adorns billboards across the city. The playboy, who later will have a relationship with Miss Belgium, is a regular customer in the nightclubs in Cairo. And he is not averse to going on a bender in Amsterdam either from time to time, though he will later deny this: 'I swear it. In one year I've only been out three times!' What is certain, however, is that he visits the Egyptian eatery The Nile in Amsterdam every day after the training. With his car double-parked right outside the door, he is often spotted enjoying the delights of a big fat waterpipe...

In his official biography, his teammate at Ajax Andy van der Meijde reveals that the top players at Ajax frequently visited The Escape, a nightclub in Amsterdam, and that Mido, the spoiled Egyptian, was the one who showed him the ropes. For example, one night Mido invited a couple of his teammates and a sexy escort girl to his home. He then asked his future wife to leave the room before making out with the escort. Zlatan Ibrahimović and Christian Chivu ignored them, but Van der Meijde was all eyes and ears. Not much later Mido fixes Van der Meijde up with the girl living next door. 'That afternoon I cheated on (my girlfriend) Diana for the first time. Without really thinking it through, I crossed a line and it turned out to be the first step on the road to living a double life,' Van der Meijde confesses. 'I suddenly realized how being an Ajax player meant having a very privileged position.' Despite Mido's excesses, however, his Egyptian girlfriend remains loyal to him and they settle down to a 'normal' married life in 2002.

The eighteen-year-old Mido has barely arrived at Ajax when he says that he wants to leave the club. Despite this announcement he is keeping Zlatan Ibrahimović out of the team because he is scoring in almost every match he plays. When, a year later, he repeats his desire to leave the club, coach Ronald Koeman starts to lose patience with him. According to teammate Jan van Halst there always seemed to be a problem: 'He was a nuisance really, only fooling around at training and criticizing everyone else in the media.' Mido is frequently a thorn in the side for the rest of the team and when the upstart player refuses to play on the left at one point, they have pretty much had enough of him. He is dropped from the squad and receives a hefty fine. He is told that he will have to fight his way back into the first team at Young Ajax. By now Koeman has really had it with the spoiled Mido, who is often seen driving at high speed into the VIP car park at the Arena stadium in his bright red Ferrari 360 Modena. Mido on this particular folly: 'Why shouldn't I drive a Ferrari? It's not like I'm buying drugs or something? And anyway, Beckham has six of them!' And when he parks his car right in front of the departure hall at Schiphol Airport and doesn't find it in the same place after returning from yet another visit to Cairo, he reacts astonished... Towed away? Why? It belongs to Mido, the famous soccer player? The Egyptian star spends money like it is going out of fashion and often races Ibrahimović on the A10 public highway. Andy van der Meijde: 'Mido could really push the boat out. Not many people know this, but one time his car went into a spin on the highway from Utrecht to Amsterdam and his Ferrari ended up on the hard shoulder facing the wrong way. He got out of the car and walked away. He then called me and said: "Hey Andy, I'm afraid to drive any further. Could you pick me up?" I didn't, of course. I'm not that mad.'

Initially, Mido is close friends with Ibrahimović and they often share their frustrations with each other. The Swede is being called a flop and Mido isn't making it into the starting eleven on a regular basis either. Despite their friendship they end up fighting with each other. One of their most infamous episodes is the so-called 'scissors incident'. At half-time during an Ajax-PSV game, an argument between the two star players becomes so heated that Ibrahimović punches Mido. He is sick of the Egyptian's constant bullying. Mido finds it rather amusing that he is the one who is keeping the Swede out of the first team. Mido, who is cutting his bandages at the time, throws a pair of scissors at Zlatan's head. The weapon barely misses its target. Zlatan picks the scissors up, grabs Mido by the neck and threatens to kill him. Koeman's patience runs out but the Egyptian hightails it back to his native country again (where nobody has ever heard anything about his antics and where he still remains a god). Koeman later says: 'Mido had already made a series of disciplinary mistakes. He stayed away from Dutch classes, didn't come to the Arena stadium in the sponsored car and didn't turn up as required at a sponsor's event.' And he wasn't exactly disciplined at the training sessions either. Mido is loaned out to the Spanish club Celta de Vigo. And Koeman would prefer never to lay eyes on him again. 'He is completely unprofessional and thinks he's a star.' And Beenhakker: 'Every coach has to deal with a completely impossible player at least once in his career. For me that was Mido.'

Ten years later, and acting like nothing had ever happened, he signs for Ajax again. Martin Jol is the new coach in Amsterdam and he has generally had good experiences in the past with Mido, even though he had to remove him from the squad once for refusing to play when they were both at Tottenham Hotspur. In the meantime, Mido has been out and about, having played for Olympique Marseille – where he would maintain close ties with the local mafia – and AS Roma, among others. In France he doesn't get to play much due to the competition for places, while in Rome he only plays twelve games for the club. With Jol at Spurs, however, he has a pretty good time in comparison. At Ajax, when Mido comes waltzing through the door again, people can scarcely believe how much weight he has put on. Although he has come from Middlesbrough on a free transfer (where he had been suspended by the club for returning from Egypt ten days too late) and says that he will play on a pay-per-game basis, all anyone can talk about is how fat he is. An Ajax supporter on their website: 'When I saw Mido play, for a second I was under the impression that the club had sent out one of the veterans to play.' Supporters mockingly refer to him as the 'kiloknaller' (kilo cracker), after a term coined in a campaign by a Dutch animal rights association against cut-price meat.

In the end, Mido only plays five games for Ajax before moving on to Zamalek (four games in one and a half seasons) and Barnsley (one game in six months). When, at the age of thirty, he still hasn't found a new club after being unemployed for six months, he announces that he will retire as a player in the summer of 2013. Six months later his old club, Zamalek, appoints him as their head coach only to kick him out again after another six months. Despite the fact that he hasn't had any real success anywhere, Mido claims that his commitment has always been unquestionable. In the end he was probably destined to become a club hopper, given his endless series of injuries and repeated refusals to honor his playing commitments. On one occasion he even refused to play when he wasn't able to park his car at the club. His lack of respect for authority became infamous. For instance, it had been an age-old custom in Egypt to always address the leader of the national team as *Captain*. During the period that Hossam Hassan wore the captain's armband, Mido refused to do so. He said that the tradition was 'idiotic'. He was the only member of the squad who would not honor this custom and his attitude caused major consternation within the team. His former youth trainer, Hesham Yakin, had warned others previously about Mido's character: 'He is a fantastic soccer player, but also a real bad egg. Whenever he didn't get what he wanted he just walked away.'

NICOLAS ANELKA

Tony Tati

Nationality: French
Born: 1979
AKA: The (Incredible) Sulk
Known for: bald head

'I DON'T CARE WHAT OTHER PEOPLE THINK. I KNOW WHAT I WANT, AND THAT'S THE ONLY THING THAT MATTERS.'

The name Nicolas Anelka will be forever linked with his missed penalty in the Champions League final of 2008. Manchester United keeper Edwin van der Sar becomes the hero of the evening after the Frenchman misses the decisive kick in the pouring rain. The Chelsea fans are furious. How can a professional soccer player not hit the target from a distance of only eleven meters? They had a golden chance to win the 'Cup with the big ears' and he goes and screws it up. Anelka, a French Muslim, quickly puts the blame on the coach, Avram Grant (an Israeli), saying that he doesn't understand why Grant only brought him on during extra time, and then after warming up for only sixty seconds. He complains: 'I had to take a penalty kick straight after coming on the pitch. Completely ridiculous! Grant even wanted me to be one of the first five penalty takers. I refused. That's why I took the seventh.' What The Incredible Sulk seems to forget is that he had been playing for 25 minutes before the shoot-out. Never mind that Beletti (Chelsea) and Anderson (Manchester) both scored their penalty kicks without even having played a minute...

Anelka has worn out more coaches during his career than he has underpants. At Chelsea, André Villas-Boas eventually becomes so fed up with him that he drops the star player to the second team. Anelka isn't even allowed to come into the dressing room any more and has to give up his parking spot. And why? The French striker is trying to make another pile of cash for himself by switching clubs. And he is a master of the well-known trick of acting rebellious. In the recent past he has already swapped Manchester United for Fenerbahce and Real Madrid for Arsenal. Once Anelka starts performing well, his brothers, who are his agents, demand a rise in salary. And when they don't get it 'The Sulk' goes on strike. When he doesn't feel appreciated he simply fails to turn up for training for a couple of days. During his time at Real Madrid, coach Vincent del Bosque is forced to suspend him for 45 days, the most severe penalty the club has ever handed down. The reason is his refusal to train because he says that the Spaniard is selecting him in the wrong position. When Anelka openly criticizes Del Bosque he is immediately dropped to the subs bench.

'The club treats me like a dog,' claims the rebel, for whom Real Madrid paid seventy-seven million dollars, in the magazine *France Football*. And after he has been handed a record fine of 800,000 dollars, he says: 'I have been polite to everyone, even learned Spanish. And what happens? They treat me like trash.' He believes that Del Bosque has it in for him and that other players like Hierro are trying to get him transferred. 'When I had to make my apologies to Del Bosque, it felt like I had to drop my pants in front of him.' While he is sitting out his suspension, he treats the journalists camped outside his front door to cake (after which he often goes off to enjoy a game of golf). The suspension was not exactly inconvenient for him. When he gets back on the straight and narrow again he wins the final of the Champions League with Real (in 2000). Nevertheless, the club decides to dispense with his services after only one season. They are disgusted by his non-stop 'trickery'.

Anelka also believes that the coach of the French team, Jacques Santini, owes him an apology. This is after Santini doesn't select him for the initial squad but later turns to him as a replacement for the injured Sidney Gouvou. 'If he gets on his knees first and apologizes to me, I will think about it,' says Anelka, deadly serious. The offended forward also has a swipe at Roger Lemerre, the previous coach of the French team. 'I want to thank him for not taking me to the World Cup in Asia, given the catastrophe that took place there. At least I was spared that.' As a result of his remarks, Anelka is not called up even once for the French squad between 2002 and 2005. But this doesn't really come as a surprise as Anelka has been regarded as a pariah in his own country for years already. He, on the other hand, feels like a misunderstood genius. He seeks support within the Muslim community. He converts and states that from now on he only wants to play in countries where a majority of the population practices his religion. He changes his name to Abdul-Salam Bilal and prays five times a day, while his teammates are usually more preoccupied with expensive cars and women. He doesn't take part in Ramadan, however, as he believes that it would make him prone to injury.

Things really get out of hand after Anelka scores his first goal for West Bromwich Albion on December 28, 2013. His method of celebration is quite odd, to put it mildly. Anelka puts his right arm down by his side and his left hand against his right shoulder. The gesture, the 'quenelle', is an inverted Nazi salute. All hell breaks loose, both in England and in France, and even politicians get involved. Valérie Fourneyron, the French minister of sport, calls it 'a shocking provocation. There is no room for anti-Semitism on the soccer pitch.' President François Hollande also expresses his disapproval and says the 'anti-Semitic character (of the gesture) cannot be denied.' After the English football association judges Anelka's gesture to have been of a discriminatory nature, he is suspended for five games and handed a fine of one hundred thousand dollars.

He says that he can't stop laughing when he first hears about the punishment.

Anelka himself is astonished at all the fuss surrounding the incident. He claims that he never meant to insult anyone. 'I am not a racist,' he says in his own defense, adding that the gesture was meant as a sign of support for his friend, the comedian Dieudonné M'bala M'bala, and certainly wasn't meant to insult certain groups in society. 'It's not against the Jews, but against the established order.' Dieudonné, a comedian with the reputation of an extremist, was responsible for introducing the 'quenelle' in France. He had since been denied access to many theaters because of his political ideas, which were viewed as being anti-Semitic. The 'quenelle' was supposedly open to interpretation, but French media had already reported that it was a genuine Nazi salute. Anelka's gesture raises fears of a new wave of hatred against Jews. It spreads quickly on the internet and is

94

adopted on the street, both by the extreme right and by migrants. Mosche Kantor, the president of the European Jewish Congress, demands that Anelka be banned from playing in the Premier League in England.

At first, however, Anelka refuses to leave West Bromwich Albion in the aftermath of the 'quenelle' controversy. And this despite the anger of Zoopla, the club's main sponsor, whose owner is a Jewish businessman. To add even more fuel to the fire, Anelka says that his relationship with Dieudonné has only become stronger because of the incident: 'Dieudonné was a friend, but now he has become a brother, even though he is public enemy number one in France.' That's when the bomb really explodes. West Brom cancel his contract and Anelka has to leave. On top of that, the English FA demands that Anelka's suspension be made effective worldwide. FIFA promises to investigate the matter. The Brazilian club Atletico Mineiro wants to sign him, but decide in the end not to make use of his services after he arrives too late in Brazil. Anelka retaliates by saying that he had never actually given his word to the club: 'I never accepted any offer.' The Brazilians are insulted and take the case to FIFA. In the end the Frenchman flees to India where he will play after he has served his worldwide suspension of three games.

Anelka already had a highly controversial track record long before the infamous 'quenelle' incident. Born in a poor immigrant area in Versailles in 1979 to parents from Martinique, he has the great fortune of being a very talented soccer player at a young age. He soon becomes part of the squad for the French youth team. However, when he is left out of the starting eleven on one occasion he immediately quits the training camp. After his professional debut with Paris Saint-Germain, he goes on to play for a long list of clubs. Conflicts with teammates, and especially with coaches, are usually the reason he moves on. At Arsenal – whom Anelka joins when he is only seventeen – his teammate Marc Overmars has to endure the wrath of the young Frenchman when he accuses Overmars of being 'too selfish' on the pitch. And also that Overmars, and Dennis Bergkamp were intentionally ignoring him during games.

Among the coaches who have to suffer Anelka's whims are the previously mentioned Santini and Del Bosque, and Roger Lemerre, Luis Fernandez, Cristoph Daum and Avram Grant. Not forgetting, of course, Raymond Domenech, who has the misfortune of having to deal with the player's bad attitude for years. Anelka even manages to get into a fistfight with Fernandez. The player thinks the coach's training sessions are boring, while Fernandez calls his star player a lazy pig. But without doubt the most infamous clash of them all is his run-in with Domenech at the 2010 World Cup. The French are having a difficult time in the group stages, and after drawing the first match things are not going well in the second group game against Mexico. At halftime the coach, Domenech, gives Anelka some tactical instructions. The player feels insulted and goes completely mad. 'Bastard, you can pick your own shitty team!'

Just before the second half begins, Domenech orders Anelka to stay behind in the dressing room. After the match, which the French lose 2-0, he becomes the first French soccer player in history to get sent home during a major tournament. While the team is preparing for its last group game and its last chance of making it to the next round – they have to beat hosts South Africa to go through – all of France is in turmoil. The press has gotten wind of the trouble in the French camp. After Anelka is sent home, the atmosphere in the squad is very tense. The players appear to be backing Anelka's stance. On the way to the last practice session before the game with the South Africans, team captain Patrice Evra gets into a fight with the fitness coach, who allegedly leaked news of the conflict in the dressing room to the media. The fitness coach resigns.

On the Sunday before the match, the players refuse to take part in training. Some of them are even considering not playing in the last group game, according to Domenech when he speaks at a crammed press conference. In the end the match goes ahead as planned, but the crisis soon takes on even greater proportions when France are eliminated. The group favorites finish embarrassingly last behind Uruguay, Mexico and South Africa. Not only Evra but also Abidal, Malouda and Gouvou are passed over for that last game. Evra even has his captain's armband taken away from him. The French football federation wants to ban Anelka from playing for the national team again. The sports newspaper *L'Equipe* reports that Anelka apparently screamed '*va t'enculer, fils de pute!*' ('Drop dead, you son of a bitch!') at Domenech, also adding for good measure that 'it's a good thing that you're leaving' (after the World Cup Domenech was to be succeeded by Laurent Blanc). No one could ever have suspected that Domenech's simple request to Anelka to stick to his position on the field could have caused so much trouble. And it didn't stop there, as the problem soon develops into a tsunami.

Nicolas Sarkozy, the president of France, says he is 'shocked' by Anelka's actions. He calls the situation 'unacceptable'. Association official Jean-Louis Valentin resigns and says he is 'sick and outraged'. Jean-Pierre Escalettes resigns as president of the French football federation. 'The country has been put to shame. Anelka's actions have set us back fifty years.' On the other side of the fence, Zinedine Zidane criticizes Domenech heavily. He thinks he is a useless coach. The former star player criticizes the players of 'Les Bleus' as well. 'They should take their fair share of responsibility and put their egos aside.' The bank Crédit Agricole, sponsor of the team, decides to stop their 'Les Bleus' advertising campaign. Fast food restaurant Quick had already announced that they would be stopping a similar campaign, one in which Anelka also appeared. Later Domenech and the football association are required to appear before a committee of French politicians. By agreeing to do so they go against the advice of FIFA, who do not tolerate any political involvement in soccer matters.

In the meantime, Anelka, the *enfant terrible*, refuses to apologize to anyone. In the newspaper *France Soir* he says that 'for a long time now there has been a ticking time bomb under the squad that was just waiting to explode.' Even before the World Cup finals there didn't see to be any chemistry at all between the international players and Domenech. 'If the bomb hadn't gone off because of me, then someone else would have set it off. In the run-up to the World Cup I had already decided to withdraw from the squad. But three of the more experienced players convinced me to stay, and so I did. The wrong decision, in hindsight.' Anelka also says: 'I played very poorly during the run-up to the World Cup and during the finals. I started to hate soccer because of Domenech, and that during my first World Cup. It's the coach who should be ashamed of himself. It's because of him we became the laughing stock of the World Cup.'

A month after the World Cup the French football federation suspends Anelka for eighteen international games. He says that he can't stop laughing when he first hears about the punishment. He calls the executives of the French football federation 'clowns', and he adds: 'This suspension isn't relevant, because my career as an international was over the moment I got sent home. The whole thing is just an exercise in saving face.'

A few months later the striker decides to forfeit his World Cup bonus payment. He is the last player to do this, however; all of the other players, apart from him and Thierry Henry, had done so much earlier. Remarkably enough, Anelka is accepted back into the fold again by the French football federation only eighteen months later. However, the new coach Laurent Blanc says he won't be selecting him for the time being. And Domenech? He strikes back more than two years later when he accuses Anelka of killing the spirit in the squad in his biography '*Tout Seul*'.

In light of Domenech's comments, one can begin to appreciate what Juan Onieva, vice-president of Real Madrid, meant when he said: 'Anelka is a child, only we don't know what age he is yet.'

GARRINCHA (MANUEL FRANCISCO DOS SANTOS)

Nationality:	Brazilian
Born:	1933
Died:	1983
AKA:	Garrincha (little bird), Mané, Allegria do povo (the people's joy), The Chaplin of soccer, Charlie Chaplin and O anjo das pernas tortas (the angel with the crooked legs)
Known for:	his small size (5 feet 5 inches), crooked legs and his 'magic wand'

'SOCCER, DRINK AND WOMEN'

All of Brazil is in turmoil in the run-up to the World Cup of 1958 because Garrincha has to have his tonsils removed. Will everything go okay? Will the 'little bird' be able to play in Sweden? In the end, the operation goes smoothly. But when he returns to the squad, which is already preparing for the tournament, it turns out that he has lost a lot of blood and shed five kilos in weight. When Pelé asks him if he is all right, the youngest member of the squad replies in all innocence that a childhood dream of his has been fulfilled: 'I got to eat ice cream after my surgery.' Spurred on by the legendary strike force of Didi, Zagallo, a seventeen-year-old Pelé and Garrincha, Brazil go on to be crowned world champions.

Another nice anecdote: when Garrincha buys a radio during a tour of Sweden with his club Botafoga at the end of the fifties, he is as happy as a child. Until he returns to the hotel and his teammates tell him that when he brings it back to Brazil it will produce nothing but Swedish sounds. He sells the radio again for half the price and is one illusion the poorer. His teammates get a great laugh out of it.

These two stories illustrate the childlike character that Garrincha will retain throughout his life. When he is an adult a test shows that his IQ is lower than that of a primary school child. Nevertheless, his life story is fascinating. First of all because he avoided all contact with the press and rarely, if ever, gave an interview, and secondly because soccer wasn't broadcast on TV as much then as it is now. The main reason, however, is that Garrincha never cared for other people's opinions of him and lived a very idiosyncratic life. A life with extreme highs and equally extreme lows...

Garrincha's grandparents were slaves and were born in Pau Grande, fifty kilometers from Rio de Janeiro, the little village where he first sees the light of day. And just like almost everybody else living there, he goes to work at the age of fourteen for a firm that cuts down trees and lays roads. Garrincha soon makes his debut in the firm's soccer team, where he quickly develops into a talented player. Soccer has yet to fire his imagination, however. While everyone else in the soccer-crazy country is watching the World Cup final of 1950, Garrincha is off fishing on his own. When he returns he doesn't understand what all the commotion in the village is about. Everyone is in tears. Brazil have just lost the final to Uruguay.

The Brazilian grows up in poverty. His father is an alcoholic and rarely has any work; his mother is the one who keeps the family afloat. They pay scant attention to their little boy, who is always playing soccer, swimming in the river or hunting little birds. What is striking is that Garrincha's legs are deformed as a result of having had polio. His left leg sticks out, while his right leg is bent in and is also more than two inches shorter than his other leg. He walks and runs with a pronounced limp. He resembles a *garrincha*, a wren - an endearing little bird that has a funny walk. His sister Rosa gives him this nickname because he reminds her of a wren. Rumor has it that Garrincha actually hated these little birds and liked catching them, plucking their feathers until they were bald and then setting them free again.

Garrincha's world is one of misery and ignorance. He discovers sex when he is twelve years old and loses his virginity to a goat - something that isn't unusual deep in the countryside of Brazil. And anyway, a prostitute would be far too expensive. He doesn't have toys as a child, his only possession being a football. He can barely read or write. Soon he is fed up with going to school. He prefers to play outside in the forest around his village. He starts drinking at the age of fourteen. Compared to his father – who puts away a liter a day – he doesn't overdo it on the cachaça, the Brazilian rum, initially at least. Later he will say: 'Eventually I started drinking everything except for poison.'

No one has even the slightest inkling that he will go on to become a great player (Johan Cruyff later calls him 'the best soccer player ever'). Garrincha leads a carefree life and marries his childhood sweetheart Nair when he is nineteen, though he keeps up a relationship with another girl on the side, too. Numerous big clubs from Rio have being showing an interest in him, but they refrain from signing him because of his disabilities. In the end, Botafogo decide to sign him for the fee of 27 dollars(!). Three days later, at the age of nineteen, he plays his first game for the team. But trouble is already brewing. It turns out that discipline isn't exactly Garrincha's best quality. He hates training, ignores tactical instructions and usually doesn't even know which team he is playing against. He displays his enormous lack of interest when he casually remarks, 'I fall asleep when we are discussing tactics.' This is also the main reason why he starts on the bench at the 1958 World Cup.

Garrincha plays soccer the way he lives his life: selfish, undisciplined, unpredictable, but brilliant as well. He plays for his own enjoyment, nothing more and nothing less. The right winger plays according to instinct, skips easily around opposing players and loves teasing opponents with moves in which he doesn't even touch the ball. Playing the ball through someone's legs, waiting for them to run after him and then playing it through their legs again becomes his trademark. Defenders invariably end up lying on the flat of their backs with their legs in the air. The fans can't get enough of it and laugh themselves silly every time he fools an opponent. During a friendly game for Botafogo in Italy, he toys with an opponent so much that, after a series of feints, the defender doesn't even notice that the ball has long since been passed to the other side of the pitch.

His destructive behavior leads to the demise of practically all of his family.

The Brazilian virtuoso enjoys his crowning moment at the 1962 World Cup in Chile, where he has to carry the hopes of the nation after Pelé gets injured and can take no further part in the tournament. He passes the test with flying colors, even though the president of Brazil, Tancredo Neves, has to move heaven and earth to undo a red card that Garrincha receives in the semi-final. Garrincha gets sent off after kicking an opponent when he was already down. While making his way off the pitch, a spectator throws a bottle at him and it bounces off the top of Garrincha's head. He is none the worse for wear and Brazil go on to capture the world title. Garrincha is crowned (co-)top scorer and best player of the tournament. When a reporter begs the taciturn player to say something – even if it's only two words – to his fellow countrymen, who are all going completely mad after the final, he says: 'Hello microphone...' before calmly walking on.

It's only after wining the World Cup that the problems really start to mount up. In 1963, he gets divorced from his childhood sweetheart Nair. He has fallen madly in love with a samba singer, Elza Soares, who is very famous in those days. The Brazilian press reveals that he has shared the bed with dozens, even hundreds of women during his marriage. He already has eight children with Nair – all girls – and it turns out he hasn't been idle during the World Cup in Sweden either. Even before the management of the Brazilian team has replaced the twenty-eight blond, female employees at their hotel with men, Garrincha has already spotted an opportunity to enjoy himself. When he returns to Brazil he gets into a fight in a bar where he is being chastised for cheating on his pregnant wife, Nair. He flees the mob in his car and knocks down his own father by accident while trying to get away. When the police arrest him he is drunk as a skunk, of course. He doesn't remember anything about the accident. A few months later his father dies as a result of his injuries. Around the same time, one Ulf Lindberg is born in Sweden but this doesn't have much of an impact on Garrincha when he hears about it. In the following years the only thing he ever does is send a little money to the child's Swedish mother from time to time. He doesn't meet his son until ten years later. In the meantime, Nair has long since passed away, completely torn up by the grief her 'little bird' inflicted on her.

At the 1966 World Cup Garrincha only shows flashes of his genius. Brazil play poorly, lose two of its three group games and the team is eliminated. This is particularly remarkable given the fact that up to that point the Divine Canaries, as Brazil are known, hadn't lost a single match when Pelé and Garrincha were in the team. Pelé even says, 'Without Garrincha we would have never become world champions twice.' Garrincha plays for Botafogo for twelve years. Various European clubs try to sign him, but he doesn't have an agent and doesn't feel like moving across the ocean. He switches to Corinthians. Again he signs the contract without even reading it, being such a poor reader. He has long since stopped being the 'joy of the people'. The player who made everyone laugh – whether a fan or not of his team – has been laid waste by alcohol and women. During the Christmas of 1982 he plays his last game, smelling to high heaven of cognac.

With his prospects in Brazil looking grim, he decides to seek his salvation in Europe after all, but no one is interested in signing a player with such a bad reputation. He gets an offer from Saudi Arabia. But he doesn't feel like playing in a country full of teetotalers. He is also having trouble with his a meniscus injury because of his crooked legs. He is reluctant to have surgery however. He believes that alternative doctors can cure his knee with their magic spells. His relationship with Elza Soares worsens after he hits her in a drunken stupor. His destructive behavior leads to the demise of practically all of his family. His mother-in-law dies after a car accident while he is behind the wheel, drunk again. He becomes seriously depressed. He attempts to commit suicide by locking himself in the bathroom of a hotel and allowing the room to fill up with gas. A chambermaid discovers him just in time. Penniless, impotent and incontinent, Garrincha tries to find a job as a coach (without success). His presence at the carnival of 1980, at which he gets to sit at the front of a float as an honorary guest, is a source of great embarrassment. He is completely numb from the medicine he is on and doesn't even notice when Pelé throws him a garland. Millions of people are shocked by the spectacle on their TV screens.

Garrincha continues to play up to three weeks before his death, still trying to earn the kind of money he had become so used to spending. He dies in 1983, only 49 years old, in a comatose condition and on a drip at an alcoholism clinic in Rio. Liver cirrhosis has taken him down. He leaves behind at least fourteen children from five or six different mothers. His reputedly 11-inch 'magic wand' also became famous and he apparently even used his 'weapon' on a nurse in the clinic. At his home, tens of thousands decaying cruzeiros are found stuffed in the mattress of his bed. His first wife, Nair, had hidden the money there after Brazil won the World Cup in 1962. Thousands of fans come to pay their last respects in the Maracanã stadium, where he is laid out. The body of the people's hero is carried on top of a fire truck, with a BotaFogo flag draped over his coffin, to his birthplace Pau Grande, which literally means 'big dick'. Hundreds of thousands of fans line the route. His grave turns out to be too small for his coffin. His tombstone, which is poorly maintained afterwards, says: 'Here lies Mané Garrincha, the joy of the people.' A local says, with a twinkle in his eyes: 'Until he collapsed the only things Garrincha did was play a bit of soccer, drink and fuck women.'

ADRIAN MUTU

Nationality: Romanian
Born: 1979
AKA: The Prince of the East and Prince of the Carpathians
Known for: traces of cocaine

'I AM NOT A SAINT AND I NEVER WILL BE.'

Adrian Mutu was crowned 'Footballer of the Year' no less than four times in his native country. The same Mutu was also banned for life twice by the Romanian football association from playing for the 'Tricolorii', the Romanian national team. The first time, after the coach of the national team Piturca catches him visiting a nightclub on the night before an international match, Mutu gets away with it. After three games the association decides to rescind his suspension. But two years later, when he is 34 years old, he really crosses the line by ridiculing the coach. When Piturca doesn't select him for the important World Cup play-off games against Greece, Mutu posts a photo on his Facebook page that is just a bit too provocative: he replaces the head of Piturca with that of the British comedian Rowan Atkinson in his role as Mr. Bean. Mutu does offer his (sincere?) apologies, saying that he just wanted to ease the tense atmosphere in the squad, but still... The Romanian football association doesn't find it at all funny. The dubious past of the 77-times-capped international player, featuring cocaine, drunkenness, red cards and a string of beautiful women, doesn't help his cause either.

Far and away the biggest scandal surrounding the Romanian is the one that blew up in 2004. The top scorer at Parma has been signed by Chelsea, but he soon runs into trouble with the club's coaches, first of all Claudio Ranieri. He calls Mutu a snake because of his subtle, clever, enigmatic and predatory instincts. 'He was a big disappointment.' And in his second season at the club, under Ranieri's successor José Mourinho, things aren't going much better. Mutu barely gets any playing time, even though he is very fit in his own opinion. 'The new signings have to play. They are being drafted into the team to show that the investment is paying off,' says the displeased Mutu in the Romanian newspaper *ProSport*. He also gets into trouble with Mourinho when he joins the Romanian team in the run-up to their match against the Czech Republic, even though he is injured and doesn't have permission to leave.

Chelsea threaten him with a fine, but this doesn't move Mutu one little bit. FIFA, through president Sepp Blatter, even lend him their support.

When he regularly starts missing training, Mourinho wants Mutu to do a doping test. The coach was already aware of the rumors regarding the use of doping that had been following his new star player long before the Romanian signed for the club. But both Mutu and his agents, including the ex-international Gica Popescu – who was thrown into prison for tax evasion and money laundering – deny the allegations. This time the coach has had enough, also because the player has been performing badly. Mutu is furious and threatens to punch Mourinho, but in the end he is caught red-handed. There is cocaine in his blood that was definitely present when he played against Aston Villa. He admits to his wrongdoing (though only at the second time of asking). Chelsea show the player no mercy; the Londoners fire him immediately for 'serious misconduct, both with regard to performance-enhancing substances and recreational drugs.'

His dismissal from Chelsea FC also has a sting in the tail. Mutu is handed a seven-month suspension by the English football association (a punishment that Chelsea regards as being far too lenient) and the Romanian star player loses his sponsorship deal with Pepsi worth one million dollars. Also, the 25-year-old striker will only be allowed to play again after he has completed a rehabilitation program. Lastly, he is fined 31,000 dollars and is told that will be tested for drug use repeatedly during his rehabilitation period. Not much later, FIFA announces that the suspension will be made effective worldwide. At a press conference Mutu asks his fans to forgive him. He denies being addicted to drugs, but he does say that he has problems because he is separated from his wife and child in London. 'I had an emotional problem. I felt lonely and sad.' He reveals that he also took drugs to 'improve sexual performance'. So, did it help? Vanessa Perroncel is probably the person most qualified to answer this question. Mutu is one of five Chelsea players (including John Terry) that the lingerie model can count in her list of conquests. In the meantime, Mutu's marriage to the Romanian TV host Alexandra Dima comes to an end after two years, and after a lot of mud-slinging (for example, she claimed that Mutu beat her). The flamboyant player doesn't seem to care. Mutu is spotted with a string of gorgeous women. He has romances with a former Miss Israel and the Italian TV star Moran Atias. He is also seen with TV host Kitty Cepraga.

Mutu goes into therapy for his drug addiction. He has to report to the clinic every day. He is even guided in that process by Tony Adams, the tough ex- Arsenal defender who had been a heavy drinker. According to the clinic, Mutu is not a real addict but someone who just takes cocaine sporadically. However, an ex-lover of the soccer player tells a completely different story to the English tabloid *The Sun*. Porn star Laura Andresan claims that Mutu had been addicted for a year already before he was caught at the doping test. She also reveals that she had a quartet together with Mutu and that he even drank her blood! 'But he was a beginner when it came to sex. Like a young boy without much experience,' according to the porn star.

Mutu enjoys a pretty comfortable childhood. His parents, both computer engineers, earn a more-than-decent living. Mutu wants to become a lawyer and later enrolls in the University of Bucharest. One of his passions is for poetry. But now that he is earning in excess of 80,000 dollars a week at Chelsea he is more interested in expensive mobile phones, women, cars and yachts. 'He has forgotten where he came from and only wants to act the prima donna,' according to a Romanian sports journalist. Things quickly go from bad to worse. He gets involved in a car chase with the Romanian police when he refuses to hand over his drivers license. When they eventually corner him they confiscate his license. And the reason behind all this trouble? A Romanian psychologist thinks the eye-catching behavior of his famous fellow countryman is down to 'severe personality disorders' and he advises the player to seek therapy. By now Mutu has also begun to acknowledge his problems. He says that he is suffering from a split personality.

Andresan reveals that she had a quartet together with Mutu.

In the meantime, the Romanian attacker complains in the *Sunday Mirror* that his career is finished. 'I might as well quit playing altogether. What am I supposed to do now? I hadn't expected that Chelsea would continue to pay me during my suspension, but I hadn't expected them to fire me either.' Regardless of the lengthy ban he is serving for the use of cocaine, many clubs are queuing up for Mutu's signature. Galatasaray and Shakhtar Donetsk make their interest known, as does the ever-decent Arsène Wenger on behalf of Arsenal, who says that a person always deserves a second chance. In the end, Juventus (coached by Fabio Capello) offer him a five-year contract, while he is still serving his suspension. And so he returns to Italy. But because 'Juve' have already used up their foreign-player quota, the club parks him at rival club Livorno who then 'sell' him directly back to Juventus, making the transfer a domestic one and thus perfectly legal.

Chelsea are not finished with the Romanian yet, however. The London club, who paid Parma 25 million dollars for Mutu, demands half of the transfer sum back from the player himself as compensation for their investment in him. And they intend to get the other half from Juventus, now that the club has been able to sign Mutu for free. The result is a long-running lawsuit that also becomes a test case because it is the first time a soccer club has demanded compensation from a player that it had fired itself. The outcome could have major consequences for similar cases in the future. A whole host of individuals and organizations become involved in the case, including the appeals committee of the English FA, a FIFA arbitration committee, a civil law judge, the Romanian players union, the FIFPro, the Court of Arbitration for Sport (CAS) and the Swiss Federal Court.

Mutu believes that his having to pay millions to Chelsea's billionaire owner Roman Abramovich is an inhuman decision. 'This sanction isn't right, because I don't think I have committed a crime that justifies such a punishment,' says the player who in the meantime has been transferred from Juventus to Fiorentina as a result of the Calciopoli (bribery) scandal in which Juventus president Luciano Moggi bribed referees to whistle in favor of 'the old lady' and against its rivals. This meant that the Turin club had won the race for the title in an illegal manner. Juventus has to hand back the titles it won in 2005 and 2006 and is relegated to the Serie B, after which an exodus of players begins.

At Fiorentina, the by now thirty-year-old Mutu is earning more than two million dollars a year, and the Romanian press estimates that his assets amount to a total of thirteen million dollars. It is clear that Mutu can't pay the fine of nineteen million dollars just like that. The Romanian is desperate for help and at one point even offers to make a large donation to charities in Romania, Italy and London (to be chosen by Chelsea) as compensation. The Londoners are not interested. For them, it's not about the money but rather the principle. Of more interest to them, probably, is the fact that Juventus received almost nine million dollars for Mutu when they sold him to Fiorentina, while they did not have to pay a single cent to Chelsea for the Romanian's signature.

At Fiorentina Mutu finally begins scoring at will again - no less than 53 goals in 89 games. However, it is precisely when the Romanian has embarked on his renaissance, and even Real Madrid and Barcelona have begun to show interest in him, that his problems come to the surface again. At a party for VIPs in his native country he punches a guest, who then has to be taken to the hospital. Mutu claims he acted in self-defense. In 2010 things get really out of hand when, after playing against Bari and Lazio Roma, he gets caught for doping once again. This time it concerns the illegal substance sibutramine, an obesity medicine that stimulates the burning of food but that also gives more energy. A lifelong ban seems imminent. But the Italian Olympic Committee (CONI) initially suspends him for only one year and then for nine months. In the end Mutu gets away with a measly six-month suspension.

After Fiorentina threaten to take Mutu to court for serious misbehavior against his employer (again) – he misses several training sessions and breaks a waiter's nose in an incident at a restaurant – the club decides that they have had their fill. He has hardly scored a goal for over a year now. AC Cesena provide a solution. The *Bianconeri* would like to buy him. After one season in which he scores only eight goals and is nominated for the 'Golden Trash Can' as the worst player in the Serie A, the striker moves to Ajaccio. The little club from France is thrilled. Mutu is the best player they have recruited since Johnny Rep in 1978. When the press ask him about his infamous past, he snaps that he is now married and has three children. '*No more comment.*' And the FIFA court eventually rules, after years of endless lawsuits, that Juventus and Livorno, the clubs who contracted Mutu after the cocaine scandal in England, must pay Chelsea 23 million dollars in compensation. Mutu is delighted with the outcome, of course. 'Soccer gave me everything in life...'

GILLES DE BILDE

Tony Tati

Nationality: Belgian
Born: 1971
AKA: The Kid and The fallen angel
Known for: his tidy, neat appearance

'I'VE HAD MY FAIR SHARE OF TROUBLE'

G illes De Bilde grew up in the Breughelpark in Zellik near Brussels, a deprived neighborhood full of tall blocks of flats. De Bilde is a real 'ket', a Brussels street kid. When he isn't playing soccer he goes around stealing and causing damage to property together with his (mostly immigrant) friends. His father is the owner of a taxi company, his mother runs a newsagents. They get divorced when De Bilde is twelve years old. 'The separation was pretty nasty. Lots of shouting, ranting, fights – stuff that makes a big impact on you when you are only twelve years old,' De Bilde later recalls. The reason is that his mother is often drunk. Nevertheless, De Bilde and his brother stay living with their mother. She pays them little attention. She suffers a stroke and thinks of little except for the bottle. As a result there is often no food at home. The kids have to make do with dog food sometimes. 'Still, I wouldn't want to change the way I grew up,' De Bilde says in his biography. His mother has subconsciously formed his character. 'I quickly became independent and I learned to trust no one but myself. I don't bow to anyone. That's what I learned in the Breughelpark.'

Soccer saves him from a life of crime. The Breughelpark is dominated by high-rise apartment blocks that tower over a large and splendid field of green located at its center. Kids are continuously chased off the park by the older boys, except for De Bilde and his friends. De Bilde: 'I learned to play soccer as the only white kid among all the black people in the area, most of whom came from Zaire. At first they were suspicious of me: a little seven-year-old kid who wanted to play soccer with guys who were at least five years older. They laughed at me and told me to scram. Africans tend to form close-knit blocks that are not easily accessible to a white person. But it didn't take long before I became one of them. They soon saw that there was more to me than your average Belgian.'

While most of his friends start drinking or doing drugs, or getting into crime, De Bilde has enough common sense to resist these temptations. He is soon being compared with the famous Belgian soccer player Rob Rensenbrink. While playing for the juniors at the Zellik club he scores 150 goals in a single season. It isn't long before Anderlecht have snapped up the young De Bilde. However, Anderlecht lose interest in him during his second year with the club's junior team. 'They thought I was too delicate. They wanted boys with a bigger build.' Despite this setback, the diminutive and lighting-fast left-footed striker will quickly rise to fame. With Eendracht Aalst, under coach Jan Ceulemans, he finishes the season as top scorer in the Second Division, and in that role he plays a big part in the club's promotion. De Bilde is so happy after the last match that he throws away his shorts in full view of the fans and celebrates the prize-giving ceremony in his underpants. His path to glory is not entirely smooth, however. In 1992 he gets into a fight with two scouting leaders who have accused his brother of stealing and he dishes out a couple of head-butts. De Bilde is handed a suspended sentence of two years.

This dent in his image has no lasting damage on his career, fortunately. Even though De Bilde is playing for an insignificant little club from the small city of Aalst, in 1994 he is called up to play for the *Red Devils*, the Belgian national team. That same season he is even voted 'Player of the year' in Belgium. Everyone is amazed; after all he has only played fifteen games at the highest level. Lorenzo Staelens thinks the award is 'ridiculous', especially because Franky Van der Elst and keeper Filip De Wilde were favorites to receive the Golden Shoe from the hands of the legendary Portuguese player Eusébio. De Bilde is headhunted by a number of top clubs, but in the end he chooses his childhood love, Anderlecht where, as a teenager, he used to shout himself hoarse with the hardcore supporters on the stadium's infamous O-side. In his first season he is joint-top scorer with Johnny Bosman. De Bilde quickly becomes the darling of the O-side. His relationship with coach Jan Boskamp, however, is a lot less rosy. He gets into frequent shouting matches with his coach, but he only really loses control of himself completely when his father is dying after having suffered a stroke. Overwhelmed by emotion, he kicks a dent in an ambulance, beats up a medic and then head-butts the medic's colleague after he tries to fend him off. De Bilde ends up in a jail cell. The next day the newspapers are full of the news.

A year later De Bilde definitively becomes the black sheep of Belgian soccer when he punches an opponent, Kris Porte, during a game. Anderlecht are losing 1-0 to

Eendracht Aalst when they are awarded a penalty. As Pär Zetterberg prepares to take the kick, De Bilde gets ready to pounce on the rebound should his teammate miss. He brushes past Porte, who then elbows him in the face and pushes him away. De Bilde reacts without thinking - 'When someone hits me, I hit them back.' Porte is lying on the ground, bleeding heavily. The photos look terrible. Unfortunately, neither the referee nor the linesman have seen anything. De Bilde doesn't even get a yellow card. The cameras, on the other hand, were certainly rolling...

The next morning, when it turns out that Porte's nose, cheekbone and eye socket have been broken by the punch, De Bilde's house is quickly surrounded by journalists and camera crews. The police don't turn up until around lunchtime and then proceed to tell De Bilde that De Porte has pressed charges and that he has to accompany them to the police station to make a statement. When he arrives there he literally has to bare all. He is told to undress and bend over for a full 'examination'. 'Humiliating,' according to De Bilde. After he has made his statement, De Bilde gets to spend another night in the cell. He is handed a suspended sentence of nine months and has to do 75 hours of community service.

He smuggles the two dogs into the country in a helicopter, flying in low to avoid radar detection.

The Belgian football association suspends him for two months and Anderlecht announce that they want to sell him immediately. Porte, who will never be able to play soccer again, demands 200,000 dollars in compensation for his injuries.

Initially, FIFA refuse to let De Bilde sign for another club while he is still serving his suspension, but in the end he is allowed to leave Anderlecht. Atlético Madrid, run by Jesus Gil y Gil, the notorious mayor of Marbella, want to sign him. 'I spent two days in Madrid and couldn't believe my eyes. Spain is a completely different world, so many strange things happen there. Take the salaries for example - and I'm not talking about the amounts but the way in which you get paid. Under the counter stuff and all kinds of dodgy financial constructions. How do you think all those clubs in the south manage to get away with mounting up such huge debts otherwise?' De Bilde has the opportunity to make so much money in the space of four years that he won't have to work another day for the rest of his life. He stands on the verge of earning a seven-figure salary - and this is back in 1995 remember. Unfortunately (for him in any case), the transfer doesn't go ahead.

Feyenoord also fail to sign him and in the end it is another Dutch club, PSV, that welcomes the scapegoat with open arms. They have been frantically looking for a successor to their former top scorer, Ronaldo. After two seasons at PSV, De Bilde moves to the English club Sheffield Wednesday. He insists that he be allowed to bring his two Dobermans, Diego and Zico, into the country with him and the club promises to make it happen. They fail to do so, however, and De Bilde has to come up with a trick of his own. He smuggles the two dogs into the country in a helicopter, flying in low to avoid radar detection. Four years later De Bilde returns to Belgium where Anderlecht embrace him once again, albeit slightly grudgingly. Coach Hugo Broos presents De Bilde with a new problem however. He can't get along with him. 'He's just so boring,' says De Bilde, who likes to drive to training in a red Ferrari and even makes a few appearances on the fashion catwalks. So he moves again, this time to Lierse SK, but decides to end his career after only one season with the club. 'I enjoy the high life too much,' is his only explanation. He chooses to worship the sun instead of a football and moves to Spain with his family.

However, in 2005 he starts playing soccer again, this time for the Belgian third division club Willebroef-Meerhof. It soon turns out that his love of dogs is still as great as ever. De Bilde fails to turn up for a game after his dog dies. He also gets himself suspended for six games after he insults a referee. In the meantime he has become a TV celebrity. He is asked to select a team that will participate in the Homeless World Cup in Australia. The team will be made up entirely of homeless people and drug addicts. A documentary is to be made for Belgian television. De Bilde: 'Why they asked me? Well, I don't come from a well-to-do background myself. Not that I've ever been homeless, but I've had my fair share of trouble in the past. Maybe that makes it easier for me to put myself in their shoes.'

Towards the end of 2008, a few months after he has finally quit playing soccer, a court in Brussels decides that De Bilde only has to pay 11,000 dollars to his on-field victim

Kris Porte. Porte is furious with the decision. 'An 11,000-dollar fine is a slap in the face for all the soccer players in this country. Now everyone has a license to do as he pleases on the pitch because you barely have to pay anything if you take your frustrations out on another player,' he says in the Belgian daily *La Dernière Heure*. In 2011 De Bilde appears before the courts again. Because of his earlier offenses, he now risks going to jail. He is alleged to have punched his wife and one of his daughters during a fight that got out of hand, and in which even the police had to get involved. De Bilde had apparently been having an affair with a Brussels Airlines stewardess for quite a long time. And it is also rumored that he cheated on his partner dozens of times, including with a famous Flemish singer and with a nail stylist. A former colleague, who wishes to remain anonymous, says on Belgian TV: 'In our circle of friends everybody knew that Gilles couldn't resist a pretty woman. Moreover, he was the one who received the most attention from women, and the only one who responded to their invitations so eagerly. He must have had dozens of lovers during that period. And his wife, Ils, didn't know a thing. During his time in the UK he even had a lover from Aalst, a nail stylist whom he flew in regularly and even gave a breast enlargement procedure as a present.' In the end the judge decides that De Bilde doesn't have to go to prison if he behaves himself for a year. He is also obliged to undergo aggression therapy. Because of the affair, De Bilde loses his job at Anderlecht TV and is fired as an analyst by the Belgian TV station Sporza. The fallen angel of Belgian soccer becomes editor of the magazine *Life After Football* - a job that must have suited him down to the ground.

ROY KEANE

Tony Tati

Nationality:	Irish
Born:	1971
AKA:	Keano, Raging Roy, and The Mean Machine
Known for:	Celtic tattoo on his arm

'YOU DON'T WIN LEAGUE TITLES WITH CHOIRBOYS IN YOUR DRESSING ROOM'

Famous around the world for his on-field antics, 'Raging Roy' was also a demon in the dressing room, never mind what he got up to beyond the bright lights of the stadium. Roy Keane had (and still has, as a coach) a real 'bad boy' reputation. For no less than twelve years he was the driving force behind the Manchester United team, but despite his enormous popularity with the fans, manager Alex Ferguson eventually showed him the door at Old Trafford in 2005.

Keane was actually a boxer before turning his attention full-time to soccer. Born in a suburb of Cork, a city in the south of Ireland, he is one of five children and his father works for the Murphys Brewery, like so many others in Cork. The family struggles to make ends meet and they don't even have a car. As a kid, Keane joins the local boxing club, for whom he goes on to box in official fights four times. 'It gave me a lot of self-confidence at a time when I needed it.' But when he has to choose between boxing and soccer, he plumps for the latter. He is not exactly a gifted player, more of a strong man. At the end of his first season at the amateur soccer club Rockmount, Keane, who is very small for his age, is voted the club's player of the year. When, to his great disappointment, he doesn't receive a single offer from any of the professional clubs in England he writes a letter to all 92 of them. In 1990 the passionate youngster (only nineteen) finally gets to play his first match for Nottingham Forest. He immediately sets the tone for the rest of his career in the away game against Manchester United when he hacks their star player, Bryan Robson, to the ground with a merciless tackle.

United manager Alex Ferguson is furious: 'How dare he behave like that at Old Trafford?'

The young professional is not afraid to assert himself off the field either. His first bar brawls may not yet be front page news, but when Keane reports too late for duty on his first trip with the Republic of Ireland team (to the United States) in 1991, the papers have a field day. While everyone else arrives on time to join coach Jack Charlton on the bus to the airport on the morning of departure, the nineteen-year-old Keane is thirty minutes late when he saunters up the street. He has come straight from the pub, together with a teammate. The flight has to be delayed. Furious, Charlton demands an explanation. The only thing the inebriated Keane has to say when he is asked how long he thinks everyone else has been waiting for him is: 'I didn't ask you to wait, did I?' When captain Mick McCarthy also makes it clear that he is *not amused*, Keane snarls at him: 'Go and fuck yourself, Captain Fantastic'. It was going to be a long trip...

Despite his scandalous tackle on the Manchester United captain Bryan Robson two years earlier, Alex Ferguson secures Keane's signature for the club in the summer of 1993 (maybe he wanted to protect his players from any further attacks...). The transfer fee of almost 7 million dollars is a record at the time, but Keane is more than worth the money. However, Ferguson also gets all of Keano's excesses off the field into the bargain, and for free. The Irishman is feared by pub-goers far and wide. He is not averse to calling people every name under the sun and spitting beer at them. While he had gotten used to being suspended by Nottingham Forest for such behavior in the past, at United the incidents quadruple in frequency. The tabloids say that he is addicted to booze but he strongly denies this. At the Irish training camp for the 1994 World Cup he gets into an argument with assistant coach Maurice Setters. Jack Charlton has to call a special press conference just to explain the situation. Keane doesn't care: 'Like a fool I played the role....' In his autobiography *The Second Half* he will later belittle Charlton by saying: 'He was a joke. His preparations for international matches were ridiculous. I found it impossible to relate to him as a man or as a coach.'

As a player, Keane had a real winner's mentality and he knew no limits. With Manchester United he grew to become the leader of the team, despite the presence of stars like Cantona, Beckham, Stam and Giggs. His motto: 'You should always commit the first offense yourself. That way you will leave a good impression straight away.'

Nevertheless it will take him almost five years of playing professional soccer until he receives his first red card. To earn it he stamps on Gareth Southgate's groin with his studs, and then does it again. As an excuse (meant to be ironic?) Keane says that defenders are not supposed to lie around on their backs. The FA suspends him for three games. Keane is only warming up, however. Over the course of the year 1995 he collects five red cards. And a year later he receives a completely unnecessary red card in an international match against Russia.

In September 1997 Keane picks up a bad injury. The night before a game against Leeds he is seen wandering through the team hotel in a stupor in the middle of the night. The game the next day turns into a real battle of attrition. Just before the final whistle Keane and his direct opponent, Alf-Inge Haaland – with whom he has been having a running battle for the entire 90 minutes – collide with each other. When Keane falls to the ground, writhing in agony, the Norwegian yells at him to get up. 'Stop faking it, you poser!' Keane, who later turns out to have torn his knee ligaments, ruling him out for the rest of the season, will not forget Haaland's words in a hurry. Bryan Robson, the former United captain and someone who knows all about heavy tackles, advises him to wait until he finds the right time and place to get his revenge. And that is exactly what Keane does.

In fact, he waits almost four years for the opportunity to present itself. In a game between Manchester United and Manchester City he commits a terrible foul on Haaland, smashing his studs into his knee at full stretch. Keane then snarls at the prone Haaland, 'Take that you c***. And don't ever stand over me sneering about fake injuries!' and spits in his face. The FA suspends him for five games and fines him 200,000 dollars. Keane doesn't understand why. After all, he says, late tackles are just part and parcel of the game. Later on however, in his autobiography, he reveals: 'I'd waited long enough. I f****** hit him hard.'

It seems the penny still hasn't dropped when Keane receives another red card only a few months later. It is his tenth in eight years - an unprecedented number. In the meantime the Irishman has won one prize after another with United, including the Champions League and the title 'Footballer of the Year' in England in 1999. His excellent play and unparalleled commitment are the main reasons why Ferguson continues to defend his poor behavior. Keane is still drinking like a fish and, only

24 hours after wining the Premier league title, he becomes the center of attention in a pub when someone sticks a glass in his eye while he is celebrating with a group of women and a few teammates, including David Beckham. He ends up spending the night not in hospital but in a prison cell, though this isn't the reason why he misses the Champions League final. He missed that match because in the semi-final he had been sent off after a tackle on Zinedine Zidane.

The World Cup in Japan and South Korea marks a new low point for Keane. Actually, the whole of 2002 is one big low point. To start with, Manchester United don't make it any further than the semi-final of the Champions League, where Bayern Leverkusen prove too strong for them. In the battle for the Premiership, Ferguson's boys come out on the losing side as well. Keane had already warned that this might happen. According to him it is all down to a lack of quality and ambition among his teammates. In his autobiography the captain says: 'Rolex watches, garages full of cars, mansions, set up for life - they forgot about the game and lost the hunger that got you the Rolex, the cars and the mansion.' That same summer, things explode completely when the Irish team is preparing for the World Cup. The ensuing clash between the coach, Mick McCarthy, and his captain becomes known as the 'Saipan incident', after the Oceanic island where the drama unfolds.

When Keane finally loses his patience with the set-up at the training camp, he vents his frustration in the *Irish Times*. He doesn't have one good word to say about the very poor organization around the squad. 'I don't want to act the star, but everything has been organized really badly by our association. The training field is as hard as concrete, and the kit and even the balls haven't arrived yet.' McCarthy, he says, maintains a 'Third World approach'. Keane wants to go home, but Alex Ferguson talks him out of it (over the phone). When Keane expresses his dissatisfaction at a team meeting he isn't supported by anyone. He feels let down and seeks out the media again. When McCarthy gets wind of what Keane has revealed in an Irish newspaper, all hell breaks loose. After a massive argument, the player is put on a plane and sent home. Keane, in turn, says that he won't play for Ireland again as long as McCarthy is in charge: And in an interview in *The Guardian* he has this to say about his former coach: 'You were a crap player, you are a crap manager, the only reason I have any dealings with you is that somehow you are manager of my country and you're not even Irish, you English c**t. You can stick the World Cup up your b*****ks.'

After the summer his newly published autobiography causes quite a stir. Haaland, who is still recovering after the scandalous attack by Keane and who will never be able to play competitive soccer ever again, is demanding 14 million dollars in compensation from the player. In the meantime Keane is sent off yet again, this time for elbowing another player in the face. The entire nation of England gets involved in discussing 'The problem'. What should be done about *Keano*? Even Ferguson, who still has the most influence over him – he has been able to stop his player from ending his career prematurely several times and even got him out of jail once – doesn't know what to do anymore. Keane expresses his regret to an English daily: 'I just can't stand losing. Trainers can shout at me '*Relax, Roy*', but I'm not like that. I know it sounds crazy, but I'm really trying to change myself.'

'They forgot about the game and lost the hunger that got you the Rolex, the cars and the mansion.'

However, even after the tumult of 2002 Keane remains a magnet for controversy. And when it's not because of his actions on the pitch it's because he is on trial for punching someone in the street or being castigated for his aggressive behavior towards referees, linesmen and opponents, including Marc Overmars, Alan Shearer, Patrick Vieira and Steven Gerrard. An example: when Vieira tries to intimidate Gary Neville of Manchester United in the players tunnel at Arsenal just before a game, Keane butts in: 'If you want to fight, don't pick on the smallest ones, pick on me!', after which he raises his fists. Keane will later justify his behavior by saying: 'When I hate someone, I play my best games.'

Off the field Keane is actually quite shy, a bloke who enjoys reading, for example. When his fellow players are busying shopping at the airport, he just sits quietly in a corner with a book in his hands.

In October 2005 Keane, feared for years by one and all, decides to quietly end his international career after Ireland fail to qualify for the 2006 World Cup in Germany.

One month later, however, there is considerably more commotion when he is forced to leave United. Ferguson takes the captain's armband off him and tears up his contract after Keane ridicules seven teammates live on MUTV, the club's own TV channel. Rio Ferdinand, in particular, is singled out for criticism after the humiliating 4-1 defeat against Middlesbrough: 'Making 120,000 pounds a week and playing well for twenty minutes doesn't give you the right to call yourself a superstar!' Keane also says that some the players ought to be sold in the New Year.

In the interview, which is quickly removed from the club's website, Keane even has the nerve to criticize Ferguson (about the facilities at a training camp). And this is all the more remarkable given that the experienced 34-year-old player has been put forward as a possible assistant and even successor to the Scot. At a training session the two protagonists almost end up going for each other's throats. Afterwards, assistant coach Carlos Queiroz admonishes the player for his behavior. In Ferguson's opinion Keane hasn't exactly shown much loyalty towards his fellow players in the interview on MUTV. Keane, in return, badmouths Ferguson and also gets into an argument with teammate Edwin van der Sar. The latter tells Keane that he needs to change his tone, upon which Keane replies that the keeper should keep his big mouth shut: 'You've been at this club two minutes and you've done more interviews than I've done in 12 years.'

By now Ferguson has had enough. Keane leaves the club through the back door and joins Celtic. Ferguson strikes back at his star player in his biography, which was published later: 'Keane ran a true reign of terror in the dressing room with his intimidating and aggressive behavior... He ruled with an iron fist and a savage tongue... His tongue was the most feared part of his body. His departure was the best thing that ever happened to Manchester United. He was a disgrace to the club.' And: 'Once, I came into the dressing room and we all had to step in to prize Keane and Ruud van Nistelrooy apart.' It also turns out that Keane had given Van der Sar's predecessor, Peter Schmeichel, a head-butt and a couple of punches during a club trip to Asia. The Dane was left with a black eye.

With his playing days behind him Keane decides to turn his hand to managing. He immediately becomes a very controversial coach. For example, he frequently kicks over chairs and is even prone to hitting his players (according to Dwight Yorke).

As a TV analyst, and also in his second autobiography, he regularly takes a pot at Manchester United and Ferguson. 'It was all about control and power for Ferguson. He has a gigantic ego.' And later: 'He made millions thanks to the class of the players.' He also refers to other players who had their fair share of problems with 'The Boss', among them Jaap Stam, David Beckham, Paul Ince and Ruud van Nistelrooy. 'Each and everyone a winner,' says Keane. 'You won't win titles when you only have choirboys in your team. These boys challenged the manager, in various ways.' *Keano* is less positive about 'Mr. Man United' Ryan Giggs though: 'If you've had a great career, that doesn't mean you're a great player.'

HARALD SCHUMACHER

Tony Tati

Nationality: German

Born: 1954

AKA: Toni, The Monster from Sevilla and 'the neurotic'

Known for: **big** moustache and 'sticky gloves'

'EGGS, POTATOES, TOMATOES, ROCKS; THEY THREW EVERYTHING THEY COULD AT ME'

S eldom has the wrath of the public been directed so vehemently at one single player than it was on a dark night in July at the 1982 World Cup in Spain. Harald 'Toni' Schumacher torpedoed the Frenchman Patrick Battiston so badly that for a second people even thought he was dead. Five years later – when calm had barely been restored – the keeper was heavily criticized again after the presentation of his book 'Anpfiff' (Kick-off) which was full of revelations about the German soccer world. Many of his fellow players felt badly let down and betrayed.

Oh, how happy the neutral soccer fan had been on that evening in Spain when Schumacher didn't get his hands on a winner's medal after losing the World Cup final, only a few days after his terrible foul on Battiston. West Germany had just lost the match 3-1 to Italy. With the Italian captain Dino Zoff embracing the cup proudly, Schumacher just stood there dazed. Mind you, it wasn't just the French who had been screaming for justice. The German keeper had become a global pariah after his kamikaze offense in the semi-final. A survey by a French newspaper showed that Schumacher was the most hated German at that moment, even more hated than Adolf Hitler. He is called a Nazi and is compared to an Auschwitz camp guard. In his own country he has to endure constant booing for weeks on end during league matches. 'Eggs, potatoes, tomatoes, rocks; they threw everything they could at me.'

The infamous semi-final between France and West Germany is a fascinating match and is being played in a very sporting manner. The French' however, think that referee, Dutchman Charles Corver, is being biased. Might that be because France had prevented the Netherlands from qualifying for the finals? 'The Blues' squander a number of chances. Schumacher almost kicks Didier Six to pieces in the penalty area. The Frenchman complains about the keeper's behavior to Corver. The Dutchman smiles at the striker as if he hadn't seen the incident at all. After half-time France dominate the game. Their coach, Michel Hidalgo, substitutes Bernard Genghini for Patrick Battiston and five minutes later the defender finds himself cast in the leading role. Michel Platini sends him off on a run with a measured pass. Battiston has only Schumacher between himself and the goal. On the edge of penalty area he shoots and then, a fraction of a second later, a terrifying moment - Schumacher comes flying out of his goal like some kind of savage.

According to his manager, Schumacher's biggest mistake wasn't what he did but rather how he reacted after he had floored the Frenchman. With Battiston out cold on the ground, Schumacher just walks around chewing on his gum as if nothing has happened. He even seems to be annoyed that the player is staying down so long. Later, in his biography, the German claims that he was afraid to go over to check on Battiston. 'Trésor and Tigana (Battiston's teammates) were already there. The atmosphere was explosive. I was cowardly.' The referee hasn't seen the incident. Schumacher doesn't even get a yellow card and not even a free kick is awarded. Years later the referee says: 'I was following the ball.' The ball in question barely misses the target. Corver consults the linesman, Valentine, who says that the offense wasn't intentional. Later Corver admits: 'In hindsight I should have given him a red card.' What's more, the FIFA rewards Schumacher with a rating of 9.4 for his performance in the game. The French captain, Platini, says it is a disgrace and calls Corver 'the twelfth German': 'We would have won if we had been given a penalty.'

Schumacher becomes the hero of the moment (for the moment...) when he stops two penalty kicks in the shoot-out after the game finishes in a draw. His country is through to the final. On the way to the dressing room Schumacher gets carried away in the jubilant celebrations that follow. When a journalist tells him that Battiston has suffered a concussion and lost a few teeth, his reaction is unusual to say the least: 'Dann zahl ich im seine Jacketkronen' (freely translated: 'If that's all that's wrong with him, I'll pay his dentist's bill for him'). He shows a complete lack of compassion. And that while the Frenchman is fighting for his life in hospital. His situation is much worse than what the journalist has told him. It turns out Battiston has broken one of his vertebrae. He is unconscious for half an hour. Platini even thought for a second that he was dead because when he was being stretchered off the field he hadn't been able to find a pulse. And Schumacher makes the same mistake for the third time when he 'forgets' to pay his victim a simple hospital visit...

At first the German newspapers keep quiet about the incident, but the matter soon escalates into a controversy of unprecedented proportions. Schumacher becomes a political hot potato. The German Chancellor Helmut Schmidt is forced to send a telegram to president François Mitterand. A joint statement follows in an attempt to ease the tension. In the meantime, the keeper disappears from public view. All contact with journalists is avoided and he stays away from parties. He can't hide from abusive telephone calls, however, and in letters strangers say they will kidnap his children and attack his club 1. FC Köln.

Why don't we employ the services of a few pretty ladies who are under medical control?

And it isn't the French who are threatening to do these things but rather his fellow countrymen...

Weeks after the incident, Schumacher finally pays Battiston a visit. The Frenchman is suffering serious spinal problems and is still wearing a neck brace. Schumacher has only this to offer by way of apology: 'Es war ein Herzinfarctspiel' (It was a game that could have given anyone a heart attack). And: 'I didn't mean to injure you, but if I had to do it all over again, I'd do the very same thing. It was the only way to get the ball off you.' Typical of a player whom the fans had always lauded for his high level of commitment. To show his first girlfriend how well he could endure pain, Schumacher once put out a burning cigarette on his arm. And whenever his team lost a game, he would go home and punch a sandbag repeatedly until his knuckles started to bleed.

The German, who was born in 1954 near Cologne, grew up in relative poverty. The Schumacher family lived in a small house and he shared a bedroom with his sister, Gaby, for eighteen years. His father worked himself to the bone in the building construction industry; his mother always told him not to be ashamed of his poor upbringing. The little 'Schumi', as thin as a toothpick, starts playing soccer as a striker. He excels in that position at first, but his knock-kneed legs soon prove to be a major disadvantage. At the age of ten he switches to keeping goal for his local club, Schwarz-Weiss Düren. Even at that early stage he is admired for his dedication. When 1. FC Köln come knocking on the door his mother turns down their offer. Her son has to get an education first. He trains to become an apprentice coppersmith. Later, before finally signing for 1. FC Köln, he finds a job repairing boilers. On his first appearances for Köln he earns himself a name for being extremely nervous. 'After that I went to see the club doctor. He advised me to think about nice things during games, like the beach, the sea and holidays.' He owes his subsequent nickname, 'Toni', to the famous Köln goalkeeper in the 1960s, Anton Schumacher, who also went through life as 'Toni'.

His star rises quickly. He wins a host of trophies with 1. FC Köln. In the national team, however, Schumacher has to fight for the number one jersey with the legendary keeper Sepp Maier. Still he makes debut for the *Mannschaft* in 1979. When Maier is injured in a serious car accident that same year, it looks like Schumacher will get a free run in the team. But the competition for that single spot underneath the crossbar remains tough. Nevertheless, Schumacher defends the West German goal at the European Championships in Italy in 1980 – despite a broken finger. They go on to win the title. Despite the Battiston affair and its enormously negative aftermath, Schumacher is voted 'German footballer of the Year' both in 1984 and 1986. In the first meeting between France and Germany since the drama with Battiston, 'The Monster of Seville' is treated to a constant shower of abuse, both verbal and physical, including Nazi swastikas, potatoes and rocks. The city of Strasbourg is turned upside down that night.

In his own country the clouds have barely lifted when things go wrong again, this time after the publication of his autobiography 'Anpfiff'. In it he takes a pop at practically everybody, including colleagues and coaches. Schumacher calls young player 'lazy bastards' and accuses them of having the mentality of civil servants and spending more time practicing their tennis or golf skills than they do on soccer. He says that the Dutchman Rinus Michels (coach at 1. FC Köln) had no sense of humor and was only interested in humiliating Germans. The players felt like slaves under his regime. 'There was never much to laugh about under coach Georg Kessler either,' he adds. And he criticizes Paul Breitner's articles in *Bild* as meaningless and weak and says that he 'would look better with a cigar in his mouth than with a pen in his hand.' He calls Karl-Heinz Rummenigge selfish, saying that 'the whole squad always has to adapt to whatever he wants.'

During the run-up to the 1986 World Cup in Mexico, the relationship between Rummenigge and Schumacher deteriorates rapidly. The keeper wants to leave the training camp after Rummenigge accuses him of trying to usurp his captain's armband. 'You can all kiss my ass,' is all that he has to say to the rest of the team. In the end Schumacher is persuaded to stay. The reserve keeper, Uli Stein, whom Schumacher hates with a passion, is not shown the same mercy however after he makes the unforgivable mistake of calling the team coach, Franz Beckenbauer, 'a liar'. Despite his poor performance in the final, Schumacher is voted second best player at the World Cup, after Maradona. He is awarded the silver ball for his efforts.

As a result of his controversial statements about his colleagues, Schumacher is immediately fired by 1. FC Köln (in February 1987). At an emotional press conference the club's enraged president, Peter Weiland, tells the press that the former club favorite has gone too far this time. 'Our club is not a kindergarten! 'Grossmaul' (big mouth) Schumacher has caused great damage to everything and everyone concerned. The German football association puts the goalkeeper's career on hold as well. Schumacher feels badly let down and he doesn't understand why they think they have to 'shoot the messenger'. All he did was 'clarify' some details relating to a number of incidents. For example, he condemns the fact that the national team had to go on a diet of pills at the World Cup in Mexico. 'They pumped us up. And not only with pills but with injections, too.' It turns out that the German team doctor had handed out over 3000 pills to the players at the World Cup. Schumacher also pleads that 'clean sex' be made available to the players during a major tournament. 'Total abstinence for weeks on end is inhuman. Why don't we employ the services of a few pretty ladies who are under medical control? There is only one risk attached to this: that your eyes will be scratched out of your head when you get back home.'

Schumacher confesses that he has used stimulants himself. 'I felt like a steam train during training sessions and during league and cup games. And you're asking me if I was the only one?' He certainly wasn't. Schumacher accuses his club of giving cough medicine containing high doses of ephedrine to players before an important game in 1984. 'We flew around the pitch like devils.' And Schumacher went even further: 'There is a long tradition of doping in the Bundesliga. For the best players at Köln, pills and performance went hand in hand. Some of the international players were unadulterated world champions at doping as well.' Among them a player at Bayern Munich, whom he doesn't name but calls a 'walking pharmacy' instead. The suspicion is that he is referring to Rummenigge.

During his last year at 1. FC Köln, he switches clubs and joins Schalke 04, who are relegated at the end of the season. He goes on to play for Fenerbahçe, Bayern Munich and Borussia Dortmund, where he was also the goalkeeping coach. In the very last game of the '95-'96 season he has to come on in the 88th minute to keep goal for the very last time, thereby making a small contribution to the club's march to the title at the grand old age of 42. Today, Schumacher is vice-president of 1. FC Köln.

DAVID BECKHAM

Tony Tati

Nationality:	English
Born:	1975
AKA:	Becks, Spice Boy, Golden Balls and Threesome Beckham
Known for:	his bashfulness, nasal-sounding voice, ever-changing hairstyles and an endless number of tattoos, including the names of his children and his wife and the full text of a song in Hebrew from the Old Testament.

'I THINK PEOPLE HATE ME BECAUSE THEY'RE JEALOUS'

Beckham has received the highest honors the English nation can bestow upon its citizens, including the Order of the British Empire. He was also made an ambassador of UNICEF and of the 2012 Olympic Games and became the face of the Malaria No More campaign and a couple of other charities. Former prime minister Tony Blair called him 'a great ambassador for the country, on and off the field.' And yet, not many of us know just how badly and how often David Beckham managed to shame the nation, his wife and his beloved children.

Who is the most famous sportsman in the world? Only a few years ago the answer to this question would definitely have been 'David Beckham'. Of all the sports-related searches on Google, his name was by far the most popular for several years in succession. Tabloid photos of him (with or without his wife Victoria) are bestsellers. In a Buddhist temple in Bangkok, fans even create a golden likeness of him. And when the statue of Saddam Hussein was taken down in Baghdad, the boy sitting on Saddam's head was wearing a Manchester United shirt with David Beckham's name and number (7). According to Ellis Cashmore, a professor in culture, media and sports, Beckham is 'the purest sports celebrity in the history of the world. Tiger Woods? Michael Jordan? They redefined their sport, and they are respected. But Beckham transcended that. He is worshipped. His fan base goes far beyond sports; many of them don't even care about soccer.'

Beckham's love for Manchester United, the club where he will go on to make a name for himself as a soccer player, is spoon-fed to him from a very young age. The parents of the player born in the cultured suburb of Chingford (East London) – his father works at installing kitchens (and is a pretty average amateur soccer player and very aggressive towards referees), his mother is a hairdresser – are huge fans of United. They frequently make the journey to Manchester for United's home games. And the very skinny young Beckham dreams of some day playing in that same *Theater of Dreams*. At his first club, Ridgeway Rovers, his coach is a certain Mr. McGhee, 'a genuine Scot with the same character traits as Alex Ferguson (who would become his coach at Manchester).' McGhee is prone to throwing tea cups and cricket balls at his players when he is angry. It isn't long before Beckham's talent starts to draw the attention of other clubs. When he is only eleven years old, West Ham United, Arsenal and Tottenham Hotspur all show an interest in the winger. Two years later, Manchester United's coach Alex Ferguson is waiting to see him after a training session. School doesn't interest the young Beckham, so the choice is quickly made. He signs a four-year contract, but he will continue living in London and train in Manchester during the holidays where he stays with a host family. In 1992, at the tender age of seventeen, he makes his debut for United's first team.

1996 turns out to be a very important year for Beckham. He has become a firm favorite at the club by the time he is called up to the England squad for the first time. But he also has something else on his mind - snaring one of the UK's most famous popstars. While preparing for an international match against Georgia in Tbilisi, he catches a glimpse of The Spice Girls performing on television. He turns to his best friend, Gary Neville, and says that he is going to marry the girl in the sexy cat suit, Victoria (Posh Spice). A few months later they share their first kiss, a moment that also marks the beginning of a continuous stream of gossip and lies about their relationship in the British tabloids. After dating for six months, Beckham asks Posh to marry him, with a 50,000 dollar three-carat ring burning a hole in his hand. They get married three years later in 1999, a year after Beckham has had to endure the wrath of an entire nation.

So what happened? At the 1998 World Cup in France, England face Argentina in an emotionally charged game, with neither nation having forgotten the mutual hatred generated by the Falklands war. His marker, Diego Simeone, antagonizes him throughout the game by snapping at his ankles whenever he can. Maybe the Argentinian has somehow heard what Glenn Hoddle, the English coach, said before the start of the tournament about Beckham's inability to control his emotions in stressful situations. When Simeone goes through him for a short cut and then kicks Beckham while he is lying on the ground, the shit hits the fan. Beckham kicks out at the Argentinian in retaliation, albeit very mildly. However, the referee spots it and Simeone gets exactly what he was looking for. Beckham is sent off while the Argentinian rolls around on the ground in apparent agony acting, in Beckham's words, 'like he's in intensive care.' Beckham will later say in his autobiography. When England are eliminated from the tournament shortly afterwards, the whole country turns on him. Fans and journalists are convinced that he is to blame. *The Daily Mirror* even prints a dartboard on its front page - with Beckham's head as the bullseye...

He goes into hiding. On the day of the Argentina match, his wife had coincidentally announced that she was pregnant, and this provides him with a welcome diversion. He flies to the USA to join Victoria in the hope that he will be able to avoid the tabloid press and the fans in his own country. However, when he lands in New York a huge press contingent is waiting for him. And it's the same story when he returns to London where twelve police officers have to escort him from the airport to his home. Supporters accuse him of abandoning his country - a doll resembling Beckham is hung from a lamp post; his telephone is tapped; the press are camped outside his front door; and a burglar is apprehended in his garden one night. He is the patsy now, and as reviled as a child molester it seems. One small comfort is that his fans at Manchester United stay loyal to him. On a church in Nottingham someone hangs a banner with the text 'God forgives even David Beckham'. He also gets some support from an unexpected source: Simeone admits that he intentionally tried to get Beckham sent off. Not that this has much effect on public opinion, however. But when the two play against each other in the Champions League two years later (Inter Milan vs. United), at least the air between the players seems to have cleared. They swap shirts and Simeone even plants a kiss on Beckham's cheek when they are walking off the field.

Manchester United win the so-called *Treble* in the season of 1998-1999: the league title, the FA Cup and the Champions League. In the Champions League final Beckham & Co are trailing Bayern Munich 1-0 with the clock ticking down, but the *Red Devils* score twice in injury time. The winning goal is scored by Solskjaer after a corner taken by Beckham. The Brit is voted the second best soccer player in the world, behind Rivaldo. And yet the majority of the English still hate Beckham. He is booed everywhere each time he touches the ball. Hostile fans scream abuse that is directed at his wife. 'They're just jealous,' says Beckham, who still can't control his emotions. When England are eliminated at the European Championships in 2000, with the supporters having booed him for the entire duration of their final game, he can't resist giving them the finger. He also loses the run of himself in the first game at the World Cup for club teams. He gets sent off in the match against the Mexican club Necaxa. *Emotions, emotions...*

In the meantime, his relationship with Ferguson has begun to disintegrate, too. According to *the Boss,* the recently married Beckham is spending way too much of his time pursuing lucrative commercial contracts on the side. Ferguson also finds his wife's influence on the player to be extremely irritating. Thing eventually boil over when Beckham asks for permission to skip training. His son is sick. But when Ferguson finds out that Victoria was spotted at the London Fashion Week show that evening, he ruthlessly demotes his star player to the reserves. After all, Beckham could have trained if Victoria had stayed at home. Beckham receives the highest possible fine (over 70,000 dollars). When the player asks his coach for an explanation, Ferguson reacts furiously. Beckham's own reaction is not all that different: 'I was pissed off that my coach talked about my wife in such a condescending way.'

It is only during a qualification game for the 2002 World Cup that *Becks* is finally welcomed back into the arms of the England fans when he scores from thirty meters with his famous 'Bend-it-like-Beckham' free kick in the dying moments of the crucial match against Greece and with the team trailing 2-1. The goal secures qualification for the finals. And he certainly can't do any wrong anymore when – complete with a mohawk haircut – he scores the winning goal in 'the war' against arch rival Argentina at that same World Cup. The bill has finally been settled it seems and Beckham says: 'The nerves, the pressure, and four years of memories were all miraculously gone.'

Life for the Beckham family is anything but ordinary and they go have to endure many ups and downs. When *Becks* had just started dating Victoria, he received an envelope in the post containing two bullets bearing his name. The attached note said, in almost illegible handwriting, that the bullets were meant for the two of them. It is not the only death threat that the popular but also controversial soccer player receives in his career. The danger becomes deadly serious when in November 2002 the SO7 (the unit of *Serious & Organized Crime Plots*) suddenly walks into the stadium at Manchester United. Barely dressed and still dripping with sweat, Beckham hears that a group of nine kidnappers is plotting to kidnap his wife and son. 'It made me sick to my stomach.'

Scotland Yard thwarts the kidnapping thanks to a tip from the tabloid *News of the World* after couple of undercover journalists infiltrated the gang. 'Not only did they know where they were planning to kidnap Victoria Beckham, but also how and when,' the newspaper says of the kidnappers' plans, which were at an advanced stage. The police also discover another plot to kidnap Victoria and her son in January 2000.

In 2003 Beckham's ten-year love affair with Manchester United comes to an abrupt end. He even has to leave the club through the back door, without getting a chance to say goodbye to either the players or the fans. After a 2-0 defeat in the FA Cup against Arsenal, Ferguson tears strips off the player and says that Beckham was guilty of the mistake that led to first goal. As Beckham tries to digest the defeat in the dressing room, Ferguson kicks a football boot at him, resulting in a deep cut above the player's eye. Beckham is incensed and goes to attack his coach, but his teammates Ryan Giggs and Ruud van Nistelrooy hold him back. 'I have never flipped so completely in my life before,' says the player in his autobiography *My story*. When the press finds out what happened – through Beckham, who is walking around with sixteen stitches in his head – the shit really hits the fan. Ferguson responds by stating his intention to sell his best-paid player as quickly as possible. 'He thinks he is more important that the coach. And ever since he got into a relationship with Victoria he has been living the life of a celebrity way too much.' Beckham in turn calls Ferguson 'The Godfather', a dictator who inspired nothing but fear in others. Barcelona flirt with him for a while, but a couple of months later it is Real Madrid who secure Beckham's signature on a four-year contract.

She is able to deliver irrefutable evidence, including an accurate description of Beckham's genitals

Success eludes him at Real Madrid, however. He does manage make the headlines after an alleged affair with his personal assistant, Rebecca Loos, which was rumored to have lasted for four months. While Loos appears nude in Playboy and gets paid 1.5

million dollars for an interview on English television, Beckham denies everything. But she is able to deliver irrefutable evidence, including an accurate description of Beckham's genitals - something you can only know if you have shared a bed with him, according to her. She rates his performance between the sheets as high as 'an eight, an eight-and-a-half,' by the way. Beckham eventually has to come clean. The Beckhams' marriage finds itself on shaky ground, particularly when more women come forward to reveal that they have also had affairs with Victoria's husband. For example, Katherine Jenkins, an opera singer, is linked to him. And Beckham was said to have declared his eternal love to the Malaysian-born model Sarah Marbeck during a Manchester United club tour, while the daughter of a Danish vicar tells all she knows about the intimate details of his underwear and body. Then there is the supermodel Esther Cañadas, the model Emma Ryan... the list goes on and on.

Very little of his image as the perfect family man is left intact by the time he decides to continue his soccer career in the United States. He receives a huge welcome there, nonetheless. Over seven hundred journalists and sixty camera crews turn up when he signs for Los Angeles Galaxy. 'I've always loved challenges,' the Englishman tells them. Mrs. Beckham is still number one at this stage, but when her husband gets acclimatized he soon gets back to his womanizing ways. He hooks up with a string of female neighbors in the expensive Beverly Hills and 'Golden Balls' is said to have cheated on Victoria with at least three of them. As a reaction, his wife briefly entertains the idea of a trial separation, according to the English tabloid *News of the World*. Sources close to her say that she can't stand her husband anymore. 'She hates his tattoos, his cursing and his stupidity. She thinks she is smarter than him and tells that to anybody who will listen.' The Bosnian prostitute Irma Nici also claims to have shared the bed with Becks numerous times (along with another girl). The story has already been published when Beckham takes her to court. He demands 25 million dollars in compensation. The judge throws out the case saying that the evidence in his defense is too weak. The prostitute's lawyer complains that his client has been harassed by people hired by Beckham and in 'a scandalous and terrifying manner.' Nici is particularly aggrieved by the fact that Beckham wasn't ordered to drop his pants during the hearing so that the court could see for itself the details of his crotch area, which she had described in such detail.

When Beckham turns 38 he decides to end his soccer career. In Los Angeles they have long since lost all patience with him. Even though he is extremely valuable as a *merchandising tool*, they regard him as being the worst buy in the history of American soccer. He is usually either injured or hanging out at parties, and mostly nowhere near California. In the off-season, he goes about filling his already bulging pockets by playing for clubs like AC Milan and Tottenham Hotspur in Europe. With his footballing days finally behind him, the attacking midfielder with the eye-catching free-kick technique, whose body is insured for no less than 258 million dollars, dedicates himself entirely to partying and promoting various products. Adidas, H&M and Motorola are just some of the companies that will probably use him as an advertising brand for many years to come. And despite their turbulent marriage and the end of his soccer career, the *Posh & Becks* dreamteam will remain the darlings of the paparazzi for a long, long time to come.

GIANLUIGI BUFFON

Tony Tati

Nationality: Italian
Born: 1978
AKA: Gigi, Superman and El Buff
Known for: hairband and black shirt with short sleeves

'I WOULD LIKE TO MEET DICTATORS'

P ress release in the newspapers at the end of September 1999: Italian parliamentarian Alessandra Mussolini, granddaughter of the former dictator, angers left wing representatives by walking around with a version of a fascist slogan from the days of Mussolini printed on her t-shirt. *Boia chi molla Buffon* ('Death to those who give up on Buffon') said the t-shirt of the blonde politician, who is a member of the ex-neo-fascist party Alleanza Nazionale. The text is a variation on the infamous fascist slogan *Boia chi molla* ('Death to those who give up') that the goalkeeper Gianluigi Buffon had displayed on his jersey the previous Sunday in a game between his club, Parma, and Lazio. After the match he flaunted the text in front of the television cameras.

Buffon's actions result in a barrage of criticism, including from the Italian Minister of the Interior, Rosa Russo Jervolino. The minister wants to put an end to the recent proliferation of extreme-right chants among Italian soccer fans. Flags showing Nazi swastikas and fascist Celtic crosses are beginning to appear more and more in the stadiums. Also, anti-Semitic chants are now being heard all too regularly on the terraces. To make matters worse, soccer players like Alberto Aquilani, Matteo Sereni and Daniele De Rossi have openly admitted to being fascist.

In 2000, Buffon makes the headlines for all the wrong reasons again. This time because of his choice of shirt number. The Jewish community in Italy is angry because the Parma keeper has chosen number 88. They say that '88' is a neo-Nazi symbol and that with 'H' being the eighth letter of the alphabet, 88 obviously stands for 'Heil Hitler'. Furthermore, Club 88 is the name of a well-known meeting place for neo-Nazis in Berlin. The commotion is enormous. A press conference is organized at which Buffon argues that he has been misunderstood. 'I chose that number because it reminds me of four balls. And in Italy everybody knows what it means to have balls: power and determination. That's exactly what I need this season to regain my place in the Italian team.' Buffon, who is only 22 years old at the time and has just missed the European Championships of 2000 because of a broken hand, does his best to limit the damage. It is clear that he is a fascist – he even admits it, albeit reluctantly – but he doesn't want to suffer the wrath of the people. 'At first I had chosen the number 00, but that wasn't allowed by the football association. 01 wasn't allowed either. So then I chose number 88.' *(The Guardian)*

Controversial or otherwise, Buffon goes on to become one of the best keepers of the world over the next few years. He even becomes only the third player in history to be part of five World Cup squads, along with Lothar Matthaus and the Mexican goalkeeper Antonio Carbajal. His transfer fee of 50 million euros when he moves to Juventus is, at the time, the highest amount ever paid for a keeper in the history of soccer. The investment turns out to be well worth the money. The Italian wins one prize after another with the club. He also wins the 2006 World Cup with Italy and is voted best goalkeeper at the tournament. In the final, although he didn't stop any penalties in the decisive shootout (Trézeguet missed for France by hitting the bar), he did point out to the referee that Zidane had head-butted his teammate Materazzi in the chest. Zidane is sent off as a result. Buffon is beside himself with joy after the victory and he walks around the pitch happily waving a fascist flag with the text 'Proud to be an Italian', just like his captain, Cannavaro.

It all began quite innocently. Born in the beautiful seaside town of Marina di Carrara, Buffon is the son of two athletes. His mother is a discus thrower, his father a weightlifter. He tries his hand at athletics for a while and also plays volleyball and basketball, but his real passion lies with soccer. At first he plays as a midfielder and scores a lot of goals, but from the age of thirteen on his natural position is under the crossbar. Only four years later he debuts in the Serie A for Parma. However, when he isn't playing, he prefers the company of fanatical, right wing 'ultras' to the luxuries of the VIP soccer player's life.

Even at this early stage in his career he is no stranger to provocation. He sports spiked hairdos and often wears a Superman shirt when keeping goal. The Cameroon keeper Thomas N'Kono has always been his idol. 'A man of the people, and that appealed to me,' according to Buffon. In Italy, and beyond, everyone knows that a lot of Italian soccer players have fascist leanings. For instance, the keeper at Torino, Matteo Sereni, even keeps a bust of Mussolini on his bedside table. Another colleague, AC Milan keeper Christian Abbiati, says he loves fascism 'because it defends family, order and the Roman Catholic Church.' Daniele de Rossie sympathizes with the fascist party Forza Nuova. And Buffon? In an earlier interview, he claimed that he would find it logical if every child had to start the school day by singing the national anthem. And in reply to the question who he would most like to meet, he says 'dictators'.

Back to the World Cup of 2006. Italy's victory was a huge surprise because just before the finals an enormous bribery scandal had broken out in the country. In the season just finished, it is alleged that no fewer than 18 matches have been manipulated. Many clubs, including giants like Juventus and AC Milan, are under suspicion. 41 people, including players, referees, officials and journalists, are under investigation. They are all charged with corruption and fraud. Buffon's name is also mentioned. He is said to have placed bets on five matches. The so-called 'Calciopoli scandal' has all of Italy in a spin.

Gambling addict Buffon is suspected of having bet as much as 1.7 million dollars in the space of eight months.

Buffon voluntarily reports to the judicial authorities and is interrogated shortly before the World Cup, together with three ex-Juventus players. In a two-hour session he continues to plead his innocence. He admits that although he has bet on games in the past, he has not done so for over a year after the Italian football association had forbidden players from doing so. 'I have always respected the rules. I have bet on foreign matches and other sports in the past because that was allowed in Italy. But I stopped immediately when it was forbidden. That was in the autumn of 2005,' Buffon tells La Stampa.

Six months after the World Cup Buffon hears that he doesn't have to fear prosecution anymore. After a closer study of the case, the prosecutor in Turin doesn't see any reason to take him to court. However, his club, Juventus – where the director Luciano Moggi played a leading role in the scandal – are stripped of the domestic championship titles they won in 2005 and 2006. On top of that, the club is immediately demoted to the Serie B. An exodus of star players (including Ibrahimović) follows, but Buffon remains loyal to his club. Juventus win the Serie B the next season by a country mile despite the disadvantage of being handed a nine-point penalty at the start of the season. Buffon claims that the scandal barely affected him. 'Despite all the things that happened to me and despite everything people say about me, it's better to be like me than like the others.'

Six years later, however, (in 2012) there is another incident. Italy is once again in the grip of a major gambling scandal, one that this time goes by the codename New Last Bet. Buffon, who had been proclaimed the 'Best goalkeeper of the last 25 years' in January, is on a training camp with the national team. The European Championships are just around the corner. He says he is not worried. 'The atmosphere in the group is good. Nobody in the current squad has been directly affected by the events of the past few days.' *(Reuters)* However, Buffon forgets to take his colleague, Domenico Criscito, into account when saying this. The police conduct a house search at the defender's home after he is accused of match-fixing. It appears that the results of dozens of matches in the Serie A and B have been manipulated. What's more, the names of top players like Luca Toni and Buffon are also being mentioned. Buffon is said to have transferred money fourteen times to a tobacco shop in Parma. Apart from selling Havana cigars and other smoking paraphernalia, the premises also housed a betting shop. Gambling addict Buffon is suspected of having bet as much as 1.7 million dollars in the space of eight months. The amounts varied between 55,000 and 220,000 dollars at a time. Fact: betting on matches is now strictly forbidden when you are a professional player in Italy. And it seems the controversial goalkeeper might have overlooked this by accident...

Buffon's lawyers go on to call their client's transactions 'money transfers with the purpose of protecting his personal property'. The substantial sums were meant to pay for the purchase of twenty expensive watches. 'The bank transfer, dated the 13 September 2010, was for the purchase of Rolex watches, which have been in the vault at Gianluigi's for months.' His lawyers defend their client by asking: 'Is it forbidden to make this kind of purchase? These are economic transactions between two people who have known each other for years, one of whom happens to be a bookmaker. The purchase fits his income, there is nothing strange about it.' The suspect himself acts as if nothing is wrong: 'I haven't done anything wrong or unlawful. It is true that I was there, but that was to sell my collection of Rolex watches so I could help a friend to buy a piece of land' *(SkySports24)*. But in Italy they know better than that. After all, the ex-professional Nicola Santoni had earlier admitted that not only Buffon but also other top players like Fabio Cannavaro and Gennaro Gattuso were hardened gamblers. Also, Buffon was said to have started a fake company together with Enzo Maresca, Mark Iuliano and Antonio Chimenti so that they could gamble under false names.

In the meantime Buffon continues to swear his loyalty to Juventus. Manchester City want to sign him and even offer top pay 82 million dollars for the keeper. Buffon could make sixteen million dollars a year at City, according to *La Gazetta dello Sport*. AC Milan and Real Madrid are also interested. Instead the keeper pleads for reinforcements at Juventus. He wants Antonio Cassano in the team, the highly flammable Roma attacker who claims to have slept with more than 600 women. And, as if he hasn't been appearing in the media enough already, Buffon also offers his opinions on the huge salaries earned by professional soccer players: 'Do players earn too much? Is a couple of hundred thousand a week too much for guys who decide matches? I actually think it makes a lot of sense that Wayne Rooney earns 300,000 a week. He has to be rewarded for his talent' *(SkySports)*. Interesting detail: Buffon, who 'only' earns four-and-a-half million dollars a year, buys the Carrarese soccer club in his hometown around the same time.

In the 2013/2014 season, Buffon makes the headlines again when he divorces his wife, the model Alena Seredova. The reason being an affair he had with a TV host. The Italian record international then (miraculously enough) decides to speak out against racism, saying that the problem should be dealt with severely in Italian soccer stadiums. The goalkeeper also supports the 'Kick it out' homophobia campaign in Italy by wearing rainbow-colored laces in his boots. Furthermore, he states to a journalist from the *Corriere Della Sera* that he has never voted for a right wing party. But why then was he waving a flag with a Celtic cross after the World Cup final in 2006 and why did he also wave back at a group of Juventus supporters who were singing *'Camerata Buffon'*? *Camerata* is the fascist equivalent of the communist 'comrade'.

JOHN TERRY

Tony Tati

Nationality:	English
Born:	1980
Nickname:	JT
Known for:	not having any tattoos

'FUCKING BLACK CUNT!'

I t is the 19th of June 2009 when John Terry is chosen as 'Dad of the Year' by a sauce manufacturer in England. Holding the trophy in his hands, the professional soccer player thanks all those present and his fans: 'It's a big honor to have been chosen as 'Dad of the Year'. I have won many trophies in my life, but I'm especially proud to have won this one. My family means the world to me.' Exactly what the father of three-year-old twins did to deserve this tribute is still a mystery to almost every Englishman. Terry has a quite few black marks in his book. And this is even before the events that would follow after 2009...

On 12 September 2001, the day after two airplanes crashed into the Twin Towers of the World Trade Center in New York, Terry is having a party with three Chelsea teammates in a hotel at Heathrow Airport. They are so drunk that they start stripping, throwing food and puking. They even make fun of American tourists in the lobby who are in tears watching the terrible images from New York on a TV screen. When Chelsea coach Claudio Ranieri is informed about what has happened, he reacts furiously. 'They have no sense of decency or respect.' The club hands them a fine equal to two weeks' salary.

The year 2002 isn't even a month old when Terry is stripped of the England under-21 captain's armband. The English FA is *not amused* about a fight in which Terry has been involved. Together with his Chelsea teammate Jody Morris, amongst others, he is said to have abused a bouncer at a London nightclub. Terry breaks down in tears during the trial. For six months the top player lives in uncertainty, but he escapes punishment this time around. The judge acquits him in August. What Terry can't deny, however, is that he urinated in a beer glass in public a month after the incident with the bouncer. The camera images from the nightclub recorded his little watery arc very clearly. And no one regards as very subtle the fact that he then threw the full glass on the floor. Terry is removed from the club. The other partygoers, his colleagues Frank Lampard, Ashley,

Joe Cole and Shaun Wright-Phillips, who is celebrating his birthday, are allowed to stay.

Terry, who grew up in the poor London neighborhood of Barking, shows his bad side once again when it turns out he is addicted to gambling on the dogs and on horse races. The player bets more than 60,000 dollars a week on average. And 'JT' is also known to have eye for the ladies despite being in a long-term relationship with his childhood sweetheart Toni Poole. He admits that he has shared his bed with numerous ladies *('eight times')*, but he promises to do better: 'I'm not going to cheat on her ever again and I want to marry her more than anything.' This particular leopard, however, is not about to change his spots. Within twenty-four hours of the above statement he has another fling going and makes use of the house of his teammate and friend, Wayne Bridge (about whom more later on). Two months later he has sex in his Bentley on a parking lot with a seventeen-year-old autograph hunter. And yet, Poole and Terry will still marry in 2007 after they have had twins. Their wedding at Blenheim Palace costs over one and a half million dollars. For their honeymoon they make use of the luxury yacht owned by Roman Abramovich, the extremely rich owner of Chelsea FC.

In 2005 *bad boy* Terry experiences an upturn in his fortunes thanks to his performances on the pitch. He wins the Premier League title with Chelsea for the first time in the club's history. He also succeeds David Beckham as captain of the English team. The new coach of the national team, Steve McClaren, has full confidence in Terry: 'I'm convinced that he will become one of the best captains ever.' However, it all goes hopelessly wrong again for the standard bearer of English soccer when he gets sent off in a game against Tottenham Hotspur after shouting *'Shut up you lippy black monkey'* at the Spur's defender Ledley King. For good measure he lets referee Graham Poll have it as well. The FA orders Terry, its 'role model', to pay a fine of more than 15,000 dollars.

Things quickly go from bad to worse. When England fail to qualify for the finals of the 2008 European Championships, the *News of the World* publishes a number of photos showing some of the England players dancing on a stage in a nightclub, together with a troupe of pole dancers. An almost comatose Terry also demonstrates that he hasn't forgotten how to urinate in public. Later, in a game against Arsenal, he really does lose consciousness when Abou Diaby accidentally kicks him in the head and he swallows his tongue. Fortunately, the speedy intervention of the team physio saves Terry's life. At the end of May 2008, he misses a penalty kick against Manchester United that could have decided the Champions League final. He slips on the wet turf just before shooting and hits the post. He cries bitterly that he 'will be haunted by this mistake forever.' The UEFA award for 'Defender of the year' that year is cold comfort to the player.

Despite this little highlight, controversy continues to stalk the Chelsea stalwart. After he parks his Bentley on a disabled parking spot for more than two hours he receives yet another fine – this time a whopping ninety dollars. And that at a time when he is earning more than 180,000 dollars a week. Even more eye-catching is the unauthorized deal the soccer millionaire makes with journalists to provide them with 'inside information' on the goings-on at Chelsea, an arrangement that will earn him 15,000 dollars for each juicy nugget he reveals. When he gets caught he claims the money is meant for charity.

The Chelsea captain pays the lingerie model one and a half million dollars in hush money to keep their affair out of the press.

However, word on the street has it that Terry has amassed major (gambling) debts. Many are left wondering whether this is also the reason why his unemployed father is revealed to be an (amateur) cocaine dealer, and why his mother and mother-in-law get caught for shoplifting after their bags are found to be stuffed with candy, clothing and cat food? Even though there is no doubting his ability as a leader both on the pitch and in the dressing room, the captain of the England team has become a much-hated figure in his country.

Things go really haywire at the end of January 2010. All of England is in the grip of a notorious sex scandal, one that threatens to see Terry stripped of his captain's armband. It has been revealed that Terry has cheated on his wife once again, this time with Vanessa Perroncel, the ex-girlfriend of his ex-teammate and good friend Wayne Bridge. The two families lived practically next-door to each other in Oxshott when the cheating took place and even went on holidays together. It is said that Terry was trying to 'help' Perroncel deal with her heartbreak after she split from Bridge. The Chelsea captain pays the lingerie model one and a half million dollars in hush money to keep their affair out of the press. Terry also tries to save his bacon by requesting that the media be banned from publishing the details of the affair. Neither of these moves succeeds. When his request is brought before the court, the judge displays a far more realistic view of the matter: 'He is only thinking about his image and sponsor deals.'

Even the more serious-minded newspapers write about the case on a daily basis, while the tabloids can't get enough of it. 'England in crisis,' screams one of the headlines in the *News of The World*, a tiny bit exaggerated to be fair. Even though Chelsea tries to support its central defender 'in these difficult times', Terry will suffer even more damage because of his illicit liaisons. He is now being hunted by one and all. In the meantime, Terry tries to silence four other lovers – among them a star of the Big Brother TV show – by offering them wads of cash. He goes into hiding, is driven around in cars with tinted windows and even rents out an entire hotel floor so that no one can camp out in front of his door. Then it is revealed that Terry got Perroncel pregnant and paid for the abortion. The Chelsea coach, Carlo Ancelotti, is at a complete loss as to what to do, though he doesn't take Terry's captain's armband off him. He eventually decides to give Terry some time off to get his private life in order. Terry immediately travels to Dubai in pursuit of his wife in an attempt to save his marriage. She, however, wants to divorce him as soon as possible. She has had enough: 'He has humiliated me for ten years,' she tells the *Sunday Mirror*.

The affair continues to sow division over the following weeks in England and in English footballing circles. Even the Minister of Sports gets involved. When Terry eventually lines out for Chelsea again he is constantly booed by the opponent's fans. They sing *'Same old Terry, always cheating'* and *'Chelsea wherever you may be, don't leave your wife with John Terry.'* Wayne Bridge's teammates at Manchester City play one of their games with the text 'Team Bridge' printed under their jerseys. The City player Craig Bellamy says to the cameras that everybody knows what kind of 'player' Terry is off the field. In the meantime it is revealed that the troubled soccer player has shared his bed with nine different women over the past eighteen months. And, according to the *Daily Star*, Miss Perroncel was said to have done the same with seven other players at Chelsea, including Eidur Gudjohnsen and Adrian Mutu. She is a genuine *soccer groupie*, a real *gold digger*.

In the meantime, the coach of the English team, Fabio Capello, is worried about the forthcoming World Cup (in 2010) and the atmosphere in the dressing room. After all, Terry and Bridge are key players in his squad. However, Bridge doesn't want to play on the same team as Terry anymore and withdraws from the English squad. 'In the best interests of the team and to prevent inevitable distractions, I've decided not to make myself available,' the already demoralized left back concludes, despite the knowledge that he would almost certainly have been in the starting eleven at the World Cup. Unlike his colleague, Ancelotti, Capello strips Terry of the captain's armband (for the time being at least) after giving him a piece of his mind. The Italian is furious with his captain. Rio Ferdinand is chosen to lead the side instead. The new captain wishes Terry well and says he 'will always support him.'

And while Perroncel continues to deny the affair and Terry misses out on more than five million dollars' worth of sponsorship contracts, he slips yet again. Capello has already returned the captain's armband to Terry when the defender is caught racially abusing Anton Ferdinand, brother of Rio Ferdinand no less. 'Terrygate' is born and all of England is up in arms once again. Eventually Terry is acquitted of all charges in court, though he doesn't deny having sworn at Ferdinand and calling him a *fucking black cunt*. The English FA is less merciful, however, and they don't believe Terry's defense. And when Capello refuses to take the captain's armband away from him for a second time, the FA overrules the coach. Capello draws his own conclusions and resigns. A year after the incident with Ferdinand, Terry decides to retire from the international scene, citing his dissatisfaction regarding the criminal case that the FA continues to pursue against him as the reason for his decision. In the end, the FA suspends him for four games and fines him 340,000 dollars. Only when the dust has settled does Terry eventually apologize for his racist remarks.

MARIO BALOTELLI

Tony Tati

Nationality:	Italian
Born:	1990
AKA:	Super Mario, Stupid Mario, MB45, Balo and The Golden Boy
Known for:	unpredictable behavior, allergy for grass, and tattoos of masks on his underarms

'A ROLE MODEL? ME? I DON'T KNOW FOR SURE, BUT I THINK I AM.'

'**F**uck you Mario, you fuckin' nigger. Go eat some bananas and get ebola, you dirty monkey.' It is the latest in a long line of insulting and racist tweets addressed to Mario Balotelli, this time from a supporter of his own club. While the account is being deleted and becomes the subject of a police investigation, the player reacts in a forbearing manner: 'They aren't used to seeing people who are different, not white, who act not as rebels but normally,' he said. 'I think what the ignorant people don't like is that people who are different are allowed to act that way. These stupid people, they get angry with me, they say horrible things, but I haven't done anything different from other people.'

In the American magazine *Time*, Balotelli is being mentioned in the same breath as Obama and Beyoncé. He is listed as one of the most influential people in the world. Others are more inclined to regard the Italian-born soccer player as the most controversial player of all time. Control? Balance? If there was one player in the past few years who *didn't* have these qualities then it was Balotelli. Dutch legend Johan Cruyff had this to say about him: 'Mario is not the problem, the problem is the education he received. If he had been schooled in a different way, he wouldn't behave like this.' And what does the player think himself? He just laughs it all off and says that he doesn't care about anything or anyone. 'I think I'm a genius, but not a rebel. I have my own life, my own world. I do what I like, without bothering anyone. I think I am more intelligent than the average person.' And in *France Football*: 'I'm the best soccer player in the world - after Messi.'

That he is a mad genius is something pretty much everyone agrees on, though not many would support the belief that he is the best player in the world after Messi. Balotelli has already played too many games in which he was completely invisible to merit such a claim. To give him his due, some of his moves on the pitch have been from another planet all right and his goals sometimes simply breathtaking, but as for the rest... A couple of years ago Balotelli asked an artist to make a life-size statue of him. He wanted to have it in his own garden and it had to portray him in the exact same pose he had adopted when celebrating his goal against Germany in the semi-final of the European Championships in 2012. Millions of fans from all around the world will undoubtedly want to be immortalized next to it. But just as many fans will do their best to stay as far away from it as possible, not to mention a whole host of (former) colleagues and coaches. The eccentric Balotelli has been the source of much misery and consternation through out his career. The bust-ups at Inter Milan alone were almost innumerable. For example, he got into a fight with Marco Materazzi – no sweetheart himself – in Barcelona's Camp Nou stadium after Balotelli displayed the absolute minimum of effort after coming on as a substitute and then gave the fans the finger after the game was over. He also crossed swords in a similar fashion with Totti, Ferdinand, Cassano and Kolarov, to name but a few. 'He definitely likes the attention,' according to Joe Hart, the England keeper in the *NY Times*. 'He doesn't act and just does what he does.'

As for his clashes with coaches - have you got a minute or two to spare? Below a very short *shortlist*, containing the most infamous incidents. His (also highly controversial) coach at Inter Milan, José *'The Special One'* Mourinho, says he could easily fill two hundreds pages of a book about him. For example, he recalls one particular incident at an away match in the Champions League only too well. Mourinho was faced with a shortage of strikers for the game against Rubin Kazan. Eto'o was out injured and he was depending on Balotelli to do the job for him. However, the player was behaving himself so badly during the game that it seemed only a matter of time before he would get himself sent off. Mourinho spent fourteen of the fifteen minutes at halftime addressing Balotelli, trying to impress upon him the need to tone it down, to stick to the rules, and so on and so on. He almost got down on his knees to beg the player to behave himself. And what happens? Mourinho: 'Balotelli gets himself sent off in the first minute after halftime...'

'He's an emotional guy,' according to Jürgen Klinsmann, the USA coach with an obvious gift for understatement. 'He can make or break a game for you. He can score the winning goal for you one moment and get sent off the next.' Massimiliano Allegri (AC Milan) believes that all Balotelli has to do is to grow up. The former Italian great Gianfranco Zola: 'People think he is crazy, but he's not. He has all the qualities you need to be a top sportsman. He has the strength, is very athletic and he understands the game. But to be successful, you need to be in balance.' The player's discipline during his time at Inter Milan was so poor that Mourinho called him a 'son of a bitch' on one occasion, adding 'I can't accept that kind of an attitude from someone who hasn't achieved anything yet.' Balotelli also acquired quite a list of *ups and downs* under Cesare Prandelli, the coach of the Italian team, who even has to write a code of conduct for his squad because of his antics. But, of course, the *enfant terrible* doesn't abide by those rules very often, which frequently costs him his place in the team. When the striker scores against Ireland after coming on as a substitute during the 2012 European Championships, he seems intent on saying a thing or two to the bench (i.e. Prandelli). His teammate Leonardo Bonucci intervenes just in time. Balotelli wanted to vent his frustration at not having been given a place in the starting line-up.

Roberto Mancini is Balotelli's coach for the longest period, during spells at Inter and Manchester City. They enjoy something of a love-hate relationship even though Mancini was no angel either in his own playing career and often drove his coaches to the point of despair. 'I understand Mario,' he says more than once. 'He is like my own child. The problem is that, because of his age, he loses his way from time to time. He is crazy, yes, but I love him because he is a good guy at heart.' Nevertheless, Mancini and Balotelli clash on countless occasions. The player is incredibly lazy during training, gets into fights with his teammates, like with Jerome Boateng after a reckless tackle, and regularly samples the nightlife on the night before a game. Mancini continues to protect and defend his pupil, but the oh-so talented player betrays that trust just as often. For example, at Manchester City Mancini begs his star player to behave himself in the last few months of the race to the Premiership title in 2012. It is now or never. Two months later *Stupid Mario* proceeds to get himself sent off at Arsenal. With the title within their grasp, he is suspended for three games. Mancini has had it with him. 'We still have six games to go, but I won't be playing him in any of them.'

It seems that all is well again after Balotelli, with his hand on his heart, promises his coach that he will try to do better. Mancini has ordered him to behave more like his teammate Carlos Tévez, who is a pretty *bad guy* himself. But the Argentinian has changed his ways and is hungry for the title. It is not until 13 May 2012 that the supporters of *The Citizens* are finally happy with their whimsical star. Manchester City score in the very last minute of the game against Queens Park Rangers to win 3-2 and claim their first title in 44 years. The assist for the winning goal comes from the foot of Balotelli, but while everyone else is celebrating wildly the Italian shows his discontent in front of the cameras. The striker is extremely frustrated because he was only allowed on as a substitute after an hour. He says that he never had any problems with Mancini at Inter and that it was because Mancini was the coach that he decided to sign for City instead of some other club. The truth of the matter is a little different, however. Mancini says he has to talk Balotelli into staying on a daily basis, and he adds: 'Now I need a psychologist myself. I've known him since he was seventeen, but he is even worse now than he was then.'

As a child Balotelli already had problems - with a capital 'P'. He is the son of Ghanaian immigrants who live on Sicily and he bears their surname - Barwuah. He suffers so badly from gastrointestinal perforations that at one point his parents fear he will die. When they can't pay the hospital bills anymore, the little Mario – only two years old – goes to live with Francesco and Silvia Balotelli, his new (rich, white) foster parents whose name he takes. He is the only dark-skinned player in the youth team of USO Mompaino, his first club. They expel him when he is only seven years old because he is uncontrollable. Despite his unpredictable character, Mario's soccer talent is unmistakable. In 2006 Barcelona want to sign him after a trial period. However, Balotelli demands more money than the club plans to spend on him, so he returns to the Serie C club Lumezzane. Hi behavior continues to raise eyebrows. For example, he refuses to celebrate whenever he scores. 'Why should I? Scoring goals is my job, right? The postman doesn't celebrate every time he puts a letter through the mailbox, does he? I will celebrate when I score the winning goal in the Champions League final.' *Balo* becomes obsessed with bicycle kicks for a while, too; every time he plays he has to try at least one or two. And it doesn't seem to bother him that some of his efforts end up going out over the sideline.

At the age of seventeen Balotelli moves to Inter Milan. A year later he becomes an Italian citizen. He doesn't want to have anything to do with his biological parents anymore. He believes they abandoned him. When they try to make contact with him again, years later, the only reaction he gives in the *NY Times* is: 'If I didn't become Mario Balotelli then Mr. and Mrs. Barwuah would not have cared about me for anything.' Remarkably, and despite his claim that he is 'African through and through,' Balotelli has not bothered to visit his parents' homeland of Ghana. He says that he has always felt different in Italy because of the color of his skin. According to his biographer, Frank Worrell, this may in some way explain his 'peculiar' behavior - Balotelli apparently suffers from a double identity crisis.

At the age of twenty-three, when in the service of AC Milan, he ranks among the best-paid players in the Serie A. And just like he did before at Inter Milan and Manchester City, he misbehaves there frequently, too. The ex-Milan player Zvonimir Boban doesn't understand him at all: 'In our time Balotelli would have had to carry Marco van Basten's bag for him and would have been given a good smack by Franco Baresi if he was late for training. He doesn't know what it means to wear the AC Milan shirt!' According to fellow *bad boy* Paulo Di Canio, Balotelli is a good soccer player but one that needs a clip on the ear from time to time. Speaking to journalists Di Canio says: 'Balotelli does not play for the team, only for himself. He is an egotist, who thinks the world revolves around him. Balotelli is just selfish. He deserves a lot of slaps.'

'In our time Balotelli would have had to carry Marco van Basten's bag for him.'

The star player continues to play innocent. When asked if he understands the criticism and anger of the fans, he replies that they should piss off. 'Everybody makes mistakes, but if I had been white, people would have treated me differently. Jealousy is a horrible emotion, but in my case people's jealousy often turns into hate, the hallmark of racism.' Most of the supporters at his various clubs are not impressed by his string of (stupid) yellow and red cards. And his sometimes inconceivably dumb behavior. Balotelli's so-called 'jokes' often get a little bit out of hand. When he gets bored during an international game and starts playing with his iPad on the bench, coach Prandelli punishes him by only letting him on as a substitute very late in the game. Double parking – one of his favorite pastimes – results in a mountain of parking tickets. In Manchester, over the course of twelve months, he collects traffic fines amounting to over thirteen thousand dollars. And he earns the wrath of the club management when they catch him throwing darts at youth players during a training session. On another occasion, in Italy, he drives into the women's prison in Brescia in his expensive Mercedes together with his brother after they spot one of the gates open. They are arrested and their only defense is that they wanted to see how ugly the inmates were. And in the run-up to the always highly-charged derby against arch rivals Manchester United, Balotelli decides to throw some fireworks down on to the street from his bathroom window. Great fun. What he fails to see, however, is that a few towels hanging from a downstairs window have caught fire and soon his own villa is threatened with going up in smoke. The fire brigade has to be called and the police have to hold him back to prevent him from going back into the burning house to rescue his stash of cash.

Of course, Balotelli is like gold dust to the English and Italian tabloids. On average, they dedicate two full pages to him every day. If it's not about Balotelli taking a pig (named Super) to the training ground, then it's probably about him dressing up as a (dark-skinned) Santa Claus and giving away money to astounded passers-by. He drives around in a Bentley painted in camouflage colors (all hos own work), engages in swordfights with rolling pins in restaurants, breaks into his own house (and gets arrested by the police) and is filmed having a remarkably hard time putting on a training jacket – the latter incident earning one million YouTube views in next to no time. During the derby between Manchester City and Manchester United, Balotelli reveals the text 'Why always me?' after he scores the opening goal. He feels hounded by the British press. And another interesting if little-known detail: a few days later he is appointed as an ambassador for fire safety by the Manchester City Council... His own particular brand of 'soccer humor' creates a huge worldwide fan base for the player, but is also the source of thousands hate mails.

At the age of 23, a rumor quickly spread that Balotelli had had a fatal accident in his Ferrari. A condolence page on Facebook entitled 'R.I.P. Balotelli' was even set up and it received thousands of reactions and likes in the space of a few hours. One day later, however, it all turns out to be a complete hoax. Clarence Seedorf is Balotelli's coach at

AC Milan for a period of six months. He says he loves him and frequently shields him from criticism – sometimes to the irritation of fellow players, the club management and fans. But when Balotelli is dropped from the team he reacts furiously: 'Life is full of fake people.' Mourinho had been on the receiving end of a similar slur in the past after saying that Balotelli was unmanageable and throwing him out of the squad at Inter. Balotelli's reaction: 'Mourinho is the best trainer in the world, but as a human he still has to learn about manners.'

In the summer of 2014 he provokes the wrath of the coach of the national team, Cesare Prandelli. At the World Cup, Balotelli only makes a half-hearted effort - what's new? He is seen as the main reason for Italy's early elimination. 'It was a big mistake selecting Balotelli,' a disappointed Prandelli says, who resigns immediately. International Daniele De Rossi rubs it in by saying: 'We need real men, not Panini stickers or characters.' Although the striker doesn't want to react to the accusations himself, Mino Raiola, his Dutch agent, does. He articulates the reaction of his pupil briefly and laconically: 'Well, being criticized is quite normal to Balotelli.' All Balotelli does is upload a typical-for-him photo to his Instagram page that shows him pointing a gun at the camera lens. The caption reads 'A little kiss for all the haters'.

Balotelli, who turns out to be allergic to dry grass (!), signs for Liverpool in the summer of 2014. The club takes all the necessary precautions, having paid 17.5 million dollars for him. Only when he has played a certain number of games and honored a number of behavioral clauses in his contract can he expect to earn a salary similar to what he was used to at Milan. However, Liverpool are completely fed up with their new striker after only two months. Balotelli is incorrigible, and lazy to boot. BBC analyst Alan Hansen on his qualities as a soccer player: 'If he performed like Lionel Messi, Cristiano Ronaldo or even Wayne Rooney, then the players would hold up their hands and let him get away with it. But Balotelli is not a world-beater.' The Italian laughs it all off, he has distractions enough himself. 'Super Mario' goes about enjoying life as usual, maintaining an endless series of girlfriends for example. He has an affair with the Belgian model Fanny Neguesha, cheats on her with a buxom British porn actress, and has an on-off relationship with Raffaella Fico. Only two months after they split up, Fico discovers she is pregnant with his child. The lingerie model, who had previously had a fling with Cristiano Ronaldo, gives him a second chance despite the fact that Balotelli cheated on her with the escort girl

Jennifer Thompson during their relationship (yes, the same Jennifer Thompson who had an affair with Wayne Rooney). To prove he is the father, Fico writes Balotelli an open letter to demand that he undergo a paternity test. Balotelli eventually complies, months after his daughter Pia is born. The test shows that he is the father. We will leave the last word to his agent Mino Raiola: 'Then he falls in love again with a new lady who subsequently turns out not to be the right one after all. Mario should focus on soccer much more.'

Remarkably, in 2015 AC Milan decide to resign Balotelli after his extremely disappointing season at Liverpool. However, he has to sign a contract that is full of special conditions. He is not allowed to smoke anymore, has to cut down drastically on alcohol, curtail his nocturnal adventures et cetera, et cetera. He solemnly swears to abide by this new code of conduct: "I know that I can not miss anything, I accept all the rules. I'm a man now and do not create problems. I will accept any decision." Within a few weeks, however, Balotelli is back to his old ways again. On the way to a game in Bari he is stopped by the police for speeding. He has been caught doing 109 km/h in a 50 km zone. The police immediately confiscate his license and so he is banned from driving, but Balotelli is more worried about persuading them not to tell his club what has just happened...

DIEGO MARADONA

Tony Tati

Nationality:	Argentinian
Born:	1960
AKA:	El Pibe (the child), El Gordito (the fatty), Pelusa (Fluff, because of his hair and nimbleness), El Diego, El Diez (the ten), D10S, Don Diego and Il Divino Scorfano (the Divine Monster)
Known for:	making the sign of the cross, big mouth, lack of feet (only 5 plus 5 inches...), tattoos of Che Guevara and Fidel Castro

'THE BALL IS ALWAYS CLEAN'

'**N**a na na na na...Live is life, Na na na na na...' For billions of soccer fans it was one of the most wonderful moments ever: Diego Maradona warning up before the UEFA Cup semi-final between Bayern Munich and Napoli in 1989. With his untied shoestrings trailing over the field, the Argentinian ball virtuoso juggled the ball effortlessly and endlessly to the sound of 'Live is life' blaring out of the stadium's speakers. From shoulder to foot, from head to thigh. Enchantment. Adoration. A packed stadium looked on in awe.

Born in 1960, the career of this legendary left-footed player is full of memorable moments. Take 1986 for instance: the World Cup, England versus Argentina. Maradona scores to make it 2-0 after dribbling past six astonished Brits. A mesmerizing goal that is voted *Goal of the Century* by the FIFA. Or take the year after that when like some kind of Messiah he helped his club Napoli win the first Italian league title in its history. And of course he also won the World Cup with his country in 1986, received the public's award for 'Player of the Century'...and so on and so on.

What most people remember Maradona for, however, is his cocaine use and the infamous 'Hand of God' episode; both cases of Na-na-na-na-na turning quickly into no-no-no-no-no... His 'Hand of God' became one of the most infamous incidents in the history of the World Cup. England had the quarter final in Mexico City pretty much under control when in an aerial duel with England goalkeeper Peter Shilton, Maradona went to head the ball but instead flicked it with the palm of his hand past the keeper and into the net: 1-0. Despite the fierce protests of the English defense, the goal was allowed to stand. At the press conference after the match the living legend defended his handball by saying that it was 'un poco con la cabeza de Maradona y otro poco con la mano de Dios' - that he scored a little bit with his head and a little bit with the hand of God. The English, especially coach Bobby Robson, were furious: 'It wasn't the hand of God, it was the hand of a villain.' Did he regret his deceit at all? No, not on your life. To *El Diego* it was 'sweet revenge' for losing the Falklands War a couple of years earlier. With the look of an innocent child he said: 'It was absolutely a legitimate goal because the referee allowed it. Who am I to doubt the honesty of the referee?'

Soccer fans are destined to argue forever more about who deserves to be called the greatest player ever - Pelé, Cruyff, Messi or Maradona. They will agree on one thing quickly though: that the Argentinian is by far the most controversial of the four. For example: when he is received by the pope after winning the World Cup in 1986 and the pope hands him a red rose, he feels insulted. The pope had said that he would have a special rose for Maradona, but it turns out to be exactly the same as the ones handed out to the rest of the team. A 'total lack of respect,' Maradona laments. Would Cruyff or Pelé have reacted like that? *Never.*

And Maradona doesn't just knock spots off the pope; he does the very same with many of his colleagues as well. Take Pelé for example. Maradona believes that the best place for the Brazilian legend is in a museum. He says that he is 'only' the second best soccer player in history, after him. And with the FIFA, the most important soccer institution in the world, he is in a permanent state of war. He hates all of those in power there. He publicly refers to the FIFA presidents Havelange and his successor Blatter as 'morons' and 'dinosaurs' after a series of corruption scandals at the organization. After FIFA punishes the Uruguayan player Luis Suárez for the biting incident at the 2014 World Cup he says: 'Why don't you just send him straight to Guantanamo?' claiming that their treatment of the player is inhuman. While he is at it, he also calls Beckenbauer and Pelé 'idiots' for saying that the punishment handed out to Suárez is justified. Controversy seems to follow Maradona wherever he goes, dogging the player who has been worshiped since he was only ten years old.

As an extremely talented youth player he leads *Los Cebollitas* (The little onions) on an unbeaten run of no fewer than 136 games. By the time he has turned twelve he is already an established 'circus act' at halftime during Argentinos Juniors' home matches. *Diegito* (little Diego) can keep a ball in the air for minutes on end and has a bottomless bag of tricks. He grew up in the Villa Fiorito slum south of Buenos Aires, a desperate place known for its open sewers, mountains of litter, high unemployment and drug abuse. His father is a Guarini Indian who makes his living as a fisherman and a snake catcher, and later on as a laborer in a mill. His mother descends from immigrants from the south of Italy. The not-so-closely-knit family consists of seven brothers and sisters. When Maradona, the *negrito* (a small, dark, poor kid), is around seven years old many people think he is a dwarf because he is so small. His size is artificially pumped up with the help of various injections and powders.

When he is only fifteen Maradona makes his debut for the Argentinos Juniors first team. 'At a stroke I became part of the adult world,' he recalls. This changes his life forever, and not always for the best. When, at the end of the 1970s pretty much every top club in Europe wants to sign him, the dictatorial Argentinian government blocks the move. It is imperative that their most important PR-instrument remains available to play in and for his own country at least until the World Cup of 1982. Maradona, who is very eager to escape the enormous pressure in his native land, explodes with anger. The World Cup in Spain turns out to be anything but a success in the end. Argentina are eliminated early on and Maradona, who was supposed to be the star of the tournament, is sent off in the game against archrivals Brazil after his frustration boils over and he aims a deliberate kick at the crotch of João Batista. 'It was meant for Falcão,' says the famous number ten in his biography *Yo soy el Diego* ('I am El Diego'), 'I just couldn't take Falcão's bullying in midfield any more. I just turned around and kicked the first person I saw.'

At his new club – he switches (after Argentinos Juniors) from Boca Juniors to FC Barcelona – things don't go too well either. Hepatitis B and injuries – including a broken leg after the infamously ruthless tackle by 'The butcher of Bilbao' Andoni Goikoetxea – don't help his cause. After clashing with his coach, Udo Lattek, it is the latter who ends up losing his job. The Argentinian proves to be a real *pain in the ass* for his coach. When Maradona doesn't show up on time, Lattek allows the team bus to leave without him. The players in the bus cheer, with Maradona's friend Bernd Schuster, who is part of his alliance against club president Nuñez, leading the chorus. Maradona is forced to follow them in a taxi. The star player is furious and he is determined not to take it lying down. He vents his anger to the management and says that Lattek is unable to motivate him. In his biography 'El Diego' he has this to say of Lattek: 'He got up in the morning, drank two beers and then sent us off running around the pitch at the crack of dawn.' Maradona also hates working with heavy medicine balls. 'One day, I simply threw one at him.' In Maradona's opinion, the German hasn't a clue about how to manage a team. *Adios* Lattek.

In the meantime 'Fluff' has become addicted to cocaine. After he has recovered from a serious ankle injury, and while playing under the influence of drugs, he shows his worst side during the final of the Copa del Rey against Athletic Bilbao (Goikoetxea's team) in 1984. After putting up with endless provocation, including from Goikoetxea, Maradona kicks out at a random opponent after the ball is already gone. His stupidity unleashes a massive fight. King Juan Carlos, who is sitting in the royal box, looks on as Maradona attacks a number of players with a series of karate kicks. But for the fences holding back the crowd in the stadium, the ensuing free-for-all would have been much worse...

Apart from soccer and injuries, the Argentinian's two seasons at *Barça* are mostly a motley collection of poorly chosen friends, parties, drugs, alcohol, orgies and venereal diseases. The Maradona clan that travels around in his wake is infamous. The number ten frequently clashes with club president Josep Luís Núñez. 'He was such a dick,' *El Diez* will later say in his biography. 'He hated Schuster, Rivaldo... He got rid of Romário and Stoichkov. All big names! He wouldn't even allow me to play in Matthäus's testimonial game.' When Núñez confiscates Maradona's passport, the Argentinian smashes one of the club's crystal trophies on the ground in protest.

As for the Catalan press, he is in a permanent state of war with them. He is homesick and feels excluded by the Catalans, who are racist in his eyes. Maradona does have unconditional trust in his long-time friend and manager Cyterszpiller - the man who would go on to deceive him on multiple occasions. Later the Argentinian refers to his time in Barcelona as 'disastrous'. He refuses the blank check he is offered in return for signing a new contract, even though he is deeply in debt because of the dubious expenses being amassed by Cyterszpiler.

On July 5, 1984 over 80,000 fans are waiting to welcome Maradona to Naples with open arms when he arrives in the stadium by helicopter. Which makes sense, because for years no top player had wanted to sign for Napoli, the club of the *camorra*. Paulo Rossi, for example, turned down their offer. But Maradona doesn't. On the contrary, he feels right at home there and he goes on to enjoy his best days as a player in Italy with Napoli. In 1987 the attacking midfielder leads the club – in a city brimming with frustration and feelings of inferiority – to the first league title in its history. The team also wins the UEFA Cup in 1988 and a second 'Scudetto' in 1990. Maradona is the club's new Messiah and even today you will find enormous murals of the player dotted around the city.

Just before the World Cup of 1986 is about to kick off in Mexico, the mounting stress catches up with the Maradona clan. The star player is forced to do a paternity test. At first he star refuses to admit that the son of Cristina Sinagra, with whom he had an affair during his time at Naples, is also his child. Later he will have to retract his denial. In Mexico, Maradona pushes his personal problems to the back of his mind. He also keeps the press at arm's length and organizes his own impromptu press conferences from behind the barbed wire around the training field. Remarkably, 'Fluff' is looking very fit. He is determined to win the World Cup this time at all costs. In the words of former coach César Luis Menotti:

A photo is published showing Maradona with his hands all over a nineteen-year-old Cuban beauty.

'Maradona without a ball is like a cowboy without a Colt 45.' His body is still full of cortisone and painkillers, thanks to 'The butcher of Bilbao'. Whether or not he uses doping during the tournament itself is never made clear, despite the rumors that someone from the *barras bravas*, the infamous Argentinian fan club, offered to supply cocaine to the players. Anyway, in the end Argentina are crowned world champions.

His wedding to childhood sweetheart Claudia Villafane in 1989 is described by the Argentinian press as the most vulgar event ever to take place in their country. Many of those invited had already seen this coming and canceled beforehand, including Maradona's friend the Argentinian president Carlos Menem. Twelve hundred guests from Argentina and abroad do turn up however to wallow in the splendor. Maradona charters a Boeing 747 to fly his famous and not-so-famous friends in from Europe. An eighty-man tango orchestra is hired to entertain the guests. The bride and groom arrive in a Rolls-Royce Phantom III and rumor has it that the car had once been the property of Joseph Goebbels, the minister of propaganda in Nazi Germany. Ninety-nine golden rings are hidden inside the wedding cake. The wedding reception, which was held in an amusement park, is said to have cost over three million dollars. Maradona is criticized by many for denying his humble origins with all this splendor. Two years previously he had been much more in touch with his roots when he paraded his newborn daughter around for all to see in a shopping trolley during a festival in downtown Buenos Aires.

On 17 March 1991, after a match between Napoli and Bari, *El Diego* tests positive for doping. Cocaine is the culprit once again. He claims he is the subject of a witch-hunt. 'I am *clean!*' he protests to anyone who will listen. He said he was the mascot of the *camorra* and that they were putting him under pressure. Photos published in the newspaper *Il Mattino* prove that he is friendly with the organization's *capo*, Carmine Giuliano. Maradona, who it is claimed has been using the drug runner Camilla Cinquegrano to transport drugs from Italy to Argentina, denies all accusations. 'All they ever offered me was protection,' he says of the *camorra*. However, he is betrayed by Pietro Pugliese, his former chauffeur and remorseful former ex-Mafioso. He confesses to the court that not only did he act as Maradona's security guard, but that he also supplied him with drugs. The evidence against him is so overwhelming that the star player takes the first available flight to Buenos Aires. 'I was kicked out of Italy like a criminal,' he grumbles. FIFA are not impressed and they slap a fifteen-month ban on the Argentinian. To top it all off, Pugliese also claims that Maradona slept with at least 8000 women during his time in Naples...

As a result, he misses out on several deals worth millions of dollars with sponsors like Fuji and Puma. Not even a month after returning to Argentina, Maradona becomes the center of a new scandal when – surrounded by dozens of journalists and photographers – he is hauled from his bed in a heavily drugged state. Has he been set up? It is suspected that the raid has been carried out to distract the attention of the Argentinian people from the scandals plaguing president Carlos Menem at the time. His family is rumored to be involved in the distribution of cocaine. The *El Clarin* newspaper says that Maradona was completely out of it when he was apprehended, but also that he was released again only half an hour after appearing before the court. After all, the 1994 World Cup is not far off and the nation expects...

During his enforced sojourn in Argentina, Maradona has to report to the courts every two months. Under no circumstances is he allowed to leave the country. So when he gets a serious offer from FC Seville (i.e. from their Argentinian coach Carlos Bilardo), special permission is required. Real Madrid are also interested in signing him. In the end he opts for Seville. He returns to Spain after a nine-year absence. The most controversial soccer player in the world at the time sees Seville as a useful stepping stone to the World Cup of 1994. He doesn't receive a warm welcome however. His new club is forced to hire private detectives to monitor his behavior after Maradona crashes his Ferrari. The club also wants to find out what exactly is going on behind the curtains at the villa he has rented from the famous bullfighter Spartacus. When he ridicules the coach, Bilardo, in full view of the fans and press by calling him a son of a bitch after being substituted, it is time for him to pack his bags again and leave Seville (after only one season).

Back in his native country, the outcast gets ready for the World Cup in the USA. His sole motivation this time is his daughter Giannina, who has never seen her father play before. But things soon go wrong again... His celebration of his goal against Greece is eye-catching to say the least. With pupils the size of dinner plates he is filmed running towards a TV camera. The doping test that follows shows that Maradona has been using ephedrine. He can pack his bags immediately after he is suspended for the rest of the tournament. Later the Argentinian will receive a ban of fifteen months. He is blind with rage and accuses FIFA of forming an unholy alliance against him with the capitalist sponsors of the World Cup. Later on he will reveal that the Argentinian players used prohibited substances before the decisive duel against Australia in the run-up to the World Cup. 'Why was there no testing for that game, while there was for all the other matches? Someone must have put something in our coffee before the game that made us run faster and play better.'

Broken by yet another perceived injustice, Maradona goes to ground back in Argentina where he plays for Newell's Old Boys and Boca Juniors but only manages to turn out 32 times in four seasons. He plays his last official match in the summer of '97. It is his umpteenth comeback for Boca Juniors after realizing time after time that he can't live without the ball and the attention. However, even in his last game he tests positive again. Prayers will not help the very religious Argentinian ('It is God's wish that I am the best') anymore. The curtain has fallen for the last time. At least on his playing career...

After his career as a player, Maradona continues to hog the limelight. His dislike for managers, businessmen and politicians is outstripped only by his loathing for journalists. The Argentinian will not even consider doing an interview for less than 50,000 dollars. He frequently attacks the pen-pushers, both verbally and physically. He even ends up shooting at them on one occasion. In that incident he wounds four people and is handed a suspended jail sentence of three years. He demonstrates his annoyance by comparing his case to that of the recently deceased Princess Diana: 'Once again I was hunted down by those *hijos de putas* (sons of bitches).' Remarkably enough, when he arrives for the closed court session in a remote village far away from Buenos Aires, thousands of locals are waiting for him in dizzy expectation. A woman holds her paralyzed baby up and asks Maradona to touch him so that he will be cured. Some of the local cops even ask him to sign their uniforms.

One of the more hilarious moments comes courtesy of his attendance at a charity tournament in Amsterdam on behalf of the management of Boca Juniors. After camping out for days in the gardens around Maradona's hotel hoping to get a glimpse of him, the huge press contingent think they finally have their chance to get face to face with Maradona at the stadium's car park. A small black van with tinted windows and a team bus eventually pull up at the grounds. Everyone expects Maradona to be in the small van, but after six people have disembarked there is no sign of 'Fluff' and the assembled media quickly turn their attention to the team bus. That bus slowly empties, too, but again no Maradona. In the meantime, he has casually stepped out of the small van, gleefully avoiding all contact with the press. Na-na-na-na-na...

His cocaine habit and his gluttony result in his hospitalization, twice. He has his first heart attack, caused by having 900 milligrams of cocaine in his body, in 2004. He is kept in intensive care for weeks in a hospital in Buenos Aires. Each day, a huge crowd of Argentinians gathers in front of the hospital fearing that their idol is destined to die young, just like the country's other heroes - Eva Perón and Che Guevara. But God saves him; at least that's what Maradona says later. Not long afterwards, however, he is struck down by another near-fatal heart attack. His eating problems – he weighed 273 pounds at the time – are resolved by a gastric bypass, after which he loses sixty-six pounds in weight. He flees to a drug rehabilitation clinic in Cuba, the country ruled by his old friend Fidel Castro, to work on his addiction. In the meantime, he entertains himself by giving (expensive) interviews and by hanging around with a host of beautiful ladies.

A photo is published showing Maradona with his hands all over a nineteen-year-old Cuban beauty. In 2007 he is even declared dead for a brief moment. Argentina and the footballing world are in shock. President Nestor Kirchner cuts short a meeting when he hears the news and the Argentinian TV stations all broadcast a black banner for hours bearing Maradona's name. The doctors are eventually forced to break their silence. The rumors turn out to be false. Maradona is not quite ready yet to meet his maker.

When he is back on his feet again he says he is going to quit doing drugs and alcohol for good. *El Diego* addresses his fans in an emotional broadcast on Argentinian television: 'It is thanks to my daughters that I've been able to kick my bad habits. I remember that when I was in a coma Giannina grabbed me by my pajamas and said that I had to stay alive for her and that she needed me as a father. That was when I thought to myself: 'this is where I have to draw the line.'

But that's not the only thing that comes out of his (often very big) mouth. All his life Maradona has been very forthright about his leftist leanings - also the reason why he has the names of Fidel Castro and Che Guevara tattooed on his legs. The Venezuelan president Hugo Chávez belongs to his circle of friends as well. Together they strongly oppose American imperialism. President George W. Bush in particular is a hated figure. When Bush pays a visit to Argentina, Maradona provocatively wears a T-shirt with the text 'Stop Bush' during a mass gathering. He screams: 'He is responsible for the war in Iraq and he is human trash. Throw him out of the country!' When the Iranian Minister of Foreign Affairs comes to visit, the Argentinian footballing genius goes even further: 'I hate everything, to my very bones, that has anything to do with America.'

Life is never smooth on the female front either for *Don Diego*. He has a long string of relationships, sometimes involving women aged thirty years his junior. He becomes a father for the fourth time when a court in Buenos Aires determines that he is the father of a girl who has since turned five years old. He already has two other children and an extramarital son in Italy, a country where he hasn't been welcome for a long, long time. The name Maradona has also become synonymous with tax evasion. According to the Italian authorities he still owes 40.7 million dollars to the taxman in that country. During many of his recent visits to Italy the ex-soccer player has frequently been detained by customs officials. This infuriates him: 'There never was a problem before and I scored more than one hundred goals for Napoli. But now, whenever I'm in Italy, they take my earrings and watches, time and time again.' When he accuses his private assistant, Gabriel Bruno, of bribery she reacts by saying that *El Diego* should look at himself first. 'If you are looking for a corrupt person, then Maradona is the first name that will appear on your list.'

While he had a fantastic career as a player, his career as a coach is a completely different story. With Maradona as coach of the national team, Argentina only barely manage to qualify for the 2010 World Cup. Just like when he was a player, as a coach he also behaves as if he is above the law. He is stuck in an almost permanent feud with officials, journalists, referees and colleagues. 'Anger is my fuel,' is his only explanation. He selects over one hundred (!) players for the Argentinian team before they eventually make it to the semi-finals of the 2010 World Cup. He says that 'no one is going to tell me what to do, not even who I should or shouldn't select. That didn't happen when I was fifteen and it's not going to happen now either.' In the semi-final Germany humiliate Argentina by beating them 4-0, despite having Lionel Messi in their team, the player who is being touted as his natural successor in terms of ball skills and the best player in the world at that time. Maradona's contract is not extended after the tournament and he is furious at this decision. He accuses president of the Argentinian FA, Julio Grondona, of lying to him. At that moment, he has already been suspended for two months and FIFA have fined him 26,500 dollars for statements he made at a press conference just before the World Cup. Immediately after his country qualified for the finals, he snapped at the assembled journalists and said that they were all whores, adding the words 'You can keep sucking it.' In England some clever guy latches on to the phrase and makes a lot of money after printing it on thousands of T-shirts. However, when Maradona expresses his desire to coach a team in England, there isn't a single club interested. He shrugs it off by saying he couldn't care less.

P.S. In 2015, 'Live is life' still sounds from the speakers of the stadium in Naples before every home match as a continuing tribute to Maradona. Na-na-na-na-na...

ZLATAN IBRAHIMOVIĆ

Tony Tati

Nationality: Swedish

Born: 1981

AKA: Ibracadabra, Ibo and Ibra.

Known for: magical skills, a lot of tattoos (including one that says Only God can judge me'), a crooked nose and a pony tail

'YOU CAN TAKE THE BOY OUT OF THE GHETTO, BUT YOU CAN'T TAKE THE GHETTO OUT OF THE BOY'

'If you buy me, you buy a Ferrari. If you drive a Ferrari, you fill it up with premium fuel, drive onto the highway and put the pedal to the metal. Guardiola filled it with diesel and went for a ride through the countryside. If that's what he wanted, he would have been better off buying a Fiat. Now I am being sold for seventy percent of my value after only one season, despite my 22 goals and fifteen assists. Friends of mine from Rosengard were so angry that they wanted to drive straight to Barcelona to wreck the place.'

Ibrahimović even blamed Guardiola for the fact that Barcelona didn't win the Champions League that year (2010) because of his stupid decisions as a coach. That said, the Swedish-born player's sojourn in Catalonia can't exactly be called successful either. He wanted to stay there for five years, but things started to go wrong after only six months. Josep 'Pep' Guardiola, the cold-blooded coach of the Catalan superpower, explains to him that they will not accept any celebrity behavior at the club. 'When I went to Barcelona they wouldn't allow me to fly by private jet. They said I had to take an ordinary plane. We are not like Real Madrid, I was told. It felt like I had returned to Ajax, like I had been sent back to school.' Guardiola also explains to the Swede that he would better off leaving his Ferrari at home. Ibrahimović doesn't get it. 'What in God's name does it matter to him what kind of car I drive?' One day, when the Swede knows that he will be starting on the bench, he drives his $300,000 Ferrari to the stadium and parks the car pontifically in front of the main entrance. Guardiola doesn't punish him and Ibrahimović then accuses him of being 'cowardly'. Later he will allege that 'the coach's balls are no bigger than those of his children.' On a previous occasion he asks the club if they could park two ambulances next to the training field, just in case he let fly at Guardiola. After being substituted early on in the semi-final of the Champions League, which they lose to Inter Milan, something inside him breaks. 'Guardiola made me feel like I was the culprit, even though he didn't say anything. He was like a brick wall. That's why I kicked a box three meters into the sky and started yelling at him that he didn't have any balls.'

With Ibrahimović it seems that you have to exude authority, otherwise he will walk all over you. And you definitely don't treat him like a lesser mortal or as somehow working class. Then you are simply asking for trouble. Guardiola managed to fulfill both of these 'negative Zlatan demands' and therefore didn't stand a chance with him. In his autobiography, Guardiola goes into great detail on Ibrahimović. On one occasion, the striker loudly threatens to rip fitness coach Lorenzo Buenaventura's head off if he doesn't declare him fit for the upcoming *El Clásico* clash with Real Madrid. Guardiola also says that he can't get the big Swede to understand that he needs to stop getting in Messi's way during games. Ibrahimović becomes so depressed during the winter break that he threatens to stop playing altogether. Afterwards he behaves like a little child, gets into endless discussions with his coach, and refuses to follow his instructions. He even suggests that some day he might lose the control over his arm and end up punching Guardiola unwittingly. He is also not impressed with the fact that Messi is now the number one striker and that he has to play out wide.

After one season, and just before the new season is about to kick off, Ibrahimović leaves Barcelona. He is loaned out to AC Milan where he continues to disparage Guardiola. 'The philosopher' or 'the wall' as Ibrahimović calls him, was not a born winner and acted like he had invented soccer. The Swede says that he has more respect for coaches like Capello, Mourinho ('He could turn a cat into a lion') and Ancelotti, who he says was like a second father to him. In any case, Zlatan has only ever shown respect to a handful of individuals in his life, including the three aforementioned coaches, his manager Mino Raiola, his girlfriend Helena Seger and Trustor, his dog. Not forgetting his mother, of course, the one who worked herself to the bone to take care of her family.

His parents emigrate to Sweden in 1970 in search of a better life. However, Ibrahimović is only two years old when they split up. His father, a Bosnian who is traumatized by the Balkan war, becomes addicted to alcohol. From that moment on, his mother, Jurka, has to work fourteen hours a day just to make ends meet. Life is not easy for them in Rosengard, one of the poorest neighborhoods in Malmö, as he explains in his authorized biography. 'We didn't hug or stuff like that. Nobody asked: 'How was your day today, darling?' There was no adult to help you with your homework or to ask you if anything was bothering you. You just had fend for yourself and were not supposed to whine if someone had been mean to you.' As a child, Ibrahimović learns to fight his own corner. He even has to buy his own football boots himself for 59 Swedish Krona (about 7 dollars) at the local supermarket. Zlatan becomes a juvenile delinquent. He throws stones at car windows and steals bikes off the street and stuff from the supermarket. 'Once I dressed up as Rambo so I could steal a soldier's bike using a giant bolt cutter.' But maybe his behavior can be explained by the fact that he has since moved in with his father, whose refrigerator contains nothing but booze. 'The hunger forced me to get up to lots of no good,' he later defends himself without a hint of shame.

Halfway through his teenage years Ibrahimović decides to quit school. He is definitely not your average Swedish adolescent. He is very insecure and has a terrible temper. The head of the school calls him 'definitely one of the five most impossible students' he has had to deal with in his thirty-three years as a teacher. 'He was the ringleader when it came to getting into trouble.' He displays the same behavior on the soccer pitch. When he is only thirteen years old he head-butts one of his own teammates. The player's father organizes a petition to have Zlatan banned from the club. It fails. Reason: as a player he is indispensable. Ibrahimović makes his professional debut when he is only nineteen. He stands out not only because of his undoubted skill, but also because of his tendency to kick out at opponents on purpose and swear at referees. A poll is taken in Sweden that shows that he is regarded as the most annoying and overrated player in the country. The well-bred Helena Seger, his childhood sweetheart who is eleven years older than him, tries her best to teach him some manners. But it seems it is already too late for that...

When he is sixteen, a trial in England with Queens Park Rangers doesn't quite work out the way both parties had hoped. When Ibrahimović holds onto the ball for too long, coach Gerry Francis tackles him. Zlatan is not impressed, tackles him back and tells the coach to *'Fuck off'*. End of trial. Two years later Arsenal show an interest in him. Coach Arsène Wenger invites the eighteen-year-old for a trial at the club. Ibrahimović refuses to come, saying that they either sign him as he is or not. 'I don't do auditions.' Ajax want to sign him as well and for once he is all ears. Ajax is his dream club. The Amsterdam club signs him for a record transfer fee in Dutch soccer at the time.

At the first training session he introduces himself by saying 'I am Zlatan and *who the fuck are you?*' However, it is not long before he starts to feel like he is being left to fend for himself and he even threatens to punch some of the other players. He is lonely and misses the warmth of his family, especially his two older sisters. Unfortunately, he has no contact with them ever since his parents divorced. The Ajax coach, Co Adriaanse, reproaches him for not realizing that soccer is a team sport. The proud Swede is unwilling to play in a 4-3-3 system. When he continues to perform poorly – and many are beginning to view his signing as a mistake – Leo Beenhakker, who brought him in, defends the striker. The supporters regularly boo him. Ibrahimović says he doesn't care: 'I play my own game. The relationship with the fans doesn't matter one bit to me.'

It seems that even at this early stage in his career Ibrahimović doesn't care about anyone or anything. Under the new manager at Ajax, Ronald Koeman, Ibrahimović (he is known by the name Zlatan only in Sweden) is given a bit more playing time. Fact is that the Egyptian Mido still is the club's number one striker. It is only in his third (and last) season that Ibrahimović manages to hold down a regular place in the team and is the club's top scorer that season with thirteen goals. In the meantime, he likes to spin around in his Ferrari on the parking deck of the Arena stadium for just as long as is takes for everyone to notice him and won't leave until everybody has done. His reputation has spread far and wide. A rumor goes around that he has bought the fastest Porsche on earth. In response he says: 'I don't think so. An airplane. Much faster.' No shortage of humor, obviously. That said, driving around in an extremely expensive Mercedes SL 55 with its own built-in phone and TV set, even though he still has to prove himself on the field of play, is a bit over the top. He also says that he will only do TV interviews for networks that he considers worth his while. He doesn't want to make time for 'Donald Duck-media'. For example, despite having agreed to cooperate on a report about his city of birth for the regional broadcaster RTV Noord-Holland, he pulls out of the deal when he finds out that the report is for a provincial channel and not a national one.

Ibrahimović becomes annoyed with Wesley Sneijder when the midfielder repeatedly tries to explain to him how the game is supposed to be played. And neither is he very friendly with Rafael van der Vaart, who he says is a 'pseudo-leader' and 'arrogant, like so many of the white players in the team'. 'Ibra' also says that Van der Vaart 'tried to play the tough guy, wanted to stand out and be the boss. There was strife between us from the very start'. Van der Vaart, for his part, is not impressed by the Swede's eccentric behavior.

They pretty much want to kill each other after Ibrahimović dishes out yet another head-butt.

Things really come to a head during a friendly international match between Sweden and the Netherlands. Ibrahimović badly injures Van der Vaart's ankle with a ridiculous tackle. The Dutchman has to come off and is lucky that he is only out of action for a month when it could easily have been half a year. According to Van der Vaart the tackle was intentional, but Ibrahimović says that this is 'nonsense'. Meanwhile, back in Amsterdam they have stopped talking to each other. A meeting is arranged to clear the air. But the Swede gets up in the middle of the conversation and says that he doesn't want to play with Van der Vaart anymore. And if Van der Vaart dares to accuse again him of mal-intent, he will break both his legs and rip his head off. The coach is faced with a choice: select Van der Vaart or select him, not both. Ibrahimović then adds that he can guarantee that Ajax will win their next game if he is selected. And that he will score two goals. And that's exactly what happens. With Van der Vaart sitting in the stands, Ibrahimović scores twice against NAC. 'Yes, we are hateful and we exaggerate,' he admits later. 'That is a character trait in our family.'

Incidentally, NAC are the opponents again when Ibrahimović plays his last game for Ajax. In front of their home support – who roundly boo him before the game because of the 'Van der Vaart incident' – he slaloms past six defenders and the keeper to score. He poetically calls his goal 'a search for space'. In full view of the cameras he shouts: *There's only one Zlatan.* So what did his teammates at Ajax think of him? The players from that period are fairly consistent in their opinion of Ibrahimović; he was a genius but crazy at the same time. He could be very friendly to you one day and then look at you as if he had never seen you before the next. Former teammate Wesley Sonck: 'Arrogant? I prefer to call it being very aware of your own qualities.' And: 'One time I got to borrow his extremely expensive Porsche. If you treat him with respect, he will treat you the same way.' Tom Soetaers, who played with 'Ibra' at Ajax during that period as well: 'We didn't necessarily have to win, just so long as he scored. Then he was all *I am Zlatan, I am the best and you are shit*'. He figured he was the king.' The absolute low point is undoubtedly the infamous 'scissors incident' in which Mido threw a pair of scissors at the Swede after he had punched him. Ibrahimović then took the scissors, grabbed the Egyptian by the throat and threatened to kill him (for more details see the chapter on Mido).

At Ajax they were relieved when he left to join Juventus in 2004. They were finally rid of their loose cannon, even though they were also well aware of just how good a soccer player he was.

For Ibrahimović, Italy represents the next step towards fulfilling his dream - no, not winning the Serie A title or Italian Cup, but rather the acquisition of a Lamborghini Diablo. Unfortunately, Juventus are owned by Fiat, so... Ibrahimović includes in his demands a 'gift' of one of the 400 limited edition Ferrari Enzos currently being manufactured, otherwise he won't sign for 'Juve'. The board members regard his demands as shameless, but they accept them in the end nevertheless. Fortunately for them, Ibrahimović pays Juventus back handsomely in titles: two 'Scudettos' in two years. It turns out, however, that the club was involved in a bribery scandal. Zlatan leaves the club after they are demoted to the Serie B and goes off in pursuit of a new dream: to play for Inter Milan, the club where he had once seen the Brazilian Ronaldo perform in all his glory.

We've already seen that he didn't get along with Guardiola at his next club, Barcelona. And Johan Cruyff, too, has his own ideas about Ibrahimović: 'He has good technique for a poor player, but poor technique for a good one.' After a season full of negative energy, the Swede returns to Italy where he will play for AC Milan. However, that didn't happen without a little cunning on the player's part. When he wanted to leave Barcelona, Ibrahimović and his agent, Mino Raiola, claimed that Real Madrid were interested. Raiola even bluffed on the radio station *Onda Cero* that his client 'is worth as much as Kaká and Cristiano Ronaldo together.' That meant a price tag of about 175 million dollars for his signature. Later on this turned out to be a clever trick aimed at making it possible for him to go to AC Milan for a smaller fee. In his biography the Swede confirms that he and Raiola 'came up with smart and dirty tricks' on a regular basis. In any event, at AC Milan he continues his habit of driving his expensive cars at high speed onto the training complex. And, just as he did with players at Juventus (Jonathan Zebina) and Inter Milan (Patrick Vieira), he gets into trouble with his teammates again. The giant Swede (6 feet 5 inches) gets into a fight with Oguchi Onyewu at a training session. The latter is an American who looks more like a heavyweight boxer than a soccer player. They pretty much want to kill each other after Ibrahimović dishes out yet another head-butt. He ends up with a broken rib himself. Zlatan knows a thing or two about 'spare ribs' by the way. He inflicted two broken on the coach of the Swedish team, Tommy Söderberg, albeit the result of an overeager hug.

Zlatan fiercely denies the popular image of him as the ultimate bad guy. In contrast to his behavior at home, where he has no qualms about changing his children's diapers, the tall striker – who has a black belt in taekwondo – is prone to kicking his teammates' behinds and heads during training. Sometimes for fun, sometimes not. His behavior during games is often dubious to say the least. The self-assured Swede believes that he is allowed to do anything he likes. He kicks players after the ball has gone, throws balls in the opponents' faces, makes two-legged sliding tackles and administers head-butts and elbows (even to the much-feared Italian 'butcher' Marco Materazzi) like they are going out of fashion. Ibrahimović has a simple explanation for his behavior: 'I have to be angry to play well.' He wants to be able to display the same anger he felt as a child. It's us against them. But this 'crazy genius' is also able to get millions of soccer fans to jump from their sofas every time he pulls off yet another ridiculously brilliant stunt, be that a casual flick of the heel or an incredible bicycle kick. The YouTube video of his wonderful bicycle kick from about thirty meters during a friendly match against England has been viewed millions of times. When a journalist says that a goal like that is actually impossible, he reacts in typical fashion: 'Fuck you, I am Ibrahimović.'

However, he does not make it to the finals of the World Cup in 2014, a bitter disappointment for himself and for soccer fans all around the world. Portugal beat Sweden in the play-offs, with Cristiano Ronaldo scoring four goals. Fortunately, his fans can still enjoy watching Ibrahimović score one spectacular goal after another in the service of Paris Saint-Germain. His arrogance (or is it humor?) will plague him in France too, however. Before a crucial match against Lyon and with the title within touching distance, he asks his nervous coach Carlo Ancelotti if he believes in Jesus. 'Yes,' Ancelotti answers, after which Zlatan says: 'Good, that means you believe in me. Nothing to worry about!' But he is just as likely to show his impossible side the very next day. For example, he is suspended again after he attacks Stéphane Ruffier with a kung-fu kick in a game against Saint-Etienne. And 'Ibra' even has two chefs at the club fired because he thinks the menu lacks diversity.

Zlatan is not amused when the Swedish newspaper *Dagens Nyheter* calls him the second best sportsman of all time in his native country. Five-time Wimbledon champion Björn Borg is the number one. Asked for his own top Swedes, Ibrahimović replied: 'I would have been No 1, 2, 3, 4 and 5, with due respect to the others.' Once again the Swede is reproached for being too arrogant. He doesn't care: *'I don't have an attitude, I just have a strong personality,'* to which he adds (with a straight face): 'They say that a person can only become a legend after they die. But I am a living legend already.'

Ibrahimović also has a few brushes with death over the course of his career. He frequently puts the pedal to the metal just a little too heavily. When he clocks 217 miles an hour in one of his Ferraris – and shakes off the Swedish police by doing so – it gives him an enormous kick. He finds it difficult when life stands still, and when it does he just has to make something happen. After Ronaldo, Messi and Neymar, he ranks among the best-paid players in the world (at the beginning of 2015). But because of his controversial behavior, he has also earned himself a place in the top ten of the most-hated soccer players. When he arrives in Paris after signing for PSG he says that he and Helena are looking for an apartment. 'And if we don't find one, we'll just buy a hotel.' Funny? There are a lot of people who would object strongly to such remarks in a world suffering from so much poverty. On the other hand, public reaction to his decision to get his upper body covered in tattoos demanding attention for the problem of famine in the world is much more positive. He spoils the atmosphere again, however, when in response to David Beckham's announcement that he is going to donate money to a certain charity, Ibrahimović says that he will do the same. But the charity he has in mind is... himself! 'After all, it is a privilege for the children of Paris to be able to go and watch the greatest soccer player on earth in action.' Ibrahimović is loved and hated in equal measure it seems. In 2015 a rumor goes around that Peter Mangs, better known as the Malmö serial shooter, once hatched a plan to kill Ibrahimović. In his new book Mangs reveals that he once spotted the player's Ferrari parked illegally in the street and cycled quickly back to his house to get his rifle. Luckily, Ibrahimović had sped off by the time Mangs arrived back on the scene.

GEORGE BEST

Tony Tati

Nationality:	Northern Irish
Born:	1946
Died:	2005
AKA:	the fifth Beatle, The Best, Bestie and George Simply the Best
Known for:	good looks, two good feet, fondness for the ladies, gap between his front teeth, and the smell of booze

'MARADONA GOOD. PELÉ BETTER. GEORGE BEST.'

Three hundred thousand fans – both Catholic and Protestant – line the road on Saturday 3 December 2005 to pay their respects as the funeral procession of George Best passes by. Northern Ireland is in deep mourning. Their superstar, only 59 years old, has died much too young. It has all the appearances of a state funeral and brings to mind the farewell afforded to Princess Diana. The day is cold and it is raining, otherwise over half a million people would probably have turned out in his honor. And endless stream of flowers and scarves rains down on the first cars in the cortege. Many cry, almost everyone applauds. Many prominent figures from the world of soccer are present, including Sir Bobby Charlton, Rodney Marsh, Pat Jennings, Dennis Law and the Manchester United manager Alex Ferguson. Best is to be buried next to his mother, Ann, at the Roselawn Cemetery. She died young too – at the age of fifty-four – of excessive alcohol consumption.

Best's life can be best described as a *rollercoaster ride*, given how turbulently the years flew by for the immensely popular soccer player. Born in one of the rougher neighborhoods of Belfast in 1946, he is the oldest of six children. He is barely out of the cradle before he starts to show an aptitude for the beautiful game. His father insists that he learns to be equally good with both feet. The small, fragile boy is fifteen years old and playing for the Cregagh Boys Club when he is discovered by Manchester United scout Bob Bishop. who utters the now famous words to United manager Matt Busby: *'I think I've found you a genius'*. Best is invited for a month's trial, but he returns home after just two days because he is homesick. Nevertheless, he knows what he wants: not to struggle as an ironworker in the shipyards like his father, but to become a famous professional soccer player.

After he drops out of school, Best debuts in the Manchester United first team at the age of seventeen. The team is called the 'Busby Babes' and all the players are young and extremely talented. Three years later, in his first full season, Best helps the club to the league title. His dribbling skills are inimitable and he scores goal after goal. When he finds the net two times in the quarter final of the European Cup against Benfica (which United win 5-1) the Portuguese media baptize the Irishman with the long hair *O Quinto Beatle* (the fifth Beatle). Best has this to say: 'I never saw myself as a genius or a popstar. I was very shy as a child, but once on the pitch I became very self-assured. I never started a game nervously. Why would I? I loved the game too much for that.'

United add another league title to their trophy cabinet in 1967. In the meantime, Best has moved into the fast lane, and not only on the pitch. The ladies start to queue up in their attempts to woo him. The footballing popstar with his fashionable suits and good looks is endlessly asked for interviews. He blends seamlessly into the spirit of the times embodied by pop groups like The Kinks, The Hollies and, of course, The Beatles. He is one of the first soccer players to be marketed as a brand, like a kind of David Beckham *avant la lettre*. He is asked to do ads for sausages, aftershave, shoes, beds, and so on. At a certain point it is estimated that his name is connected to no less than 78 different brands. Best jokes: 'My agent said that we would even be able to sell elevators to people in bungalows just by using my name.' In the meantime, the parties start stacking up for the young star. He even loses his undisputed starting place in the team for a while because of them. Journalists dive into his private life looking for juicy stories. At a certain point, playboy Best is in the tabloids more often because of his performances off the field than on it.

29th of May 1968 - the date on which Best crowns the greatest season of his career. Manchester United win the European Cup for the first time in their history. The 'machine', as they are called, with stars such as Bobby Charlton, Nobby Stiles, Denis Law and Best, is known for its attractive style of play. They beat Benfica 4-1 after extra time, including a brilliant solo goal scored by George Best. After winning the title, the beer flows freely. Best is voted 'European Footballer of the Year' for 1968. He is only twenty-two years old and is the youngest player ever at that time to be awarded this honor. Northern Ireland and England go all gooey on him.

However, his fall from grace proves to be just as dramatic as his rise to fame. Best is convinced that many more trophies lie ahead for him and the club, but Manchester United fail to win anything in the years that follow. Later on Best will claim that this was because 'no new players were brought in and the team got too old.' 'Bestie' is driven by a desire to win everything and it begins to look like he will not succeed in that goal anymore with Manchester United. It might also be the reason why 'the fifth Beatle' starts drinking more after all the success. On top of that, Best, who is quite shy by nature, is starting to experience more difficulty in dealing with his celebrity status. The young man who had always liked a drink or two soon loses the plot completely. Depression and suicidal thoughts follow each other in quick succession. Sometimes he can be found in the pub at eight o'clock in the morning. He doesn't know when to stop, drinks until he falls over and often misses training sessions for days in a row. 'I loved to win, so if I couldn't do it on the field I just did it in the pub instead.' His club and the English FA suspend him time and time again, but Best remains completely uncontrollable.

In 1972 he flees to Marbella in Spain in the middle of the season. He says that he doesn't ever want to play soccer again. He tells the journalist John Roberts, who has followed him there, that he thinks that Manchester United are 'just not good enough' anymore. Best is also completely fed up with the British tabloids, who keep sniffing about in his private life and writing stuff that is simply not true. In his last two seasons at United he doesn't get to play all that much, respectively only nineteen and twelve times. He scores only six goals in those two years. In 1974, and at the age of 27, the club decides to release him. Reduced to tears and extremely bitter, Best joins the Jewish Guild club in Dunstable Town, South Africa (for a total of five games per year). In the meantime, United are relegated to the second division.

But Best is not finished yet. Not with soccer and not with partying. He devours women just as gleefully as most Brits digs into their fish and chips. Soap stars, models, Playboy bunnies, stewardesses, singers, Miss UK's and no less than four Miss Worlds all pass the revue. 'People claim that I have dated seven Miss Worlds, but there were only four. With the other three I didn't show up.' Wild stories regarding his sex life start to do the rounds - that he slept with seven different women in the space of 24 hours, and with a mother and a daughter at the same time. To the allegation that he had already slept with over a thousand women before 1969, Best dryly replies: 'It was a lot more than that.' Trainee professionals at Manchester United even have to send locks of Best's hair off in envelopes to satisfy the demands of his admirers. The player himself thinks this is just swell. On a live TV show he says candidly and with no shortage of pride: *'I like screwing.'* He misses an important game against Chelsea because he decides to stay in bed with a certain gorgeous actress. His coach Matt Busby tries to reason with him now and again, while at other times he reprimands him sharply. Busby has already handed him a lot of fines and eventually he prohibits him from chasing after women, saying that Best needs to see a psychiatrist and then try to settle down quickly to a more normal kind of life. Then, suddenly, Best gets engaged to a Danish woman, Eva Haraldsted, who he has only known for two weeks. She later takes him to court because of his refusal in the end to marry her. The court orders Best to pay a fine of 750 dollars for breaking off the engagement. Busby explodes with rage and doesn't know what to do with him anymore.

Best, for his part, just continues on doing whatever he feels like. One night, after he has ordered yet another bottle of champagne from room service in a hotel, an employee finds him lying in bed covered in banknotes. Lying next to the soccer player is the current Miss World, barely dressed. *'George, where did it all go wrong?'* are the legendary words the employee speaks while Best pops the champagne in front of him. Another famous line associated with Best goes: 'I spent a lot of money on booze, birds and fast cars. The rest I just squandered' Never a truer word was spoken. Even though he earned only about 550 dollars a game at the time, his commercial activities more than compensated for the shortfall. At one stage Best is pulling in 150,000 dollars a year, a phenomenal amount for that time. But his flamboyant lifestyle also costs him a fortune. Best gambles heavily on card games and horses, and he also trades in his beloved sports cars for a new model every few months. After yet another marathon session at the blackjack table, Best wins such a large amount of money that he goes out and buys a very expensive Jaguar MK2 the very next morning. The car even has built-in picnic tables.

Bankruptcies and regular fights with customers in bars and casinos are almost inevitable. Best is threatened by a gangster when he finds out that his sweetheart took off with him. He orders a gang member to break the player's legs. Best escapes injury when the henchman refuses to carry out the order; it turns out he is a big fan of the soccer player. *'Bestie'* also receives a death threat on another occasion. When the rumor goes around Belfast that he lent 7500 dollars to the Protestant leader Ian

Paisley, Catholic paramilitaries declare that the player has become a legitimate target. They plan to kill him during a game against Newcastle United. Best gets wind of it and doesn't want to play, but the club says he must line out. He barely touches the ball throughout the entire match. When nothing happens in the end, the club coolly claims that the threat never existed.

At the end of the '70s Best hightails it again, this time to America. He is determined to leave the booze, crashed cars, bar fights and suffocating media behind him once and for all. In *The Approved Biography of George Best* he says: 'I was so popular that when I went for a piss people would follow me to shake my hand.' At first, he likes the quiet life on the other side of the ocean. In Los Angeles, where he plays for the Aztecs, he can walk the streets more or less anonymously. Nevertheless, Best soon falls back into his old alcoholic ways. 'I lived near the beach, but I didn't see it that often. This is because to get to the beach I had to pass a bar first.' He opens his own sports bar, *Besties*, together with a teammate. It quickly becomes a favorite haunt of British expats and soccer fans. And Best likes to indulge them by giving out free rounds...

On a live TV show he says candidly and with no shortage of pride: 'I like screwing.'

Everywhere where the Aztecs go there are huge crowds of women waiting for Best at the airport. When Guus Hiddink, who plays with him at the San Jose Earthquakes, sees Best's pecker he is not very impressed: 'I sure hope he can do some tricks with it, because it's nothing to write home about.' His liver gets worse all the time. Best claims that he once lived on nothing but alcohol for 26 days in a row. The Northern Irishman pays countless visits to the Vesper Hospital in his many attempts to cure his alcoholism. Nothing helps. Eventually, life doesn't interest him anymore. 'When you're an alcoholic, drink is your whole life. Nothing else matters.' (from *Blessed*, one of his autobiographies). His best friend, Mike Summerbee – together they own a fashion store in Manchester – also knows that the cause is hopeless. 'George was George, unchangeable, ungovernable if you like. I'm told it is often the price of genius.'

Best says one of his lowest points was the time he stole money from a woman on the beach. When she has to go to the toilet, Best grabs a fistful of dollars from her handbag and runs to the nearest pub for more booze. Before that, he had stolen jewelry from his girlfriend, Marjorie Wallace, who was Miss World at the time. Still, the *enfant terrible* continues to play some incredible soccer. While playing for the San Jose Earthquakes he fools the entire defense and scores a mesmerizing goal. A call-up for the 1982 World Cup is suddenly on the cards, but the idea proves fanciful in the end. Guus Hiddink, who was his roommate at the time, confirms that Best was still a fantastic player then. 'I have never seen anyone who could bamboozle you with both feet like he could.'

In the meantime, Best has gotten married to Angela MacDonald-Janes in Las Vegas. The marriage lasts for eight years. Later he will go on his knees to propose to the model Alex Pursey, but that relationship doesn't work out either. His alcohol addiction frequently results in violence, also directed at women. Pursey, for example, was beaten by him a couple of times: 'He thrashed me numerous times.' Once he gave a barmaid a broken nose, though he will be acquitted of any wrongdoing later. 'He actually never grew up,' according to first wife Angie, also the mother of his son Calum. 'And I couldn't look after two babies. So the first one had to leave.'

Around Christmas 1984 he is incarcerated in Pentonville Prison for three months for drunk driving and hitting a police officer after he tried to take his drivers license off him. He is unable to meet bail. However, the upside is that this gives him the chance to play for the prison's soccer team. After he is released, Best ends up in hospital several times and eventually he is given a new liver. He receives almost four thousand letters while in hospital and they cheer him up a little. One of his most famous statements at the time: 'In 1969 I gave up women and alcohol - it was the worst 20 minutes of my life.' Also he says: 'My problem is that I get bored quickly. Then often I end up in a bar, where everyone knows me. Everyone buys me drinks and yeah, you know how it goes. Sometimes I change into a monster. Actually, the only time I stop drinking is when I sleep.' In her autobiography, Alex Best, who was his wife for ten years, describes how she once woke to find Best cutting off her hair in the middle of the night. 'He used to scribble on my skin with a black marker while I was asleep as well.' She finally bid him farewell after Best gave her a black eye, cut her with a knife and inflicted several bruises on her body, all in the same day.

Despite all of the above, Best is still regarded by many as one of the best soccer players ever. In Pelé's and Sir Alex Ferguson's opinion he was the greatest player ever to have lived. In 1976 the journalist Bill Elliot finds himself sitting next to Best on the Northern Ireland team bus on the way to the Feyenoord stadium in Rotterdam. When he asks Best who he thinks is the better player, Cruyff or himself, the Irishman answers by asking if he is joking. At the first opportunity in the international game between the Netherlands and Northern Ireland, he purposely goes looking for Cruyff and plays the ball through his legs. Best then runs on with the ball and his fist in the air in triumph, basking in the afterglow of what he had just done. The Dutch player Willy van de Kerkhof would later say that it was the only game in which he had been 'turned completely inside out' by an opponent. In 2000 Best is voted 'British Footballer of the Century.' This despite the fact that as a Northern Ireland player he never got to play at either the European or World Cup finals. Best dies five years later in 2005. As a side effect of the medicines he uses to combat his alcohol addiction, Best develops an infection in his kidneys. His last wish is that *The News of the World* publish a photo of him with the headline *'Don't die like me'* printed above it. His wish is granted. The photo, in which he is hooked up to a maze of tubes and his head is completely yellow, is the last image that millions of soccer fans will ever see of him.

PAUL BREITNER

Tony Tati

Nationality: German

Born: 1951

AKA: Der Afro, Red Paul and The Intellectual

Known for: Leftist leanings, beard and Afro hairstyle

'I DON'T WANT TO BE AN EXAMPLE TO OTHERS'

Many people remember Paul Breitner only as some kind of left-wing loony who also happened to be a soccer player. Most Dutch people, however, will never forget him for his role in the 1974 World Cup final, when Cruyff & Co lost 2-1 to the West Germans. Gerd Müller scored the winning goal after Paul Breitner had equalized in the 26th minute through a penalty awarded after a blatant dive by Hölzenbein. Because Müller had already missed a few penalty kicks in the previous rounds, Breitner took on the responsibility in the final. *'Wir hatten alle die Hosen voll, aber bei mir lief's ganz flüssig,'* he would later say. Meaning: all of the Germans shit their pants, but for Breitner it came in a more liquid form...

The Dutch fans were even more incensed by Breitner's wild celebrations after the match, including trying to provoke Willem van Hanegem by dancing like a madman in front of him. The World Cup of 1974 was the absolute career highlight for the perpetually controversial Breitner.

Breitner's name has long been associated with his leftist ideas. When he was sixteen, the Cuban revolutionary Che Guevara made a big impression on him and his ideas would shape much of Breitner's development. When a mob of journalists interview him a couple of years later he can't resist the opportunity to provoke them. 'Who do you admire the most?' 'Mao!' 'Which book are you reading?' 'Marx!' 'What is your biggest wish?' 'Defeat for the Americans in Vietnam!' And, full of pride: 'Mao has given rice to eight hundred million Chinese people.' That the dictator Mao also caused the death of tens of millions of his fellow countrymen seems to be beside the point to him. When playing for West Germany he refuses to sing the national anthem. The reason he gives is that 'it breaks your concentration.'

So how did he become so extreme in his thinking? Breitner, who was born in 1951, started his career at SV Kolbermoor. Then, while playing for ESV Freilassing, he was discovered by Bayern Munich. He had already developed a deep mistrust of the German football association by then. While playing for the German U-18 team, he was once told after a game that he had to go to the hairdresser. He had a lot of hair, in a kind of Afro style. Breitner refused. The gentlemen insisting on the haircut first needed to explain to him what the point of cutting his hair would be.

Shortly afterwards, Breitner was called up for military service. He was sharing an apartment with fellow Bayern player Uli Hoeness at the time. When he refused to join up the military police appeared on their doorstep at two o'clock in the morning. With Hoeness doing his best to keep them busy, Breitner ducked into the coal cellar to hide until they left. This happened a couple of days in a row until the military police threatened to hang 'wanted' posters in the neighborhood. That way he could be arrested in the street if they found him. Breitner surrendered and was immediately driven off to the barracks. While his Bayern teammates were playing soccer, as punishment he had to clean the toilets at the military base.

Breitner goes on to enjoy an impressive soccer career. In 1971 he secures a starting place in the German team. In the meantime he has been transformed from an attacker into a defender, albeit against his will. A couple of months later he gets his first taste of success when Bayern win the German Cup and he makes his debut in the national team. However, he finds out pretty quickly that life as a professional soccer player is not all it's cracked up to be. 'It's all just one hotel after another, and one airport after another.' Playing for Bayern, a club known for showing off and being flashy, doesn't quite gel with his leftist ideals. There is no room for any hint of socialism; it's all about the money. He is soon fed up: 'I have to keep my ideas to myself because of the fans, but at least my friends know that I'm still the same person.' His teammates frequently make fun of him in the beginning, but once he has explained his opinions to them they calm down and henceforth judge him on his performances alone.

When Bayern Munich win the title in 1972 and Breitner is photographed dancing naked by the pool, the knives come out. The coach of the national team, Helmut Schön, refers to his behavior as pornography, while the Bayern president, Wilhelm Neudecker, hands him a large fine and even looks into the possibility of selling his radical star player.

Breitner's answer to all this is to say that 'this shit club can't even organize a decent party.' Having won the league title and the European Cup in 1974, the battle for the world title awaits him. But Breitner wouldn't be Breitner if he didn't cause some kind of turmoil. Together with Uli Hoeness he leads the calls for a players' bonus of 56,000 dollars each if Germany become world champions. Breitner openly criticizes the weak attitude of his teammates when they don't dare to back him up. In the training camp in the run-up to the tournament Breitner even packs his bags twice to emphasize how important he thinks it is that his demands are met. Franz Beckenbauer and Gerd Müller convince him to stay after a long conversation with him in the middle of the night. The association promises to pay each player 40,000 dollars if they win. But the peace is only temporary. After the triumph over the Netherlands in the World Cup final Breitner says that he never wants to play for the national team again. He says that Schön treats his players like amateurs, that they should receive higher bonuses and that the DFB, the German football association, is a mess.

Some of the squad would fill themselves up with whiskey, partake in the wildest adventures in bed and then come walking into training the next morning feeling like shit.'

But the soccer player with the leftist tongue has his comments thrown back in his face. Breitner is called a salon socialist. He makes a lot of money, lives in a big house and drives expensive cars, including a Maserati. On top of that he is in trouble with the captain of the German team, Beckenbauer. In 1974 Breitner moves to Real Madrid. He has had it with the constant stream of criticism in his native country. He is delighted that he can leave Bayern, where he doesn't have any friends anymore apart from Uli Hoeness. He describes the club as 'an aristocracy based on nouveau riche money'. He says he will never return, doesn't feel like a German anymore and even less like a Bavarian. The latter comment does not go down very well. Most Bavarians want his name taken off the World Cup role of honor. Breitner couldn't care less. The only thing he isn't happy about is that he can't take his expensive sports cars to Madrid.

In Spain, Breitner enjoys the best period of his career. He becomes friends with his flamboyant fellow countryman Günter Netzer. Together they man the midfield; Netzer as the chief and Breitner as his deputy, always with his socks around his ankles. In the meantime, Breitner is enjoying the good life and he doesn't have to worry about anything except his family and playing a couple of games. Real's Latin playing style is also better suited to his personal pursuit of freedom. He terms it 'interesting' that Franco is still alive (the dictator will die in 1975). Franz Beckenbauer doesn't understand his thinking at all. 'He just blows with the wind. Not too long ago Breitner was calling the Spaniards fascist pigs.' The money that Breitner makes by playing soccer is only a means to achieving a higher goal: a school for children in need. His dream is to run such an institution himself one day. In the meantime, he wins the league title with Real.

On a more amusing note, Breitner gets a small role (two minutes screen time) as sergeant Stark in *Potato Fritz*, a spaghetti western. Less amusing to Breitner, however, is that he hasn't seen any of the 1.6 million dollars that Real paid for his signature. He says it is against the law. 'It is a breach of human rights and basic human dignity.' Breitner goes to the media and insults several directors at Bayern. Nevertheless, he decides to return to Germany, the country with which he maintains a love-hate relationship. At Eintracht Braunschweig he criticizes his teammates and accuses them of being amateurs. He says it is a backward club where they talk nothing but bullshit. With Beckenbauer having moved to play for the New York Cosmos in the meantime, nothing now stands in the way of a return to Bayern for Breitner. He soon gets into trouble again when he is caught wearing a microphone under his shirt during a game for a documentary film. And is soon in trouble with officialdom after he yells 'kiss my ass' at a referee. He is not suspended, however, the main reason being his increasing power at Bayern.

After mediation by Netzer and his teammate Karl-Heinz Rummenigge, the prodigal son returns to the national team. He apologizes to the DFB for his negative remarks in the past and promises not to call the assistant coach, Jupp Derwall, a 'shifty character' in public anymore. But Breitner will remain a source of discontent. Having previously participated in an advertising campaign for cigarettes, right before the World Cup in 1982 he receives a ludicrously large fee of 84,000 dollars for having his hair cut for a cosmetics company ad. The whole country is up in arms at the salon socialist's antics once again. 'What's the problem?' he asks in the magazine *Der Spiegel*, 'I can decide for myself what I do or don't do, can't I? And just because I might have changed my mind over the years, does that mean I have to keep on explaining myself to everyone?'

With Breitner as their driving force – if only because of his ability to attract ladies to the training camp – Germany make it into the final of the World Cup but end up losing 3-1 to Italy. He scores the Germans' consolation goal. The group game against Austria is remembered for less noble reasons however. Breitner is partly responsible for allowing the game to precipitate an enormous scandal. After the Germans go 1-0 ahead both teams more or less grind to a halt in what became known as 'The Disgrace of Gijón'. The two countries make a deal so that they can eliminate Algeria, who are dependent on the result of this game. The match is marked by an endless series of backpasses and uselessly long goal kicks by the keepers. At a certain point the German commentators even advise their viewers to switch off their TVs. The Algerian fans wave white handkerchiefs and even banknotes at the 'actors' on the pitch. The Dutch newspaper *de Volkskrant* calls it 'soccer porn'. Breitner, who walks around with the ball at his feet for most of the match, was said to have made a secret agreement with the Austrians, according to Harald 'Toni' Schumacher in his biography: 'He and Overath were already well-known as troublemakers back in those days.'

Injury puts an abrupt end to his career just six months after the World Cup. He is only 31 and had won the Golden Ball for 'Footballer of the Year' only the year before, just beating Beckenbauer to the prize. The award barely interests him however. Smoking and playing poker are more important to him. 'He could drink everyone under the table,' according to teammate Schumacher. 'On the pitch he had the biggest personality, but off the field he didn't really set a good example. Some of the squad would fill themselves up with whiskey, partake in the wildest adventures in bed and then come walking into training the next morning feeling like shit. Breitner did all those thing as well, but with one difference: at training he was always fresh as a daisy. Incredible.'

Breitner never had many friends and after his active career he disappears from the radar completely for a couple of years. He doesn't want to have anything to do with soccer anymore for a while. No hotels, airplanes or nagging about his leftist leanings. He finally becomes 'human' and finds peace reading books about Socrates and Cicero. He also donates a large chunk of his earnings to helping disabled children and makes new enemies when he reveals the salaries being earned by the top players in German soccer. Breitner says that he and his colleagues are actually underpaid. 'We are the biggest actors in the world, but aren't paid as actors at all. On top of that we put our bodies on the line to earn that money; serious injuries are not unusual in professional soccer.' He accuses the managers at the top of lining their pockets at the expense of the players. Breitner threatens to take on the system and take everyone to court. He lashes out at teammate Berti Vogts, whom he reproaches for being hypocritical after Vogts states, with a straight face, that doping isn't an issue in the Bundesliga. Breitner: 'Especially at the beginning of the season, everyone talks about it. New players tell the others what they used at their previous club. Doping is just as normal in soccer as it is in other sports.' He also criticizes *'Kaiser'* Franz Beckenbauer year in year out and calls him 'the undertaker of German soccer' because of his reign of terror. Because of these and other incidents, he earns himself the dubious title of most unsympathetic soccer player of all time.

Breitner shows up again in 1998, after the World Cup that went so disastrously wrong for his country, as a potential candidate for the job as coach of the national team. He isn't on the list for long; seventeen hours to be exact. After DFB president Braun has announced Breitner's interest in the job, a storm of protest breaks loose. Breitner: 'I also knew that Braun wouldn't be able to guide me through the executive committee of the association. Too many people were afraid of me.' After the brief 'will he or won't he' appointment, Braun retracts his statements when it is revealed that Breitner may have passed on confidential information from a phone conversation to a third party. Insiders know better. Breitner retaliates by calling the DFB a 'backward association bereft of ideas'.

His later role as a columnist and analyst suits Breitner better. In that role, respectively for *Bild* and the German TV channel *Sat.1*, he frequently aims his harsh criticism at other (ex-)players. During the European Championships in Sweden, he also appeals to the coach of the national team, Berti Vogts, to send his star player Jürgen Klinsmann home. He says that he doesn't want to become a coach himself and even turns down an important position at Bayern Munich. What the *enfant terrible* does enjoy is scouting new players and playing with the Bayern All Stars. And the former revolutionary and anti-establishment figurehead even takes up an offer to become an ambassador for UEFA. Breitner: 'That image has always stuck with me, but I was taught never to blindly accept authority.'

ERIC CANTONA

Tony Tati

Nationality: French
Born: 1966
AKA: Le Roi, The King, King Eric, King Cantona, The Karate Kid,
Eric the Red, Canto and Mad Eric
Known for: proud gaze, temperament and his turned-up collar

'YOU ARE EITHER WITH ME, AND THEREFORE MY FRIEND, OR YOU ARE MY ENEMY'

The pretty tame match between Crystal Palace and Manchester United on 25 January 1995 is exactly 56 minutes old when all of a sudden it explodes into life. After a long goal kick from keeper Peter Schmeichel, the ball sails over the heads of Eric Cantona and Richard Saw. The Frenchman has become increasingly irritated by Shaw's marking throughout the game and now he finally loses it. He aims a sneaky kick at the defender's shin, but it doesn't escape the attention of the linesman. The referee, Alan Wilkie, draws a red card immediately. Cantona is sent off for the fifth time in his career. 'The King', who always plays with the collar of his shirt turned up, folds his collar down as he trudges off having seemingly accepted his punishment. But then, as if bitten by a snake, he suddenly lunges at a spectator with a kung-fu kick. The hooligan, who had been charged with armed robbery three years earlier, recoils in defense but he should have expected this reaction after shouting 'Go home, you French motherfucker!' at the player. You don't insult Cantona like that, he is way too proud to tolerate such treatment.

The consequences of Cantona's actions are enormous. Any other player would have been thoroughly ashamed of himself after being shown a red card and disappeared directly the dark depths of the stadium. Not Cantona. However, he quickly finds out what lies in store for him. First of all, the Frenchman is arrested straight after the game. He has to go to the police station, where he is interrogated at length. He even has to spend some time in a cell before being released on bail. The French FA strips him of the captaincy of the French team not long afterwards. The British tabloids don't show

Cantona much mercy either. *The Sun*, for example, dedicates twelve full pages to the incident. The FA suspends him for nine months – the longest suspension handed down to a player in England in thirty years – and he is fined fifty thousand dollars and given 120 hours of community service. The case is even brought up in the British House of Commons.

And his own reaction? At a specially organized press conference, Cantona offers an extremely short and enigmatic explanation for his aggressive behavior: 'When seagulls follow a fishing boat, it is because they think sardines will be thrown in the sea. Thank you...' And with that he departs, leaving everyone in the room completely astounded. A few years later, in an interview with the BBC, Cantona would say that he had few regrets about anything he did during his career. And he definitely wasn't sorry about his famous kung-fu kick. Above all, he was proud to have made his fans happy: 'I play with passion and fire. I have to accept that sometimes this fire does harm.'

Partly due to Cantona's absence in months following the 'kung-fu incident', United fail to win the league title; the only time in the five years he played for the club that this happens. But Cantona is and will remain an icon. He is even chosen as 'Player of the Century' by his club, above other star players like George Best and Ryan Giggs. By that time Cantona has already quit playing, even though he is only thirty years old. He will later say that he regrets that decision. But it's not the first time he decides to hang up his boots. The career of the temperamental Frenchman is a tale of countless ups and downs. His reckless behavior at Crystal Palace isn't the only reason why Cantona became known as one of the most controversial players in the history of soccer.

Cantona grows up in the suburbs of Marseille, where the locals don't just feel different to other French people but also superior. His father is a psychiatric nurse and painter, his mother a seamstress. They are immigrants from Sardinia. They have great difficulty making ends meet and even have to live for a time in a cave that was once used by the Germans in WWII. This unusual abode was apparently chosen as a home in the mid 1950s by Cantona's great-grandfather, who was a stonemason and who had fought on the side of Franco during the Spanish Civil War.

Cantona starts playing soccer at the local SO Caillolais club, where stars like Jean Tigana and Roger Jouve had been in the youth academy before him. The young Cantona plays as a keeper at first. Only later will it become clear that he is more suited to the role of striker. Cantona starts his professional career under the famous Auxerre coach Guy Roux and quickly earns himself a reputation as an extremely difficult character with little self-control. Then, all of a sudden, he quits the game and joins the French army to complete his military service. When he returns to the club, Cantona is loaned out to Martigues because he apparently misses the warmth of the south. Auxerre are only too happy to be rid of the intransigent troublemaker. However, he returns to Auxerre one year later and actually becomes a club favorite. Almost as if some kind of miraculous change has occurred, the superbly talented player suddenly becomes the fittest member of the team and is capable of deciding the outcome of a game all by himself. But the dark side of his character slowly begins to emerge, too. At the end of his spell at Auxerre he is handed a heavy fine after giving his own keeper (Bruno Martini) a black eye. He is also suspended for three months after an idiotic attack on a Nantes player.

In the meantime, Cantona makes his debut for the French national team. Against West Germany he even scores the only goal for *Les Bleus* in a 2-1 defeat. But he soon goes too far again when he insults the French coach Henri Michel on television. He calls him the worst trainer in the world and 'a big pile of shit'. The French football federation suspends Cantona for a year. Much worse is to follow, however, after he signs for Olympique Marseille. The Frenchman, who was bought for the record sum of 3.7 million dollars, stays at the club for two seasons.

After a whirlwind start, his performances for Marseille rapidly deteriorate. The problem it seems is that he doesn't see eye-to-eye with the coach, Raymond Goethals. 'That man is small, very small. When he dies, only a very little grave will be dug for him.' After a friendly game against Torpedo Moscow in which Cantona kicks the ball into crowd and throws his shirt at the referee, his club suspends him for a month. Club president Bernard Tapie says that Cantona will never play for Olympique Marseille again. He is loaned out to Bordeaux, who in turn loan him out to Montpellier. There he helps the team to win the French cup but once again he finds himself in trouble with his teammates. He throws boots around the dressing room and even knocks team captain Jean-Claude Lemoult to the ground in a tussle and calls him an 'ass licker'. At first the club management is intent on firing Cantona, but in the end all they do is suspend him for ten days.

In 1991 the French sports newspaper *L'Equipe* writes: 'Eric Cantona est mort' (Cantona is dead) after the star decides to quit playing soccer for the second time. The reason is yet another suspension – this time for two months – handed down by the French football federation. They initially suspend Cantona for four weeks for throwing the ball at a referee. However, when he appears in front of a disciplinary committee he calls them a bunch of idiots, upon which the suspension is promptly doubled. He is completely fed up with the footballing world and even goes as far as to buy his way out of his contract for 1.4 million dollars. Luckily, Michel Platini is still a big fan. The newly appointed coach of the French team asks him to return to the international fold. It's time he dedicated himself to the game again. To stop now while having so much talent would be a mortal sin. Cantona ('Comparing Platini to Goethals is like comparing Mozart to a busker') only follows that advice partially. He wants to pull on his boots again, but this time only in England where, according to him, they play 'real' soccer. He sees a psychoanalyst in an attempt to curb his aggressive behavior and says later on that the decision to go and play in England can be attributed entirely to his shrink.

He refuses to do an extra week's trial at Sheffield United after already having played for the club in a friendly match. The petulant Frenchman then signs for Leeds a week later and promptly helps the club to win the league title in 1992. The Leeds coach, Wilkinson, says he is a brilliant player but one who sadly lacks the temperament needed to succeed in English soccer. 'I have never had to spend as much time on a player as I do on him. He has the temperament of a child.' Cantona's reaction is as short as it is simple. 'He should keep his mouth shut. I was the boss at Leeds, Wilkinson was never in charge. I was the one who entertained everyone. When the fans found out that I was leaving the club, they came and smashed the windows. But that's just the way I am, I need a change every now and then.' In the end it turns out that the real reason for his forced (!) transfer is that Cantona had bedded the wife of Lee Chapman, his teammate at Leeds.

His new employer is Manchester United, a club that up to that point had not won a league title for 25 years. The club is in eighth place and has only won two out of their last thirteen games. Cantona arrives in the middle of the season after only one phone call and a meeting that lasted no more than an hour. He is signed for the measly fee of 1.5 million dollars, 'a steal' as they say in England. The alarm bells are soon ringing in Manchester, too, however. When Leeds come to play United, the visiting fans try to provoke him and he responds by spitting at them. In his autobiography, fellow player

Bryan Robson calls Cantona 'a complete idiot', and says that 'he has only ever caused problems at his previous clubs.'

Manager Alex Ferguson, whose neck is already in the noose, has taken a huge gamble with his most recent signing. But it pays off in the end. 'He stuck his chest out, lifted his head and survived,' recalls Ferguson with pride. 'Cantona was born to play for the club.' Manchester United go on to win the title that year. And they follow that up with three more titles in the next four years. With his turned-up collar, Cantona lords it over the playing fields of Britain like a king. He plays on instinct, and it almost seems like soccer is an art form to him. The fans, who dub him The King, idolize him, and even more so when he states in public: 'I was born in France but I don't feel any connection with that country. I feel like an Englishman.'

In his autobiography, fellow player Bryan Robson calls Cantona 'a complete idiot.'

Cantona doesn't rule only on the field but also in the dressing room. He learns from his colleagues at United how to play the game with the media and with sponsors, and also how to be more open-minded and better as a professional. Teammate David Beckham in his autobiography: 'He had an enormous aura around him. When he walked into a room, everything stopped. Every morning I was excited about being able to train with him. Every time we were in the dressing room I watched him; I watched everything he did and didn't do so I could find out how he prepared for a game. Everybody was in awe of him.' And: 'When we went to the premiere of one of the Batman movies, we were supposed to go dressed in black. Eric arrived wearing a white suit and shiny red Nike sport shoes.'

Cantona quickly becomes a cult hero and makes full use of the freedom granted to him by Ferguson. Finally enjoying success again, at United they shrug their shoulders at his numerous red cards, like those picked up against Swindon Town, Arsenal and (in particular) Galatasaray. In relation to the latter: with the Heizel stadium drama (where 39 fans died) still fresh in the memory, Manchester travel to Istanbul. The place is ablaze with fireworks. 'I had never experienced such a hostile atmosphere before,'

Ferguson comments later. The game at Old Trafford had finished 3-3 and Galatasaray smell an upset. In 'the hell of Istanbul' Cantona is sent off just before the final whistle after insulting the referee, Kurt Röthlisberger, by saying that he has been bribed. While the players are leaving the field after the match has finished 0-0, Cantona receives a blow from the baton of a police officer. 'Eric went completely nuts in the dressing room,' fellow player Roy Keane recalls in his autobiography. 'While everyone else just wanted to get out of there as quickly as possible, Eric was intent on finding the cop. And Eric, a pretty strong guy, meant it. He really wanted to kill him. It took the entire team to hold him back.'

Two years later, his kung-fu kick at Crystal Palace will make Cantona even more (in)famous. He is now public enemy number one. The Frenchman just about avoids getting sent to prison for two months, but it looks like the curtain is now definitely set to fall on his career. United fail to win the title that year. He returns briefly to United after Ferguson travels to Paris to talk to him. The newspapers write: *'The lunatic is back on the grass'*. After his last season (in which United win the title) he hangs up his boots for good. He is only thirty years old. His departure from United is as unexpected as his arrival. He informs the club chairman of his decision on a Thursday and hands him a letter to be read out to the team in the dressing room the following Sunday. By which time he will be sunning himself on a beach somewhere.

Later on Cantona becomes captain of the French beach soccer team. And as coach of the team he wins both the European Championships and the World Cup. He remains firmly in the public eye and is often the center of discussion. Cantona tries his hand at acting and directing. He gets a part as a *stud* in an erotic movie in which his character loosens his belt at one point and says: 'Be warned. It's still in sleep mode.' In another movie, 'The Force' he plays a tough criminal who has to endure a strip search in prison. He still seems to relish his role as the 'bad guy'. In his native country he continues to insult anyone and everyone whenever the opportunity arises, including the coach of the French team, Domenech, whom he calls a 'rotten fish' and a 'slimeball': 'His kind are always licking people's butts in the hope of getting a job. They always know someone who knows someone who knows someone else...' On another occasion he says 'I fuck the pope in his ass' live on TV and calls the two journalists on the same show a couple of idiots. In 2010 he appeals (unsuccessfully) to the French public to withdraw all their savings from the banks after president Sarkozy plans to raise the retirement age. In *Le*

Parisien Cantona also takes a swing at FIFA president Sepp Blatter and UEFA president Michel Platini: 'When you have to choose between the plague and cholera, it's best to get it from the doctor.' As far as Cantona is concerned, it is a choice between two evils. If one of them has to become the boss of world soccer's governing body, then he would rather it was a former player. Even though his active career is over, Cantona never tires of offering his unvarnished opinion.

Looking back on the press conference with the famous phrase about seagulls he says: 'My lawyer told me I had to say something so I just made it up. The journalists began to analyze my statement, but it didn't actually mean anything.' One British journalist 'translated' his statement as: 'I'm definitely not going to account for my behavior. So get the hell out of here!' Cantona never had any regrets about the kung-fu incident: 'You never see that kind of thing, no. But that's just me. It was a lovely feeling, the best moment in my career. I did it for our fans. A lot of fans hate having those kinds of idiots in the stands. Finally they could be happy that someone stood up to them.' And, in another interview: 'If I feel like kicking a supporter, I will do so. I'm not a role model.'

RENÉ HIGUITA

Tony Tati

Nationality: Colombian

Born: 1966

AKA: The Scorpion, El Loco (the lunatic) and Sweeper Keeper

Known for: long, curly black hair

'I AM NOT A PERFECT BEING, I AM JUST A POOR SINNER'

R omário claimed that all keepers were either crazy or gay, but most soccer fans just stick to the 'crazy' tag. And René Higuita certainly fits into that category. The Colombian didn't get his nickname *El Loco* for nothing; a moniker he earned primarily because of his antics on the field, not off it, where he was often even 'crazier'.

It is 2010 when the Colombian keeper bids a tearful farewell to thousands of fans in his hometown of Medellín, the cocaine capital of the world. Big names from Colombian soccer, such as Faustino Asprilla and Carlos Valderrama, also turn up to play. They see the 43-year-old keeper score from a free kick, and he also repeats his famous 'scorpion kick'. Even when their hero allows the ball to slip under his body into the net on purpose, his fans cheer him on. They love the man and the way he always seemed to play for fun. In his emotional farewell speech Higuita says: 'I hope we will live in peace, that we can all look each other in the face, shake hands, hug and that the hostages return to their homes. This is what I ask of the authorities and the armed groups.' And on his alleged ties to the Colombian drug lord Pablo Escobar: 'I am not a perfect being. I am just a poor sinner.' As is well known, the country of Colombia, aka 'Locolombia', was ruled in the 1990s by the drug cartels who never hesitated to murder politicians, journalists or judges.

In 1989, Higuita wins the Copa Libertadores with his club Atlético Nacional. It is the first time a Colombian team has won this prestigious trophy. Higuita stops no less than four penalty kicks in the decisive shoot-out against Olympia. His playing style is remarkable, to say the least, though many rather prefer to call it reckless because of his penchant for dribbling the ball up to the halfway line and sometimes even further.

After a game against England in 1988, Bobby Robson, the England coach, says that he has never seen a keeper like him before in his whole life. 'He rushed out of the penalty area to tackle Gary Lineker. And he bamboozled Peter Beardsley by teasing him with the ball before dribbling it back into the penalty area and picking it up. Unbelievable.' By way of explanation the *Sweeper Keeper* says that all he wants is to be remembered as a player who could add a bit of magic to people's everyday lives.

And he could score goals too. In 380 club games the extravagant keeper scores 25 times. He played 68 times for Colombia and he scored three goals for them. He insisted on taking his team's penalty kicks himself, and would run all the way up the pitch to take free kicks around the penalty area as well. And the clown even scores from those too! In addition to 'El Loco', Higuita has also earned the nicknames 'Sweeper Keeper' and 'The scorpion'. He received the latter nickname after a truly remarkable piece of goalkeeping during the game against England in 1995. A boring friendly match at Wembley is looking like it will end without any goals. The hosts are camped in front of the Colombian's penalty area. When Jamie Redknapp suddenly thinks he has fooled Higuita with a smart chip shot and the ball is sailing over the keeper's head, he dives forward, sweeps both his feet up behind him and kicks the ball back into the field. Tens of thousands of spectators can't believe their eyes. 'It's something that you will only manage to do once,' Higuita says after the game, a mischievous look in his eyes. 'I can do a lot more of those tricks, but I usually leave them behind in the dressing room.'

The Colombian coach, Francisco Maturana, almost had a heart attack during the World Cup in 1990 thanks to the nerve-racking antics of Higuita. Deep into injury time in the quarter finals against Cameroon and with Colombia trailing 1-0, Higuita takes possession of the ball 25 meters from his own goal. He tries to dribble around Roger Milla but the 38-year-old wily veteran doesn't let himself be fooled, robs the ball from Higuita and heads for the open goal. In his desperation, Higuita tries to take him down but the harm is already done. The flamboyant keeper becomes instantaneously world famous but Colombia are out of the tournament. After the game everybody expects to see a very angry Maturana when he faces the cameras, but instead he says: 'There was no reason to be angry because Higuita was only expressing the spirit of the Colombian people.'

The soccer-crazy country of Colombia is still trying to come to terms with its early elimination from the World Cup when Higuita gets himself into some real trouble. One year after the tournament, he is secretly filmed paying a visit to the infamous drug baron Pablo Escobar. At that moment, Escobar is staying in a luxurious prison somewhere in the mountains of Colombia. Though everyone says it is a disgrace, the keeper himself doesn't express any regret at all. Through his lawyer he dryly states that 'Escobar has paid for many people's funerals. He also took care of the construction of floodlit soccer fields and even provided whole neighborhoods with houses. Something that the government neglected to do.' What the rest of the world doesn't know at the time is that Escobar, who always presents himself as very charming, has become a kind of Robin Hood for many in this very poor country. He appears to be generous to a fault. And the fabulously wealthy drug dealer is also secretly the owner of Higuita's club, Nacional. In Colombia, organized crime has been dictating for years what goes on, both on and off the pitch, in Colombia.

A couple of years later, Higuita is arrested when he is caught speeding through the streets of Medellín on his motorbike with a gun in his hand

In an attempt to escape an angry public, Higuita signs for the Spanish club Real Valladolid but only plays for them for one season. His European adventure is not a success. He quickly finds himself relegated to the subs' bench and after that one season there isn't a single European club interested in him. 'In Europe, it's only the result that counts. Nobody dares to sign a keeper who takes that many risks,' he laments in *Marca*. Back in Colombia, Higuita lines up for Atlético National again. And again he comes face to face with the drug cartel of his 'friend' Escobar. When the eleven-year-old daughter of another mafia big shot, Luis Carlos Molina, is kidnapped and Escobar is the main suspect, Molina calls in the help of the keeper. He is the ideal intermediary for handing over the ransom of 300,000 dollars to the kidnappers in a fast food restaurant. Higuita will later be thanked for his services with a gift of 50,000 dollars. What the helpful keeper 'forgets' for a moment, however, is that accepting such a gift is forbidden by law in Colombia. And he has actually been hired for the job by Escobar, who is wanted everywhere. He is accused of calling Roberto, the brother of Pablo Escobar, on the phone when he was in prison. The conversation has been tapped and it turns out that Higuita asked Roberto to give him another chance in the Nacional team after he had been punished for striking a journalist.

Higuita is arrested and sent to the La Modelo prison in Bogota. He faces a jail sentence of ten years. Behind bars he sees his country qualify for the World Cup thanks to their unbelievable 5-0 win over the 'mighty' Argentina. After five months in jail, the keeper has had it. He goes on hunger strike. Two months later, in January 1994, he is released after paying a handsome bail. His release has nothing to do with his impending death by starvation, but rather with the fact that the authorities failed to process the charges within the time period allowed. His wife and two hundred fans are waiting for their hero when he walks out of the prison. He will later say that his time in prison was the best time of his life. 'I discovered another kind of loyalty there, the kind you find among so-called delinquents, drug dealers, and terrorists. I got to know their hearts, their noble hearts.' He defends his role in delivering the ransom by saying: 'I'm a soccer player, I didn't know anything about any kidnapping laws.' Maybe Higuita thought he was above the law somehow, being a famous goalkeeper.

Higuita is plunged into mourning when Escobar, who had become the world's biggest drug dealer, was shot dead while being arrested during the keeper's time in prison. After all, Escobar was like a second father (or more aptly Santa Claus) to him. He gave the goalkeeper gifts of cars, trips, houses and many other things that Higuita needed. After all, he was born into tremendous poverty and was raised by his grandmother after his unmarried mother died a couple of years after he was born. For many, soccer offered the only escape route from the ghetto. Those who were left behind generally fell victim to drugs (in a country that supplied sixty percent of the worldwide stock of cocaine).

In the meantime, Maturana has started preparing his team for the 1994 World Cup. It looks likely that he will be taking Higuita to the tournament in the USA. The coach believes that the way Higuita participates in games as a keeper is an important and integral part of Colombia's tactics. However, a couple of months before the start of the World Cup it becomes clear that Higuita will not be given permission by the Colombian authorities to leave the country. The USA government also refuses to give him a visa. Higuita can forget about participating in the world's most prestigious soccer tournament. He is furious. The authorities' admission, later on, of procedural errors and 17,000 dollars in compensation do nothing to appease him. 'They denied me the chance to be with my family, my country's team,' the keeper reacts bitterly. In the end, Colombia are eliminated in the first round, despite people like Pelé having tipped the team as one of the favorites to win the tournament. It seems that they missed Higuita - the *Sweeper Keeper* who could defend his 18- yard area with such aplomb.

Both Colombia and Higuita go through a difficult period after the World Cup. The defender Andrés Escobar (no relation to the famous drug lord) is riddled with bullets in a fight a couple of days after the squad's return. Escobar had scored an own goal in the game against the United States, ultimately leading to Colombia's elimination. It is whispered that his death may have something to do with illegal gambling in the underworld. Higuita returns as first choice keeper for Colombia at the 1995 Copa America, in which they finish third. A year later he announces his retirement from the international scene. He has been feeling out of shape for quite some time already. For reasons that are still unclear, in 1996 he is the victim of an attack in which a bomb is dropped on his house. Higuita is slightly wounded. His family is not at home at the time. The keeper says it is a complete surprise to him and that he didn't think he had any enemies. A year later he is the target of another bomb attack. This time there is a 'logical' reason: he has just announced he will be joining the Mexican club Veracruz.

A couple of years later, Higuita is arrested when he is caught speeding through the streets of Medellín on his motorbike with a gun in his hand. In 2002, while playing for Deportivo Pereira, he is suspended for six games when he tests positive for cocaine. He turns out to be a repeat offender. He also tests positive at a doping control while playing in Ecuador for Aucas de Quito. He is fired immediately. Higuita soon finds himself in financial trouble and as a result he agrees to take part in a reality TV show. He also undergoes plastic surgery because he 'no longer wants to be ugly René, but handsome René'. He begins to harbor political ambitions. For example, he wants to become mayor. 'I want the people to understand that delinquents generally leave prison thirty to forty percent more idiotic than when they went in. Prisoners aren't rehabilitated and nobody teaches them the norms and values they need as an individual.'

When his 'scorpion kick' is voted the best soccer trick of all time it provides a much-needed ray of light in the ex-keeper's darker hours. He has this to say about his dubious past: 'I was only a survivor in the war that was going on in our country. I've paid for the consequences. I thank God for all the obstacles I have encountered in my life. Thanks to him, I've also survived them all.'

PATRICK KLUIVERT

Tony Tati

Nationality: Dutch

Born: 1976

AKA: Paddy, The Panther, Pantera Generosa (generous panther), the Black Bergkamp, Black Magic, Nightclub Patrick, Don Quichot and Party Pat

Known for: barbed wire tattoo on his right upper arm

'AND THEN I JUST BLEW A FUSE'

Although Kluivert was known as the 'Black Bergkamp' during his period at AC Milan, he was frequently booed by the fans. But not so much because of his dubious past as for not scoring enough goals. He scored only six times for the club in the Serie A. His teammate Costacurta said it was due to his attitude: 'He didn't have the mentality of a great soccer player. He should have listened more to some of the older players. Then he might have become a star.' It seems that Kluivert earned the nickname *Il Bergkamp nero* primarily because Dennis Bergkamp had played just as poorly as he did during his period at the city's other club Inter Milan.

Those who remember Kluivert's excellent start to his career at Ajax will certainly recall his goal against AC Milan in the Champions League final of 1995. He comes on as a substitute fifteen minutes before the end and scores the winning goal in Vienna. He is only eighteen years and 328 days old, making him the youngest player ever to score in a Champions League final.

The young Kluivert comes from a modest background, though as a kid he never really lacks for anything. Together with Edgar Davids, he learns how to play soccer on the little square in the Naardermeerstraat in Amsterdam. At the Schellingwoude club he scores at will, so it is no surprise when his talent is discovered early on. When he is seven years old Ajax get him to join their youth academy. Kluivert scores high marks in the club's famous TIPS system (Technique, Insight, Personality, Speed), with 'P' (for personality) being the only area in which he scores poorly. The academy's coaches find him to be rash and impulsive, which explains his tendency to get booked quite often.

His rashness comes bursting to the surface on 9 September 1995, only four months after his famous goal against AC Milan. Together with a friend, he drives to a fashion show in a borrowed and uninsured BMW M3 cabriolet. He is a bit late because he forgot the shoes he wants to wear during the show. In Amsterdam he crashes into a car as it is pulling out onto the road. Having failed to put on his seatbelt, Kluivert is thrown forward and hits his face against the windscreen. The Putman couple in the other car, however, fare much worse. The woman is heavily injured and the man is killed. The official estimates of how fast Kluivert was driving vary widely. He claims that he was doing 70-75 kilometers per hour in a 30 km zone. Witnesses, on the other hand, say that they saw wheels of his car leave the road as he raced over the bridge towards the Putman's car at around 100 km per hour. Other estimates vary between 70 and 90 km per hour. In the end he is charged with involuntarily manslaughter. Kluivert has to perform 240 hours of community service and is banned from driving for almost two years. The court's leniency causes a national outrage. Kluivert goes into hiding. The press search high and low for him. He receives racist and threatening letters, and even a death threat. The Kluivert family considers leaving the country and moving to Curacao.

His standing in the public eye continues to plunge. Most people simply can't believe it when they read in the papers that Kluivert has turned out for the Ajax reserves in a match against Feyenoord on the very same day that the Putman funeral is being held. In his defense the player says he hadn't heard anything about the funeral. What he does admit, however, is that he drove through an orange/red light on the night of the accident. The whole country is soon baying for his blood again. The club management at Ajax bans him from driving for the foreseeable future. Eleven years later, on a Dutch TV show, the host reproaches him for only ever sending one text message to the Putman widow since the fatal accident. Kluivert doesn't know what to say, eventually confirms this, and says that he finds it difficult to make contact with the family. In the meantime, he has fulfilled his community service by doing odd-jobs for elderly people.

The '96/'97 season is a poor one for the player and he decides to leave the Netherlands. Rival supporters have been taunting Kluivert with chants of 'murderer'. Public opinion and the media turn completely against him after a new incident on 10 May 2007. Together with three friends, Kluivert goes for a couple of drinks in the Sinners discotheque in Amsterdam. And, as is often the case, he is quickly the subject of female attention. Kluivert refuses all offers until the very persistent Mariëlle Boon climbs into a taxi with him and his friends. According to the driver, there is a lot of messing around in the overcrowded car. Kluivert grabs the girl's breasts. Against her will, according to

Boon. Back at Kluivert's house the four of them all have their way with her. Kluivert's girlfriend, Angela, just happens to be in hospital with pregnancy complications. When Boon later accuses the four of them of rape, all hell breaks loose. Is she doing it just to get attention and money or is she really traumatized? Kluivert's relationship is on the rocks. Both sides hire the best lawyers around. The day before he signs for AC Milan, the public prosecutor says that there is not enough evidence to charge Kluivert. Ajax throw a farewell party in his honor before he leaves for AC Milan, but 'that was all the support they offered me,' says a disappointed Kluivert.

He leaves AC Milan after only one season. Kluivert: 'The club had very little consideration for the problems in my private life.' The fact is, however, that he only scores six times in the Serie A. He is thrilled when he hears that FC Barcelona (coached by Louis van Gaal at the time) want to buy him. In Spain, things finally start working out for him again. The goals begin to flow and the successes follow. But he still allows himself to be provoked too often. He calls the referee Manuel Díaz Vega a 'hijo de puta' (son of a bitch) and is suspended for four games. He even risks being suspended for twelve games by taking revenge on Jesús Diego Cota of Rayo Vallecano after the Spaniard grabs him full in the crotch. Kluivert loses it. He punches Cota full in the face and is punished in retrospect based on the TV images, the first time this has happened in Spain. Eventually he gets away with a suspension of five games. He refuses psychological counseling. The Dutchman says he is too down to earth for that. In the meantime, his past comes back to haunt him. When Barcelona go to the USA for a training camp, Kluivert is not allowed to enter the country because of his conviction for the fatal accident in the Netherlands seven years earlier. He lacks the required visa. Only after five days of feverish deliberations does he manage to get through the gates of Boston airport.

By the time the 1998 World Cup comes around, Kluivert is already pretty fed up

He admits to cheating on his wife on a number of occasions, but only for the sex, not for love...

with the Dutch team. His teammates regularly mouth off in his direction and for a moment he considers retiring from the international scene altogether. In the opening game of the World Cup he lets a Belgian opponent, Lorenzo Staelens, get under his skin. During the match Staelens whispers in Kluivert's ear that he is a rapist and a murderer. Kluivert wags a finger in his face and shouts: 'Don't say that, don't say that!' He is extremely angry and walks up to the Belgian and elbows him in the chest. Staelens falls to the ground as if he has been hit by a Scud missile. Referee Collina immediately pulls the red card. Kluivert is suspended for two games and he misses the group games against South Korea and Mexico. The Dutch coach, Guus Hiddink, is *'not amused'*. Kluivert reacts in the Dutch media by saying: 'After Staelens had committed yet another foul on me, I looked him straight in the eye and saw the hate. He provoked me several times and then I just blew a fuse.' According to Staelens, Kluivert was also guilty of verbal abuse: 'All kinds of things get said all the time on the pitch, but he went too far.' Afterwards it turns out that Staelens made a pact with his teammate Mike Verstraeten. 'We knew it was easy to aggravate Kluivert. Why wouldn't you capitalize on that? He was the best player in the Dutch team.'

Back in Spain, Kluivert loses his self-control again. This time because he is the target of whistling and monkey chants because of the color his skin. During the away game against Real Mallorca he reacts by making the Black Power sign with his fist, the one that American athletes used during the Olympic Games in 1968.

Only one year later he is front page news again on the day of the friendly game between Denmark and the Netherlands. It is alleged that Kluivert, Frank de Boer and Edgar Davids organized an orgy in the players' hotel the night before with the striptease dancer Kira Eggers and a couple of her friends. Team captain De Boer says it is all one big lie: 'I didn't see any women.' But the coach, Louis van Gaal, later reveals that at around half past ten on the evening in question he had to have nine or ten women removed from the hotel to protect his players from possible temptation. Even though Van Gaal hasn't actually seen the women with his own eyes, he says that the information is from a trustworthy source. In the end, Van Gaal allows the three players to take part in the game against the Danish. However, the coach decides to leave the Dutch set-up shortly after that, in particular because of the 'unprofessional attitude' of his players. The Netherlands had already failed to qualify for the 2002 World Cup by then.

Party Pat has something of a reputation with the ladies. In public he says that he is proud of the beautiful body of his girlfriend (and later his wife) Angela. But insiders also know that he didn't always take his relationship with her very seriously. Around the same time as the 'incident' in Denmark, Kluivert's name is mentioned in connection with another orgy. This time five Barcelona players (Kluivert, Phillip Cocu, Frank de Boer, Gerard and Thiago Motta) are said to have spent the night before the game against Rayo Vallecano with a number of high-class prostitutes. The Spanish TV channel that broke the story, *Tele Madrid,* has to back down in the end when it cannot provide any proof. They are ordered to pay each of the players 100,000 euros in damages.

In the meantime, Kluivert keeps up his hectic nightlife and even becomes co-owner of the Carpe Diem Lounge Club in Barcelona, where he is soon lord and master of proceedings. According to the Spanish media, he often hangs out there until the sun comes up. He drinks a lot, though he doesn't become an alcoholic. His shenanigans don't do his relationship with his wife Angela any good. There is no shortage of girls, and he admits to cheating on his wife on a number of occasions, but only for the sex, not for love... His performances in his final season at Barcelona suffer accordingly. He is also injured a lot. He has acquired another new nickname, Don Quichot, because of his constant battles with his poor image and his injuries. After five years with the club, he leaves Barcelona when the *socios* (the fans) send him a clear message from the stands that they don't want the former club darling around anymore. The new management want to get rid of him, too, as his salary of 6 million euros a year is too much of a burden on the club's budget. At first Kluivert agrees to have his salary cut in half, but in the end he is put on the transfer list.

His career starts to slide after leaving Barcelona. Newcastle, Valencia, PSV, Lille... In four season he plays 64 games for these clubs and scores only fourteen goals. He is mockingly called 'Nightclub Patrick' by the Newcastle fans. Everywhere he plays he is frequently spotted out on the town. In 2014 he goes to the World Cup in Brazil as the assistant coach of Louis van Gaal. However, his name appears in the news again, this time because of his ex-wife. It is rumored that Angela has fallen for Edgar Davids. Well, at least that's what the gossip columns say. The fact is that the same Angela got into a relationship with a criminal, a certain Danny K., who shares her belief that

Kluivert doesn't take good care of his children; the three sons he has with Angela, to be exact. Angela even attacks Kluivert's new wife, Rosanna, on one occasion because of it. She will later be sent to prison for alleged money laundering. She is one of ten people that are arrested in connection with a major inquiry into organized crime. The previously mentioned Danny K. and the top Dutch criminal Willem 'The Nose' Holleeder are among the prime suspects. The public prosecutor suspects Angela of using the money to pay for expensive holidays to the Maldives, Curacao and Dubai, among other things. Angela is said to have laundered a staggering total of 880,000 dollars. At the beginning of March 2015 she is sentenced to seven months in prison, three of which are subsequently suspended.

CRISTIANO RONALDO

Tony Tati

Nationality: Portuguese

Born: 1985

AKA: Crybaby, The Portuguese wunderkind, Ronnie, CR7 and Mr. Magic Feet

Known for: 'perfect' appearance, narcissism, arrogance and having no tattoos

'I LOVE BEING WHO I AM'

Seldom has a soccer player been so hated as Cristiano Ronaldo dos Santos Aveiro. While the Portuguese native goes about collecting one prize after another, he also manages to arouse the hatred of millions of soccer lovers with his 'mannerisms'. Jealousy, no doubt, plays a role in this. Apart from his extremely fat bank account, Ronaldo also exerts an extraordinary attraction on women, and he has had more than his fair share of flings as a result.

In the summer of 2014, the English comedian Joe Weller decides to try a little experiment. As a true look-alike of the famous soccer player he goes to the local park. With his slick-backed hair, tanned skin, and Real Madrid outfit he sets about approaching a number of ladies. The response is overwhelming. In addition to lots of hugs and kisses he also gets his hands on several phone numbers. Of course, this would have been no surprise to the real Cristiano Ronaldo. He is well aware of his own sex appeal, a fact that is borne out by his statement in *The Guardian*: 'I'm frequently booed because I'm handsome, rich and a good soccer player. On the other hand I get a lot of attention as well, yeah.'

To be honest, jealousy is not the only reason why the Portuguese is booed so often. Despite his claim that this only drives him on ('I play better because of it'), the statistics tell a different story. At international tournaments, such as the World Cup finals, Cristiano often performs well below his own high standards. In 2006 he suffered the wrath of the English fans and media when he got Wayne Rooney sent off in the quarter final of the World Cup. Rooney, a teammate of the Portuguese at Manchester United at the time, had clearly stamped on Ricardo Carvalho. But after Cristiano went to the referee to complain loudly, and then winked in the direction of the Portuguese bench when Rooney was shown a red card, an unmerciful witch-hunt was set in motion. In England, he was followed by the media for weeks and booed at every single away match. As for Rooney, he threatened to chop him in two at the next United training session.

'Wayne, please, may I have your autograph?' When Rooney arrives for the first training session after the incident, a United fan asks for his autograph. Rooney hesitates for a moment, but then grants the fan his wish. The autograph hunter was wearing a Portugal shirt with the name of Cristiano Ronaldo on the back... It may have been that in the meantime Rooney, who also has a *bad boy* reputation, may have remembered that he was also guilty of endlessly harassing the referee, Elizondo, during the match against the Portuguese. 'He never stopped complaining; came to me all the time with 'ref this, ref that,' Elizondo would later tell the *BBC*. 'Constantly protesting. He reminded me of my children.' When Rooney arrives in the dressing room, his fellow players give him a pair of boxing gloves as a present. He laughs at the joke but refrains from testing them out on his colleague Cristiano. To the American sports channel *ESPN* he says: 'I understand that Cristiano did everything to win. Besides, I tried to get him booked in the first half as well.'

Back to Ronaldo. His image is not exactly squeaky clean either, to say the least. He has a reputation for diving at even the slightest physical contact. Fans would turn red in anger, clench their fists and throw beer cans at him every time they saw the hurt look on his face and his hands imploring the heavens in despair at the latest tackle. Ronaldo – who had been called a *crybaby* as a child – endlessly begged the referees for help, as if the whole world was against him. The Danish referee Claus Bo Larsen once called him the biggest cheat he had ever come across on the pitch. After refereeing his last competitive game (AC Milan-Ajax), he reflects thus on a career that spanned fourteen years: 'Cristiano Ronaldo was the most annoying player. He is always out to get a cheap free kick. We tend to talk before games about how he would go down so easily. We know how not to be biased. When he would lie down after failing to win a free kick, he would smile at me because he knows I don't fall for his theatrics.'

Phil Neville, a teammate at Manchester United, says that the squad put a lot of work into persuading Ronaldo to stop doing his fake dives: 'In training at the time you had Keane, Butt, Scholes, and every time he got the ball they kicked him and they kicked him – not just once, they kicked him every day, every week, all season.' Gary Neville, another teammate and Phil's brother, told *BBC Radio*: 'Ronaldo is a bully. He bullies the weakest defender. He does it all the time. Because of Ronaldo, a lot of things changed at United. He just decided his own position, which was based upon where the space was and who was the weak link. He would go and win us game after game.'

Ronaldo experiences more than his fair share of trouble with fellow players and coaches. They often said he was a spoiled brat, especially when he expressed his incomprehension any time he was substituted in a game. José Mourinho, his coach at Real Madrid, had a poor relationship with his fellow countryman because, according to Mourinho, 'he would refuse to follow my instructions. He rarely thought of the interests of the team.' The star player also argued a lot with Ruud van Nistelrooy during training sessions at Manchester United. They would shout at each other constantly and the Dutchman even kicked Ronaldo on one occasion and almost ended up in a fistfight with him. Luckily their teammates were able to pull them apart. Van Nistelrooy was often openly annoyed after he had embarked on another futile sprint, with Cristiano hogging the ball just for show. The Portuguese also dished it out to opponents, too, his elbows and legs flying. And when 'his' Real Madrid lost to Barcelona it became almost standard practice for him to whine about it being a conspiracy. 'We had to play against twelve. It is always the same. They (i.e. the referees) never let us away with anything. Maybe they (the Spanish football association) want Barca to become champions. I don't know what's going on anymore.'

His poor image doesn't help him when it comes to winning the Golden Ball for player of the year either, or so Ronaldo believes himself. Although he was voted the best player in the world a couple of times, in his own opinion he would have beaten his main rival, Messi, to the prize more often if his image was as impeccable as the Argentinian's. Giullem Balague, an expert on Spanish soccer, claimed that Cristiano was very derogatory towards his colleague off camera. Apparently he even called him a *motherfucker*, a charge denied by Ronaldo, of course. In public all he says is: 'Messi and I are as different as Ferrari and Porsche.' But Royston Drenthe, a teammate at Real Madrid, supports Balague's view that the Portuguese player was obsessed with Messi. Drenthe: 'All that being compared to Messi. He gets up with it and goes to bed with it on his mind. If Messi scores three goals on Saturday, Cristiano has to score four on Sunday. Otherwise he will be pissed.'

Ronaldo knows only all too well that he has a bad image. Of his misbehavior and mannerisms on the pitch he has this to say: 'It all is down to my emotions, my enormous drive to win and to be the best. But if you are my friend, I will let you into my home. When you spend the day with me, you will know that I hate to lose.' The latter is confirmed by Edwin van der Sar on a Dutch TV show: 'He was always first to arrive at the training ground. Did exercises to make his ankles stronger. Did ab crunches before training. He was really driven during training. Of course he had his tricks, like when you touched him he immediately went down. All the stuff you see in a game as well. But after training he always wanted to practice his finishing, practice free kicks, which became his trademark, of course.'

Cristiano cried and cried the day he left his parents' house to join Sporting Lisbon at the age of eleven. Everyone could see what amazing talent this skinny little kid had and that he would have to leave the island of Madeira, 400 miles from the Portuguese mainland, to fulfill his potential. His parents, who had to support three more children, were poor. Their house was so small that the washing machine was perched on the roof. His father was a gardener and groundsman at the local soccer club. And an alcoholic. The young Ronaldo skipped school a lot because all he wanted to do was to play soccer out on the street from early in the morning until late at night.

After he joined the youth academy at Sporting Lisbon he was confronted with the biggest test of his life. 'His heartbeat was very irregular,' says his mother, Dolores. 'Because of that he had to undergo a special, but very risky, laser treatment.' With his life hanging by a thread, heart surgery saves his career. Dolores: 'Even when he wasn't on the field, his heart beat very fast. Luckily the doctors at Sporting quickly found out what was wrong. And shall I tell you a secret? Since his surgery he runs twice as fast as before.' His mother also reveals in her autobiography that she wanted to abort Cristiano before he was born. 'But the doctor didn't support my decision.' So she drank warm beer and 'ran until I dropped' in an (unsuccessful) attempt to terminate her pregnancy.

Only sixteen years old, the agile and lightning-fast Ronaldo puts himself center stage with a spellbinding performance for Sporting against Manchester United. José Mourinho, fellow countryman and coach: 'It was like watching Marco van Basten's son playing. He was an attacker with beautiful moves and fantastic technique.' He uses his first salary as a professional to pay for the rehabilitation program for his addicted brother. Two years later United sign him. When Ronaldo flirts with Real Madrid –

229

which happens repeatedly, angering many of the United fans – the manager Alex Ferguson slams the door in his face. He lets his star player know that he would rather shoot him than sell him to Real. In the end, not even the Scot can stop him leaving (after six years at United). The transfer sum is more than 100 million dollars, the highest amount ever paid in professional soccer. 80,000 fans show up for Ronaldo's presentation in the Bernabéu stadium. The striker immediately has his legs insured for 100 million euros. In the meantime, he sets up his own clothing line and lives the life of a celebrity.

'Spanish, Brazilian and also Eastern European women are the best. And Portuguese aren't that bad either.'

Ronaldo is front page news when he fathers a son in 2010. It comes as no surprise that the identity of the mother is unknown, initially. The child – named Cristiano Ronaldo Jr. – is the result of a one-night stand with a waitress. The mother is paid 11 million dollars to sign a confidentiality agreement. The star player soon earns a reputation for being a terrible playboy and a womanizer. In *Bild* (2009) his mother tries to paint a completely different picture of her world-famous son: 'He is a well-behaved and loyal boy. If I believed everything other people say about him then he would have been with over a hundred different women already. I know better.' But mothers often don't know the full truth about their siblings. Her son says that one of his favorite pastimes is 'dating'. Okay, he usually gets a friend to make the initial contact for him, but after that he is well able to finish the job himself.

He likes to wear very expensive clothes, with expensive labels attached, of course. Patrice Evra, his teammate at Manchester United, once said: 'I always have to laugh at Cristiano because he is the only one in the dressing room with a little mirror in his locker. He spends hours putting gel into his hair. And he loves his body (chest: 109 centimeters, thighs 64 centimeters, fat percentage 8 percent). That's why we call him the playboy.' Alex Ferguson: 'The players used to throw jockstraps, boots and all sorts at him. It never bothered him one bit. They need to win, these guys: the ones that are cultivating their egos a little bit... Dealing with an ego doesn't bother me.'

And who doesn't remember the European Championship game against The Netherlands in 2012 when the vain creature came back onto the field after halftime sporting a completely different hairdo to the one he had when he left the pitch only fifteen minutes before? Ronaldo even sends his own hairdresser to Madame Tussauds every month to comb the hair on his wax likeness exactly the same way he happens to be wearing it himself that month. As a child he was already quite narcissistic. His godfather Fernão Sousa: 'He has always been quite vain. Everything had to be neat and tidy. Hair neatly parted, shirt tucked into his trousers.'

He has no time for alcohol. After the early death of his father (aged 51) all Ronaldo ever drinks is Red Bull. 'My father was an alcoholic and that cost him his life.' The Portuguese isn't into drugs either. He has seen up close the results of his brother Hugo's addiction. His only vice, it seems, is women. There are doubts expressed about his sexual preferences - what are the plucked eyebrows, varnished nails and Louis Vuitton handbag all about? Not to mention the photo taken in 2015 of the Portuguese star sporting an obvious erection in his swimming trunks on a yacht in the company of his equally 'slick' male friends? However, a quick look at the list of drop dead gorgeous women with whom Cristiano has shared his bed points to only one conclusion. All of his conquests say that he is attentive and romantic, and they are especially fascinated with his athletic body, which he maintains meticulously. The Portuguese has had flings with Paris Hilton, Maria Sharapova, Gemma Atkinson and Kim Kardashian. He has a preference for models, usually a couple of years older than him. On the Portuguese TV show *FamaShow* he is quite open about all this: 'Spanish, Brazilian and also Eastern European women are the best. And Portuguese aren't that bad either.' And, flashing a big smile: 'I thank God that I get to travel the world so much.'

The unveiling of Ronaldo's statue in his birthplace Funchal is the cause of great hilarity. It turns out that the statue has an enormous bump in its shorts. 'Typical' is the most common reaction on social media, where people ridicule him and his well-endowed statue; he being, after all, the man who has seduced so many women and also cheated so often on many of them. His wily ways are often discovered and published for all to read. He was said to have cheated on Irina Shayk, his girlfriend of five years, with a certain

'Miss Bum Bum' from Brazil in 2013. The player denies everything, of course. Just like he denies his involvement in dozens of other affairs and an alleged rape incident in 2005 when, together with a friend, he was said to have assaulted a woman in a hotel in London. Even Scotland Yard has to be called in to investigate. In the end, the case is thrown out because of insufficient evidence. Cristiano also features in the news when he has an affair with the Ukrainian model Alyona Haynes. The brunette's husband, the millionaire John Haynes, discovers almost fifty text messages from 'Mr. Ronaldo' on her phone. Haynes: 'He destroys marriages. She even lay next to me naked while sending text messages to him, like 'Do you miss me babe? I miss you!'

The English tabloids have always been known for their rich imagination, but in October 2007, when *The Sun* publishes a story that reveals how Ronaldo and his teammates (and best friends) Nani and Anderson hired five call girls through an escort agency, the Portuguese player's goose looks well and truly cooked. The orgy was said to have taken place at his home, in and around his swimming pool, with the players eager to celebrate the first win of the season with some high jinks. The ladies, however, are less than satisfied with the 'performance' of the top athletes. Tyese Cunningham tells the *News of the World*: 'I've slept with about 200 clients and I've never been treated with such little respect. They didn't care about our feelings. They didn't even talk. They just moved our bodies into the right positions.' The party lasts for six hours and it turns out that the ladies have the pictures to prove it. One photo shows Anderson stark naked in the bath. Later the gentlemen are given an 'S&M session with no limits'. At five o'clock in the morning the party ends, possibly with a *happy ending* for the gentlemen. Anderson and Nani tell the ladies to be quiet when they are leaving as their teammate is already in bed, out for the count and thoroughly exhausted.

ACKNOWLEDGEMENTS

This book is the result of an endless amount of research, interviews, my own experiences and the cooperation of many correspondents and journalists.

I am very grateful to the following for their help: Cynthia Boot, Govert van Iterson, Gijs de Swarte, Esther Sinnema, Steve Reid, Philipp Danneels, Jeroen Walstra, Omar Kanteh, Carlos Vejar, Angela Capo, Wouter Pennings, Erol Elman, Kees Jongboom, Ernst van de Reep, Katinka Zeven, Arnie Henderson, Tony Tati, Ferdi Gildemacher, Peter Veenhoven, Jack Spijkerman, Maarten Beernink and Doede Jaarsma.

Special thanks to Daan Schippers and René Pförtner.

Sources (in random order): ANP, DPA, FHM, Voetbal International, Elf, Sporza, de Telegraaf, Algemeen Dagblad, de Volkskrant, Het Parool, HP De Tijd, Sportgeschiedenis. nl, Elsevier, Hard Gras, DeOndernemer.nl, SkySports, SkySport24, The Guardian, The Independent, The Observer, The Telegraph, Mirror, Daily Star, Four Dimensional Football, Sportweek, Der Spiegel, Süddeutsche Zeitung, Frankfurter Allgemeine Zeitung, WDR, AFP, L'Equipe, France Football, France Soir, Le Figaro, Gazet van Antwerpen, La Dernière Heure, Vandaag.be, Guido.be, Libertatea, Clarín (Argentina), Diario Marca, Gazzetta dello Sport, Corriere della Sera, Sportinglife, Sports Illustrated, CNN, SkySports, NY Times, FourFourTwo, Worldsoccer.com, Wikipedia, The Irish Times, La Dernière Heure, DerStandard.at, Shortnews.de, Andere Tijden Sport, El Clarín, FIFA.com, NOS, La Stampa, Ekstra Bladet, Manchete, A Bola, L'Equipe, El Tiempo, Metro News, ESPN, TV America, Reuters, AP, Urgente24... and a countless number of biographies and other books about soccer.

NEXT BOOK
'Sex, drugs and sports' will be the next book to be published by Eye4Sports. Expected release date: May 2016.

ABOUT THE AUTHOR

Author Maarten Bax (1960) has been a sports journalist for over 25 years. He has worked in the Netherlands and beyond and met many of the *bad boys* in this book himself. 'My most memorable experiences? There are a lot of them. I had many conversations with Ibrahimović when he was still quite young, and I also had a few interesting run-ins with Kluivert and Davids. And when you live only one hundred meters up the road from Romário in Rio de Janeiro, you're bound to pick up a few juicy bits of information. Unfortunately, I never got to meet other colorful characters, like George Best and Garrincha, simply because they died far too young.'

Thanks in part to previous books he has written on the subject, Bax is widely regarded an expert when it comes to *bad boys*. His authorized biography of the famous soccer twins Frank and Ronald de Boer was something of a warm-up before he gained momentum with the first biography ever written about a hooligan, the now deceased Joark of the Ajax F-side. He also wrote a book about aggression in Dutch soccer after the tragedy involving linesman Richard Nieuwenhuizen, who was kicked to death after a match. He is the author of the (only authorized) biography of the infamous former world kickboxing champion Badr Hari.

* Bax is frequently asked to give lectures and presentations about errant sportsmen in which he explores their psyche and their often reckless behavior. For more information: info@eye4sports.nl